THE PURITAN EXPERIMENT

New England Society from Bradford to Edwards

THE PURITAN EXPERIMENT

New England Society from Bradford to Edwards

Francis J. Bremer

With an Introduction by ALDEN T. VAUGHAN

St. Martin's Press   New York

Library of Congress Catalog Card Number: 75-38013

Copyright © 1976 by St. Martin's Press, Inc.

All Rights Reserved.

Manufactured in the United States of America.

09876

fedcba

For information, write: St. Martin's Press, Inc.,

175 Fifth Avenue, New York, N.Y. 10010

cover: photograph by Frank Scherschel of
The Plymouth Embroidery, designed by Pauline
Baynes, 1970. Courtesy of Plymouth Congrega-
tional Church, Minneapolis, Minnesota.

for
Heather and Kristin
and
Bobbi

PREFACE

The Puritan Experiment is designed as a map of the major features of New England Puritan history from its English origins to the Great Awakening. There are probably more good books in this field than in any other area of American history, but they reflect scholarly interest in a single colony, problem, town, or controversy. This study was conceived after numerous encounters with students in which I was unable to respond satisfactorily to their requests that I recommend "one book" to introduce them to colonial New England. *The Puritan Experiment* is a survey intended to answer that need, for those who want to familiarize themselves quickly with the field as well as for those who wish an introduction for more extensive study.

In the following pages I have tried to depict the multiple concerns of the colonists and the many facets of their lives. Religion plays a central role in the story because it was at the center of life for most sixteenth- and seventeenth-century Englishmen and Americans—Puritans in particular. In describing the varied aspects of colonial existence, I have attempted to avoid concentrating exclusively on Massachusetts. This largest and most influential of the New England colonies has always drawn the most scholarly attention. But the Puritan attempt to create a Christian Commonwealth was not confined to the Bay. It commanded the attention of settlers in Hartford, New Haven, and other corners of New England and of many Englishmen who never left their homes. The story is spread over large areas of the Anglo-American community. I have described the evolution of the Connecticut and New Haven colonies, as well as that of Massachusetts, and demonstrated the relation of colonial events to English history. Rhode Island provides an interesting laboratory in which the radical tendencies of colonial Puritanism can be seen achieving their own fulfillment; that colony's seventeenth-century history is also examined in the following chapters. New England north of Massachusetts was of less consequence to the Puritan experiment and enters only briefly into the story.

It is my hope that students who use this book will achieve a fuller understanding of Puritan society in the New World, and, in particular, that they will be helped to resist the natural inclination to impose their twentieth-century biases upon the seventeenth-century colonists. I have tried to elucidate the context in which the Puritans lived and to explain, by reference to that context, actions unpalatable to modern sensibilities, including the persecution of Baptists, the enslavement of blacks, and the execution of Quakers and accused witches. To understand is not to condone. Students of colonial New England will undoubtedly wish that the colonists had done some things differently, but before they form such judgments they must first seek to perceive the Puritans—their beliefs and their actions—from the perspective provided by a knowledge of the world in which they lived.

Just as Puritanism was largely shaped by its sociocultural environment, so too is any work of scholarship. This volume could not have been written without the efforts of the many scholars whose names are found in the text itself and in the suggestions for further reading. I am obliged to teachers and students who have provided a sounding board for my ideas as well as many insights of their own. Among the former, Raymond Cunningham and Robert Handy deserve to be singled out; among the latter David Jaeger, Daniel Richter, and Steven Ward. My colleagues at Thomas More College have provided friendship and encouragement. And I owe a very special debt to Alden T. Vaughan, who has encouraged me in this project, criticized early drafts of the chapters, and made innumerable helpful suggestions for improvement of the manuscript. Finally, I am deeply indebted to my parents and to those who have endured on the home front—my wife, Barbara, and my children, Heather and Kristin.

INTRODUCTION

Almost half a century ago a professor at the University of Chicago warned a promising graduate student not to specialize in Puritan New England. "All the hay of New England Puritanism has been threshed," Perry Miller later recalled; "I would wreck my career, even before it commenced, crawling through the dry stubble hoping to pick up stray gleanings."[1] Fortunately for historical scholarship in general and Puritan studies in particular, Miller persisted. His doctoral dissertation was subsequently published as *Orthodoxy in Massachusetts, 1630–1650*; he followed it with two magnificent volumes on *The New England Mind*—the first on Puritan thought in the seventeenth century, the second on the transition of New England from an isolated bastion of Puritanism to an integral and increasingly secular part of the British empire.[2] Through those three books and several perceptive essays, Perry Miller revolutionized the interpretation of a topic that had been debated by historians—professional and amateur—since the 1630s.

Perry Miller's version of early New England's history and thought supplanted a view put forward a generation earlier by the progressive historians and their intellectual allies. Writing in an era deeply suspicious of religious and philanthropic motives, scholars such as Vernon Louis Parrington, and publicists such as Henry L. Mencken, rejected the Puritans' theological rhetoric as a mask for more mundane (usually economic) concerns.[3] James Truslow Adams, whose *Founding of New England* (1921) earned a Pulitzer Prize in history, epitomized the interpretation that Miller challenged. Adams had made little attempt to explain Puritan theology or to probe below the surface of the New England mind. Instead Adams emphasized "those economic and imperial relations which are of fundamental importance; for the one outstanding fact concerning any American colony in the colonial period is that it was a dependency, and formed merely a part of a larger and more comprehensive imperial and economic organization."[4]

Miller took issue with Adams's fundamental assumption that *thought*, when important, pertained to economic or imperial problems. In the preface to *Orthodoxy in Massachusetts*, Miller acknowledged that he had "attempted to tell of a great folk movement with an utter disregard of the economic and social factors." He admitted that he thus opened himself "to the charge of being so very naïve as to believe that the way men think has some influence upon their actions, of not remembering that these ways of thinking have been officially decided by modern psychologists to be generally just so many rationalizations constructed by the subconscious to disguise the pursuit of more tangible ends."[5] Or as Miller put his case in the first volume of *The New England Mind*, "I am . . . concerned with defining and classifying the principal concepts of the Puritan mind in New England, of accounting for the origins, inter-relations, and significances of the ideas."[6]

And so Perry Miller restored the theological and philosophical elements of Puritanism that an earlier generation had put aside as window dressing. Together with the works of Samuel Eliot Morison and other scholars, principally at Harvard, Miller fundamentally altered twentieth-century perceptions of the New England Puritans' religious and secular ideas, their social and cultural vitality, their humanism, and their humanity. In 1921 James Truslow Adams seemed to have said all that was worth saying about Puritan New England; by 1956, when Perry Miller's collection of essays, *Errand into the Wilderness*, appeared, Miller seemed to have said all that needed saying in refutation of Adams and in support of a newer and more valid interpretation. (Because of its brevity and broader scope, *Errand into the Wilderness* probably had a greater impact on students and general readers than the more profound but more intimidating *New England Mind*.) One can imagine professors cautioning their students against venturing into a fallow field.

If such advice was given, it was certainly not taken. The two decades since Miller's last volume on early New England have witnessed a flood of new books and articles. In some cases recent scholarship has amplified or revised what Miller wrote about Puritan modes of thought and expression. In other cases historians have explored issues that Miller ignored—matters of family structure, community growth, ethnic relations, political evolution, or economic diversification.[7] The scholarly outpouring on these and other topics has been enormous. In 1966 a leading historian suggested that "we already know more about the Puritans than sane men should want to know," and called, half-seriously, for a moratorium on the subject.[8] Yet in 1970 alone, eleven important books were published on seventeenth- and eighteenth-century New England, prompting another scholar to observe that "colonial New England has become, perhaps, the most thoroughly studied segment of world history."[9]

Readers addicted to Puritan studies have welcomed each addition to an increasingly sophisticated analysis of early New England. But nonspecialists can only sigh resignedly as every new title further complicates an already intricate field. For this latest wave of historical scholarship has had no overview, no synthesis into which a reader can fit new pieces in an ever expanding intellectual puzzle. The older syntheses—J. T. Adams's, for example—reflect outmoded perspectives. Samuel Eliot Morison's *Builders of the Bay Colony* (1930) remains a delightful and informative assortment of biographical essays, but it does not address a variety of questions that engage today's scholars. Edmund S. Morgan's *Puritan Dilemma: The Story of John Winthrop* (1958) is widely and rightly acknowledged as a splendid introduction to New England Puritanism, but the narrative necessarily ends with Winthrop's death in 1649. Other, more recent, introductions to early American Puritanism are admirable for their own purposes but do not fill the need for a comprehensive historical survey of the early New Englanders' thoughts and actions.[10]

The Puritan Experiment meets that need. Its chronology stretches from the roots of the English Puritan movement in the sixteenth century through New England's Great Awakening in the eighteenth. Its geographical scope covers all the New England colonies, including the northern outposts, without slighting the formative events that so often occurred in Massachusetts. And the book's topical range encompasses all the issues of current scholarly concern—political, social, cultural, and, most pervasively, religious.

Because this volume is intended as a synthesis, it does not argue strongly for a single interpretive framework or espouse an overriding theme. Yet the book has an organizing structure. As the title suggests and the text amplifies, Francis Bremer—who has himself contributed to the mounting research on Puritanism—views early New England as a unique experiment in English colonization, an experiment that was primarily religious but had profound social, political, and economic manifestations. Within that gently imposed framework, Bremer integrates the latest scholarship, summarizing where consensus exists and delineating the arguments where historians are still at odds. With this book as a guide, novices and professionals alike will find their way more quickly and surely through the labyrinth of New England's early history.

ALDEN T. VAUGHAN
Columbia University

[1] Perry Miller, *Orthodoxy in Massachusetts, 1630–1650* (Cambridge, Mass., 1933; 2nd ed. 1961; Harper Torchbook ed., New York, 1970), p. xxxi. Miller earlier gave a similar version of the episode, with a slightly different metaphor, in *Errand into the Wilderness* (Cambridge, Mass., 1956), p. viii.

[2] Perry Miller, *The New England Mind: The Seventeenth Century* (Cambridge, Mass., 1939; reissued 1954); *The New England Mind: From Colony to Province* (Cambridge, Mass., 1953; reissued 1962).

[3] Vernon Louis Parrington, *Main Currents in American Thought: The Colonial Mind, 1620–1800* (New York, 1927); H. L. Mencken, *A Book of Prefaces* (New York, 1924).

[4] James Truslow Adams, *The Founding of New England* (Boston, 1921), p. ix.

[5] Miller, *Orthodoxy in Massachusetts* (Torchbook edition), p. xxv.

[6] Miller, *The New England Mind: The Seventeenth Century*, p. vii.

[7] Much has been written about Miller, his influence, and his shortcomings. Among the best evaluations are "Perry Miller and the American Mind: A Memorial Issue," *The Harvard Review*, II (Winter–Spring, 1964); Robert Middlekauff, "Perry Miller," in Marcus Cunliffe and Robin W. Winks, eds., *Pastmasters: Some Essays on American Historians* (New York, 1969); Michael McGiffert, "American Puritan Studies in the 1960s," *William and Mary Quarterly*, Ser. 3 XXVII (1970), 37–60; and David D. Hall's introduction to the Torchbook edition of *Orthodoxy in Massachusetts*.

[8] Edmund S. Morgan, "The Historians of Early New England," in Ray Allen Billington, ed., *The Reinterpretation of Early American History* (San Marino, Calif., 1966), pp. 41f.

[9] John M. Murrin, "Review Essay," *History and Theory*, II (1972), 226.

[10] See especially Darrett B. Rutman, *American Puritanism: Faith and Practice* (Philadelphia, 1970); and Larzer Ziff, *Puritanism in America: New Culture in a New World* (New York, 1973).

CONTENTS

PART ONE

THE RISE OF PURITANISM

1 | THE ORIGINS AND GROWTH OF THE PURITAN MOVEMENT

On 6 February 1566, in the reign of Queen Mary, Bishop John Hooper was brought to Gloucester, the seat of his diocese, where he was burned at the stake. A confirmed religious reformer, who had traveled to the centers of continental Protestantism during the reign of Henry VIII, Hooper had returned to England upon the accession of Edward VI to work for further reform of the English church. His opposition to the wearing of clerical vestments had resulted in a quarrel with Archbishop Cranmer and a brief period of imprisonment. But whatever his differences with Cranmer, he stood firm with the archbishop against Roman Catholicism—and with him was a victim of the Marian persecutions.

Almost seventy years later John Winthrop, lord of Groton Manor and a respected member of the English gentry, gave up his ancestral home, his status, and the comforts of English life to lead a Puritan exodus to New England. The decision made by Winthrop and the thousands who followed him was fraught with danger. Many who ventured to America never got there, falling prey to shipboard diseases or North Atlantic tempests. And those who reached the New World could take little comfort from the record of those who had preceded them. The mortality rate in the Virginia colony had been horrifying—between 1619 and 1625 over two-thirds of the 6,500 English colonists had perished from disease, Indian attacks, or starvation.

In 1649 representatives of the English people, including Vincent Potter—one of those who had followed Winthrop to Massachusetts and who subsequently returned to England to fight the Lord's battles against Charles I—signed a warrant condemning their king to die.

It was a sign of how far England had come since the reign of Henry VIII and the beginning of the English Reformation.

When we ask what Puritanism was, we are seeking to understand the nature of a faith that had profound significance for tens of thousands of Englishmen and Americans in the sixteenth and seventeenth centuries. We are probing for what it was that strengthened John Hooper's resolve to die rather than recant, that motivated John Winthrop to risk his life and his family's security in an attempt to erect a godly state, and that firmed the resolve of Vincent Potter to overthrow and finally to execute his sovereign, Charles I. The chapters that follow attempt to describe what Puritanism meant at various times and in different settings, primarily in seventeenth-century New England. It should constantly be kept in mind that Puritanism, like any vibrant and living ideology, adapted itself to its times, and that if it is valuable to understand what Hooper, Winthrop, and Potter had in common, it is equally important to place any one incident or series of incidents in the broader context of the evolving Puritan tradition.

THE HENRICAN AND EDWARDIAN REFORMATIONS

Where does the story of the Puritans and Puritanism begin? Marshall Knappen, in his classic study *Tudor Puritanism*, opens his discussion with the reactions of William Tyndale to the Henrican reforms. And while Knappen has been taken to task by some scholars for this early dating of the movement, his approach has the merit of identifying as the earliest and most constant characteristic of Puritanism the belief that the Church of England had not been sufficiently purged of the theology and worship of Roman Catholicism. As the clergyman-founder of Connecticut, Thomas Hooker, later phrased it, Henry VIII's "mistake [was that] he cut off the head of Popery, but left the body of it yet within his realm!" That, of course, was about what the king had intended. For while the Reformation on the continent was, from its inception, primarily religious in intent and leadership, England's alignment with Protestantism was begun by its monarch for essentially political reasons.

The church in England upon the accession of Henry VIII was divided into twenty-seven dioceses, each with a bishop at its head. Administratively, these dioceses were grouped into two provinces—York in the north and Canterbury in the south—each under an arch-

N

TUDOR
ENGLAND

········· County boundaries

Miles

0   40   80

Berwick

Northumberland

Newcastle

Cumberland   Durham   Durham

Westmore-
land

York

York

Lancaster

Lincoln

Carnarvon   Flint   Chester   Derby   Nottingham   Stoke

Denbigh

Merioneth   Stafford   Norfolk

Mont-   Salop   Leicester   Rutland
gomery   Hunting-   Cambridge

Cardigan   Radnor   Warwick   Northampton   don   Cambridge

Brecknock   Hereford   Worcester   Bedford   Suffolk

Pembroke   Cam

Carmarthen   Gloucester   Oxford   Bucks   Hertford   Essex

Mon-   Oxford   Middlesex   London
Glamorgan   mouth   Berks   Kent

Surrey

Somerset   Wilts   Hants   Sussex

Taunton

Devon

Exeter   Dorset

Cornwall

bishop who had oversight not only of his own diocese but also of the others in his province. While officially coequal, the archbishop of Canterbury held greater political and ecclesiastical influence than his counterpart of York because of his proximity to the center of government and the inclusion in his province of the great universities of Oxford and Cambridge. Both archbishops were traditionally responsible only to the pope for their conduct of church affairs, and this ecclesiastical loyalty had often in English history irritated relations between the monarchy and the papacy. That friction reached its peak in Henry's reign.

English Catholics, including such internationally respected scholars as Thomas More and John Colet, had frequently criticized the operations of the church in England, pointing to the clergy's sparse education, an abundance of superstitious practices, and the mismanagement of church finances. But when Henry asserted his independence from Rome and married Anne Boleyn, he had no intention of reforming ecclesiastical abuses. His motivation was essentially political, just as the pope's refusal to annul Henry's prior marriage to Catherine of Aragon had as much to do with international considerations as it did with canon law.

Nevertheless, despite his own continued belief in Roman Catholic dogma and his acceptance of its devotional practices, Henry—again for political reasons—was forced to make occasional accommodations to Protestant religious reform. Isolated from Catholic Europe, the king at times relaxed his pressure on English reformers while he sought support from Protestant nations, just as he persecuted the reformers when the aid of foreign princes seemed less necessary. Given the unstable nature of the Henrican religious scene, some Englishmen of strong Protestant sympathies found it more effective to work for reform from overseas, applauding the king for having moved away from Rome, but criticizing him for not having traveled far enough down that road. William Tyndale and John Hooper were but two members of the exile community who imbibed Protestantism from continental reformers and printed religious tracts to be smuggled into England for the enlightenment of their countrymen.

When Henry VIII died in 1547, reconciliation with Rome was seen as possible and potentially painless by many observers, so little had Henry affected the nature of the English church. But the rapid pace of religious change in the brief reign of Edward VI made clear that a reversal would never be painless—and perhaps not even possible. The archbishop of Canterbury, Thomas Cranmer, was chief architect of the new policy. Demonstrating much more initiative than he had in the previous reign, Cranmer established contacts with John Calvin of Geneva, Luther's lieutenant Philip Melanchthon, and other continental reformers; he attempted to draw those leaders together in an international Protestant conference to iron out the differences between the various communions; he invited reformers Peter Martyr and Martin Bucer to Oxford and Cambridge respectively, thus ensuring that future generations of English clergy would reflect a Protestant theological orientation. Under his guidance the Church of England was moved closer to the practices of the "best reformed churches." Clerical marriage was officially approved; a Protestant Book of Common Prayer was published in 1549, followed by a more reformed Second Edwardian Prayer Book in 1552; images were removed from the churches, and communion tables in the naves replaced church altars; one month before his death the young king endorsed the Forty-Two Articles of doctrine, which reflected the Protestant view on all points at issue in the church.

Not all Englishmen approved of these new directions. Catholics, of course, hoped for a return to the Roman fold and resented every step away from that goal. But even in the Protestant camp there was dissension. John Hooper and John Knox wanted faster and more thorough change. The former had developed a strong reformed orientation during his exile under Henry. Returning from Zurich in 1549 he had cooperated with Cranmer in the archbishop's early program of reform. But he soon chafed over the slow pace set by Canterbury. His radical stance led to his imprisonment for three weeks when he preached against the clerical use of vestments in worship, which he believed were symbolic of the concept of a sacrificial priesthood. Hooper outwardly conformed and was installed as bishop of Gloucester in 1550, but he remained an influence for more thorough purification of the church. John Knox, in exile from Scotland for his radical Calvinist views, played a similar role in the Edwardian church. Had the king not succumbed to tuberculosis at an early age, Hooper and Knox might have formed the nucleus of a loosely organized Puritan opposition to the hierarchy. As events transpired, one became a Marian martyr, the other a Marian exile.

MARY TUDOR AND THE MARIAN EXILES

The five-year reign of Mary Tudor (1553–1558), Henry VIII's daughter by Catherine of Aragon, was a testing time for English Protestantism. Her attempt to restore Catholicism to England kept the fires of Smithfield burning with the flesh of martyrs and sent about eight hundred of her Protestant subjects into exile. While her persecution of dissenters was no harsher than that to be found elsewhere in Europe at the time (as well as in England in her father's reign—albeit on a smaller scale), her victims were immortalized by one who fled to fight another day. John Foxe's compilation of their stories in his *Book of Martyrs* served to strengthen the faith and confidence of the surviving English Protestants.

Many of those dissenters spent the five-year reign of Queen Mary in the centers of Reformed Protestantism. More welcome in communities such as Zurich, Basle, and Geneva than in Lutheran territories, the exiles there established their own churches and entered into dialogue with figures such as Heinrich Bullinger and John Calvin. But even in exile English reformers could not agree among themselves; their debates on the continent foreshadowed the issues that would divide the Church of England after their return.

The English church had been founded without a clear ideology and had been in the midst of evolution when Edward died. Some among the exiles sought to continue that process, working to model their forms of worship more closely upon those of the continental Protestants among whom they lived, to aid in the formation of a universal "reformed way." John Knox and William Whittingham, among the exiles, looked to Geneva as their model and urged it on their colleagues. Others, opposed to this internationalist ideal, strove to preserve the "English face" of the church in exile, arguing that to depart from the religious system of the 1552 Prayer Book would be to betray the cause for which Cranmer, Hooper, and others were dying.

For the most part these émigrés gathered according to ideological bent, so that each group pursued its own direction. But the differences in the broad exile community were given focus by the dispute that racked the English church in Frankfurt. In 1554 that congregation did away with clerical vestments, congregational responses, and other survivals of Catholic practices and drew up a Calvinist creedal discipline. Alarmed by these developments, the more conservative exile group at Strasbourg successfully persuaded the Frankfurt church to appoint one of its members as pastor, sent Edmund Grindal to demand conformity to the old English standards, and finally dispatched Richard Cox to influence the Frankfurt reformers, who had by then ignored the Strasbourg remonstrances and chosen John Knox as one of their pastors. Invited to join the congregation in 1555, Cox assumed leadership of the anti-Knox minority, disrupted services, played upon the magistrates' fears of Knox's political theories to have him banished from the city, and drove out his followers. The Prayer Book party thus triumphed at Frankfurt, and Knox and his colleagues settled in Geneva, where they drew up a Confession of Faith that accepted predestination and identified the three marks of the visible church as proper preaching, correct ministration of the sacraments, and ecclesiastical discipline. In the beliefs and practices of Knox's Geneva congregation of exiles can be detected the hallmarks of Puritan ideology as it was to emerge in the following decades.

ELIZABETH

When Queen Mary died in 1558 she was succeeded by her sister, Elizabeth, who restored Protestantism to the realm and, through her longevity, ensured its permanence. To staff her church the new queen looked to the returning exiles but found that they demanded a role in the structuring of the new church. The result was a compromise. Elizabeth had sought a return to the type of church symbolized by the 1549 Prayer Book; the exiles were committed to the 1552 Prayer Book at the least, with many seeking a much more Calvinistic practice. The Elizabethan Settlement of 1559—which essentially restored the 1552 Prayer Book with a number of conservative amendments—was dictated by the politics of the situation and designed to contribute to the solidity of Elizabeth's grasp on the throne. It was not a settlement for all time, but was viewed as temporary by those who made it, so that much of the era's religious history focused on attempts to modify it.

The early years of Elizabeth's reign saw also the emergence of Puritanism as a movement to further reform the queen's church. Few of the returning exiles were satisfied with the new religious regime, but most (probably five out of six) were willing to work within it—if not in positions of authority that would require them to enforce unpalatable decrees, at least in parish posts. Some were unwilling to compromise at all, however, and attached themselves as chaplains to private households, served as itinerant lecturers, or assumed other positions outside the official structure and discipline of the church. From the activities of the dissatisfied clergy arose the Elizabethan Puritan movement.

The dissidents strove initially for a liturgy purged of "popish remnants." According to historian Patrick Collinson, "Apart from the vestments, the surplice and the outdoor dress of the clergy, the first and foremost of their gravamina, the puritans would object with monotonous consistency to signing with the cross and addressing interrogatories to the infant in baptism, baptism by midwives, the rite of confirmation, kneeling at the communion and the use of wafer bread, the giving of the ring in marriage, the purification of women after childbirth, the retention of such terms as 'priest' and 'absolution,' the observance of saints' days, bowing at the name of Jesus and 'equisite singing in parts' and organs. More radically, some of them would complain of the 'longesomeness of the service' which seemed out of proportion in a Reformed Church and implied a subordinate place for the sermon."

That Puritanism grew to include a challenge to the episcopal structure and to develop a distinctive theology was primarily the responsibility of the queen, whose attempts to suppress dissent only resulted in the broadening of its attack. The nature of the church helped to make such opposition possible despite the queen's displeasure. Organizationally, the division of the realm into provinces and dioceses remained as it had been in the reign of Henry VIII. But his confiscation of the monasteries and the dissolution of religious orders had led to the creation of a large number of congregations free from episcopal supervision. The rights to the tithes of many parishes had originally been assigned ("impropriated") to the monasteries or religious orders, which had the associated right of appointing a stipendary curate to serve the parish. These rights of impropriation were given or sold by Henry to lay supporters, who in turn could sell them or transfer them, as they could any other property. Thus, in Elizabeth's time many clergy were appointed by laymen, and the support of some of these laymen assured the Puritans of a number of positions free from episcopal supervision. Further complicating attempts to suppress the Puritan clergy was the sympathy they received from some bishops, who could be counted upon to overlook much. The movement also enjoyed the support of many prominent laymen, including influential figures at court such as the Earl of Leicester, Sir Walter Mildmay, and Sir Francis Walsingham. Moreover, the government itself was inconsistent in attempting to suppress Puritanism in the southern counties while recognizing its value in the north, where Catholic influence remained greatest.

The quarrel between Elizabeth and her Puritan subjects began in earnest in 1565 and centered at first on the same dispute over the use of vestments that had caused the rift between Thomas Cranmer and John Hooper. The Puritans, accepting the continental Protestant argument, contended that the use of vestments set the minister apart from his congregation and was symbolic of the Roman Catholic concept of the priesthood. Criticism of vestments had been widespread in the Convocation of 1563 (the clerical assembly that met during sessions of Parliament and was that body's ecclesiastical counterpart). In 1565 it became evident to Elizabeth that many of the clergy were not wearing the prescribed vestments and she instructed her archbishop of Canterbury, Matthew Parker (who had been a fugitive in England during Mary's reign and thus missed the liberalizing influence of exile), to enforce the regulations. The beneficed clergy of London were particularly affected by Parker's campaign, but throughout the realm many were deprived of their livings for refusing to conform.

Irked at the bishops' reluctance to make reforms—and at their obstruction on such issues as the use of vestments—the Puritan clergy tried to improve the church through Parliamentary action. A series of religious reforms were proposed in the Parliament of 1566, but they were dropped when the queen made known her displeasure at the legislature's interference with church affairs. But Parliament had declared Elizabeth to be Head of the Church, and there would always be some members who believed that Parliament consequently had authority to alter the church settlement. In 1571 another reform bill was introduced; its sponsor was imprisoned for his efforts. Still hoping for relief, two of the clerical leaders of the movement, John Field and Thomas Wilcox, published *An Admonition to Parliament* (followed shortly by a *Second Admonition to Parliament*), which appealed unsuccessfully to the Parliament of 1572.

The call for parliamentary relief caused Parker, at the behest of the queen, to launch a major suppression of nonconformity. More clergymen were deprived of their posts, and some sought refuge on the continent to avoid facing more severe penalties. But then, when hopes of relief were seemingly exhausted, Matthew Parker died in 1575 and was succeeded by Edmund Grindal. Though not quite a member of the Puritan movement, Grindal had been one of the more progressive of the Elizabethan bishops. He had accepted office from the queen with reluctance and in the hope that he could thus bring about needed changes. With his promotion to the see of Canterbury, that theory would be tested.

It soon became apparent that under Grindal's direction conformity to the standards of 1559 would be loosely enforced. More positively, attempts to root out "papists" were speeded up, and steps were taken to encourage a preaching ministry. Grindal began to initiate reforms of ecclesiastical abuses, and the English-translation Geneva Bible, printed with Calvinist annotations for household use, which Parker had in effect suppressed, was given an English printing.

Hopes for reform were also given support in the early 1570s by the growth of prophesyings. Adopted by the Puritans from continental practice, the prophesyings began as mechanisms for the continuing education of preachers. Two or more learned ministers would moderate at a regional conference, examining the remainder of the clergy on matters of faith. These soon became well attended by the laity as well, particularly in areas starved of preaching, and by the 1570s were being encouraged by a number of bishops, including Grindal, who saw in them a means of improving the quality of the clergy.

In 1576 all of these progressive tendencies of Grindal's early archbishopric were checked by Elizabeth's command that prophesyings in the province of Canterbury must cease. The gulf dividing the queen from Grindal—and the Puritans—became obvious. Elizabeth wanted a conservative church that would bolster the crown. In her view, three or four preachers were sufficient for a shire; she was content with a ministry capable of reading the Scriptures and reciting approved homilies. Grindal dissented, stressing the importance of the Word—and was suspended.

The removal of Grindal from authority marked another turning point for the Puritan movement. Hope of episcopal-directed reform was seemingly dead. As episcopal vacancies opened thereafter they were filled by men who were less sympathetic to the Puritans and more inclined to please Elizabeth by taking action against nonconformists. Foremost of these new church leaders were John Whitgift and John Aylmer. Whitgift, who had been numbered among the dissenters in his student days, had eventually cast his lot with the establishment, rather than jeopardize his career. With the eclipse of Grindal, Whitgift became in the late 1570s the most important figure in Elizabeth's church and, on Grindal's death in 1583, was elevated to Canterbury. Aylmer, who worked in close concert with Whitgift, was bishop of London and president of the High Commission—the ecclesiastical court which under Aylmer began to focus on the cases of Puritan dissenters.

The Puritan leaders who had taken comfort from the progress of reform under Grindal were stunned by his suspension. Some began to organize themselves in a new fashion and on a new theory. Bishops having proven an obstacle to reform, the idea of a church without bishops gained currency in some quarters of the movement. Presbyterianism, which had been developed out of Calvin's ideas by his Geneva successor, Theodore Beza, was first advocated in England by Thomas Cartwright, Lady Margaret Professor of Divinity at Cambridge, in 1570. His lectures on that subject cost him his position. Seeking refuge in Geneva, Cartwright had received a further exposure to Presbyterianism. Returning to England later in the decade, he joined with other dissenters who had organized themselves into self-governing classes, or conferences. The various conferences were united by the correspondence network that radiated from John Field in London. Thus a church had emerged within the church.

Not all Puritans supported the classical movement, but Archbishop Whitgift's efforts to force subscription to the Prayer Book generated further sympathy for the presbyterians. In 1584 the shadow church organized by Field and Cartwright formed the backbone of another attempt to force change through Parliament. Canvassing for sympathetic candidates, the Puritans succeeded in electing a reformist minority to the House of Commons. They also conducted a survey of the ministry in seventeen English counties, which produced an effective rebuttal to Whitgift's denial of the need to upgrade the clergy. But once more the queen thwarted the Puritans' political success. More Puritan clergy therefore joined the classical movement, which reached its peak during the period 1586–1588. At least two national synods were held in that period, the first in conjunction with yet another unsuccessful attempt to influence Parliament.

The year 1588 is remembered as a glorious one for England and for English Protestantism, and the defeat of the Armada was certainly applauded by Anglican and Puritan alike. But, for the Puritans, 1588 also inaugurated a series of setbacks that led to still another shift of direction in the movement. John Field, the organizing genius of Elizabethan Puritanism, died in March of that year. Death soon thereafter purged the Queen's Council of the officials who had blunted so many efforts to purge the church of Puritanism: the Earl of Leicester in 1588, Sir Walter Mildmay in 1589, Sir Francis Walsingham in 1590. These losses were irreparable, and never again would Puritanism have such influential friends at court. Then, while searching for the author of a series of satirical attacks on the bishops, published under the pseudonym Martin Marprelate, Whitgift's agents found evidence of the extent and strength of the classical movement. In 1590 Thomas Cartwright and about ten other Puritans were arrested and brought before the Court of High Commission. When lengthy attempts to prove a case against them failed (as it did also before the civil Court of Star Chamber), they were released in 1592 after pledging to cease their efforts to alter the church. The Elizabethan presbyterian movement was at an end.

In the remaining decade of Elizabeth's reign there were no major conflicts between the hierarchy and the Puritans. But the absence of public controversy did not mean that Puritanism was quiescent. Rather, the energies of the movement were directed elsewhere, in the elaboration of a theological stance and in ministering to the souls of Englishmen. Puritan spokesmen such as William Perkins had begun to set forth their own formulation of an essentially Calvinist viewpoint, which was different in emphasis from the intellectual orientation of orthodox Anglicanism.

Most important to the growth of Puritanism during the last decade of the century—and indeed throughout the entire history of the movement—was the increasing lay strength that the reformers gathered from their pastoral work. Initially a clerical movement of limited size, Puritanism became a major force in Elizabethan England because its spokesmen devoted themselves to the needs of the populace. Oxford and Cambridge universities sustained the movement by training preachers of Puritan leanings. Sympathetic to the work of Field, Cartwright, and the other organizers of dissent, most of these university-trained Puritans were not radicals themselves but preaching "physicians of the soul," absorbed in their pastoral life and responsibilities. Some served as pastors under lay patronage and were immune to the crises of the reign. Others achieved a degree of freedom as lecturers, hired to preach the word in parishes with an inadequate beneficed pastor, to supplement the preaching available in a particular community, or to counteract the preaching of orthodox clergymen. Protected by local authorities in many cases, these preaching clergy proved impervious to all but the most determined efforts to silence them. Although less concerned with matters of government than their more prominent brethren in the movement, their impact on the church was perhaps greater.

Puritan theologians and pastors made important inroads among Englishmen in the closing years of Elizabeth's reign. At the same time, their challenge was ably taken up by Richard Hooker, whose *The Laws of Ecclesiastical Polity* provided the supporters of Anglican orthodoxy with a lengthy, scholarly, and persuasive defense of the established church order. Whereas the Puritans were following Calvin in emphasizing man's depravity and the necessity of carefully following the path laid out by God, Hooker argued that reason was a gift of God, the creative use of which was as important a source of guidance as revelation. In thus arguing that "the light of natural understanding, wit, and reason, is from God" he set forth a more rationalistic view of man and argued for a larger scope for human choice than the Puritans were willing to accept. In Hooker's works, most church ceremonies were described as matters where God allowed man to choose whatever form he willed, in contrast to the dissenters' argument that the order of worship was dictated by God in the Scriptures.

The Anglican theologian's works proved attractive to those for whom Puritanism seemed to deny human creativity. Hooker's views allowed for a steady expansion of Anglican liturgical ceremonies and a return to church ornamentation. Under the Stuarts they also provided a foundation for the elaboration of an Arminian emphasis on man's spiritual abilities by such churchmen as Richard Neile and William Laud.

THE STUART MONARCHS: JAMES I AND CHARLES I

The death of Elizabeth in 1603 brought James VI of Scotland to the throne as James I of England. Having been raised and ruled in Presbyterian Scotland, it seemed likely that James would be responsive to the demands of the English Puritans. Certainly the prospect of an attentive ear was behind the circulation by the Puritans of the Millenary Petition (named for its presumed one thousand signers) asking the king for reform of the church.

Responding to the Puritans' plea, James agreed to hear their spokesmen in a conference at Hampton Court. There, as historian Mark Curtis has demonstrated, the king did express some sympathy for the Puritan case. He agreed on the need to end nonresidency in the clergy, to upgrade the quality of the ministry, and to make changes in the catechism and in the Book of Common Prayer. Thus, while he resisted suggestions for alterations in the governance of the church, he did yield to the Puritans in other areas.

But implementation of these concessions was in the hands of the bishops, and James's fear of Puritanism's political implications led him to keep anti-Puritans in the episcopal sees. When Whitgift died in 1604 he was replaced by Richard Bancroft, even more of an enemy of the nonconformists than his predecessor. In hands such as these, and with an indolent monarch like James, the decisions of Hampton Court were largely ignored. Instead of relief, the Puritans received further persecution. Whereas Whitgift and Aylmer had first demonstrated the repressive potential of the High Commission, Bancroft turned it into an instrument of true coercion. William Ames, candidate for master of Christ College, who was forced to go into exile in the Netherlands for refusal to wear vestments and to use the cross in baptism, was only one of many whom Bancroft made to pay for their nonconformist views.

While James may have been responsive to some parts of the Puritan program, his bishops were dedicated to thorough suppression of the movement. The irony of the situation in the Anglican church became apparent in 1618. Representatives of the Church of England were dispatched that year to the assembly of Calvinist theologians at Dort, ordered by the king to join with the orthodox majority in opposition to the challenge of the followers of Jacob Arminius, who had sought to temper the rigidity of predestination. But in the first two decades of the seventeenth century there had already appeared in the Anglican hierarchy a group of prominent leaders who themselves represented a viewpoint that called for a combination of a somewhat Arminian view of man's ability with an increased emphasis on the efficacy of the sacraments. These men, led by Bishop Richard Neile and his protégé William Laud, also stressed greater emphasis on the authority of the king, believed that the office of bishop was of divine institution, and wished to restore what they saw as "the beauty of holiness" in church worship. While James was not sympathetic to many of these ideas until the closing years of his reign, his son and successor, Charles, was a firm convert to such High Church views. This Laudian program tended to mark the Anglican church as more distinct than ever before from the Reformed churches of the continent, with which the Puritans had always sought accord.

The rise of the Arminian "High Church" faction to leadership in the church, delayed only slightly by the tenure of William Abbot as Bancroft's successor, was inevitable with Charles's support of William Laud. The theological differences between orthodox and Puritan members of the church, which had previously been implicit (and even nonexistent in some cases), became ever more visible in the 1620s, as the essentially Calvinist orientation of the church was reversed. Under Charles I, predestinarian teaching was forbidden at Cambridge in 1626 and at Oxford two years later. In 1628, William Laud was appointed bishop of London and five years later, archbishop of Canterbury. In the eyes of many, the Church of England seemed to be drifting back in the direction of Rome.

Concurrent with this trend, another binding tie in English religious life was dissolving. Under Elizabeth, English foreign policy was militantly anti-Catholic—and no matter how she disappointed their hopes for religious reform, Puritans regarded their queen as the "Protestant Deborah," leading England to her rightful place as the champion of international Protestantism. But under James I and Charles I the government showed a new willingness to treat with Catholic powers. Negotiations were begun by James to marry his heir to a Spanish princess, and Charles's eventual marriage to a French princess shocked his subjects. More significantly, James and then Charles refused to aid the Protestant cause in the Thirty Years War, which broke out in Germany in 1618 and in which the religious future of Europe was popularly believed to be at stake.

As the 1620s came to a close the English church was displaying a far different profile from that it had worn during the reign of Elizabeth. But if the establishment was different, so too was Puritanism, which had grown into a movement increasingly widespread and more clearly alienated from the nation's civil and ecclesiastical leadership.

2 | PURITANISM, ITS ESSENCE AND ATTRACTION

During the three-quarters of a century from the reign of Edward VI to the early 1620s, the critical voice of Puritanism had steadily developed, largely in an escalating response to the intractability of the establishment and to alterations in the official stance of the church. By 1630 reconciliation of Puritan and orthodox Anglican viewpoints was probably impossible. But to concentrate upon what the Puritans opposed would be to do them an injustice and would make it impossible to discover the source of their appeal to the English laity. Puritanism was more than a mere reaction to Anglican worship and ceremonies. It was also a theological system in its own right, with considerable attraction for sixteenth- and seventeenth-century Englishmen and Americans.

Describing what the Puritans believed is a difficult task made even more arduous because Puritans regarded themselves as Anglicans. As members of the Church of England, which they were trying to change, and unable to enforce their own orthodoxy on members of their movement, the Puritans developed an ideology with discernible central thrusts but with nuances that often differed from individual to individual. Thus, when the opportunity finally presented itself for Puritanism to become institutionalized—in New England in the 1630s and in Old England in the 1640s—the movement's diversity gave rise to bitter debates over matters of faith and polity.

To say that the Puritans were Calvinists is to begin to place them on the theological spectrum. But having made that claim one must take care to qualify it. While Calvin was the single most important theological influence on English Reformation thought (the *Short-Title Catalogue* of books printed in England reveals that between 1548 and 1660 more of Calvin's works were published than of any other author), he was by no means the only one. Puritans, like Anglicans, drew on the writings of the fathers of the Catholic church, including Augustine and Aquinas, and on the leading spokesmen of the Reformation. Luther's ideas were studied, and some were appropriated. Almost as influential as Calvin were the other theologians of the Reformed tradition with which Calvin was associated.

The Puritans read all Christian authors, but they used their works as aids in understanding the Scriptures. The Bible was, for the Puritans, the only divinely inspired Word of God. In the pages of the Scriptures were to be found the standards of doctrine and the true way of worship specified by God for the use of his saints. The Old and New Testaments were thus the source of standards of behavior, belief, and worship. The writings of later Christians were important—as was one's own experience—in that they enabled men to uncover and expound the meaning of God's revelation. Believing that they were illuminating the meaning of the Scriptures, the Puritans shaped a message that spoke to the needs of their followers and their times, a message designed to explain the nature of God and man and the relation between them.

PURITAN THEOLOGY: GOD AND MAN

Puritan speculation about God began with the assumption that man could not actually understand the deity. The very nature of infinite being was such as to be beyond the comprehension of finite minds. The essence of God is hidden, all that we can attain is a knowledge of those aspects of his being which he has voluntarily revealed in his dealings with men. From this revelation of his power, man can draw certain conclusions about God, but the Puritan minister followed in the footsteps of Augustine, Calvin, and others in warning his congregation against confusing human images of God with the true nature of the deity.

Having made this disclaimer, the Puritan theologians went on to describe God's actual conduct in his transactions with man. They were most impressed with the divine sovereignty. He had created and he maintained the universe by exercise of his will. He directed all things to an intelligible end (though his providential design might not always be intelligible to man's corrupted intellect). As William Perkins expressed it, "God must first will a thing before it can be just. The will of God doth not depend upon the quality and nature of a thing, but the qualities of things in order of causes follow the will of God. For everything is as God wills it." Nothing in the creation had power to influence the will of the creator, nor could God in any sense be bound by the natural order he had created.

But if God's sovereignty was his most impressive attribute, the Puritans spoke frequently of his benevolence. In one sense, of course, they recognized that the attribution of benevolence to God was meaningless, since the deity was the source of all goodness and everything he did was by definition good. The Puritans, however, meant more than this. They understood God to be benevolent because of all he had done for man—despite man's total unworthiness.

Man was part of God's creation and was made in the image of God. The relationship between God and the first man, Adam, was described as a covenantal bond. In the words of the Puritan Westminster Confession, "life was promised to Adam, and in him to his posterity, upon condition of perfect and personal obedience." But "our first parents" violated this covenant and "fell from their original righteousness and communion with God, and so became dead in sin, and wholly defiled in all the faculties and parts of soul and body." The effects of this original sin were borne not only by Adam and Eve but by all men thereafter. The Puritans differed on how generations after Adam came to bear the guilt of original sin—some adopted the Augustinian theory that it was a product of inheritance, while others saw Adam as the representative man in whose guilt and punishment all men shared. But they were agreed in their assessment of the effects of original sin. Physically: suffering, illness, and death became part of the human condition. Spiritually: all of man's faculties were disoriented and his soul corrupted. After being a God-centered creature, man became self-centered. The human will lost its inclination toward good. Incapable now of recognizing his need for a proper relationship to God, man instead sought gratification of his senses. Physical pleasures would not satisfy man, but he could not realize this nor break his thralldom to Satan. Only God's intervention could restore man's proper relation to the deity and to nature.

The Puritans believed that even when man's conduct was judged to be good by his neighbors it might be wrongly motivated—by self-interest, for example, rather than by a desire to please God—and was consequently evil. Thus, man after the Fall is by nature sinful, and for sinning against the just God man is deserving of eternal damnation. *All men deserve damnation*—this was a central belief of the Puritan, confirmed by his observation of his fellows and by his awareness of the darker impulses of his own nature. But God in his benevolence chose to save some men in spite of their unworthiness.

His choice was arbitrary, but it was also unnecessary. Such was the gulf that divided the almighty God from depraved man that nothing in man's nature or in his conduct required God to reprieve any man from the sentence merited by his sins.

But God in his goodness absolved some men and women from their guilt. How many was debatable—perhaps only a very few, though in a godly community it might be a sizable majority. "Because," according to Ames, "God determined this order by himself before any actual existence of things, it is called not simply destination but predestination." This doctrine appalls most modern sensibilities. For the Puritans, however, it was comforting evidence of God's love. Whereas most moderns assert the essential worth of man, the Puritan was scripturally and experientially convinced that he and his fellow men were fundamentally depraved and deserving of damnation. That God went beyond the dictates of strict justice to elect some men to be saved was a source of hope and a basis for thanks.

PURITAN THEOLOGY:
THE COVENANTS OF SALVATION

At the time that God created Adam, man's salvation depended on his own actions. God pledged eternal happiness to Adam and his posterity in return for man's absolute obedience to the will of God. The Puritans labeled this commitment the Covenant of Works. In the Fall, man broke the covenant and lost his opportunity to merit salvation. The consequences of his sin could only be reversed by divine action. God provided that release in what the Puritans referred to as the Covenant of Redemption: the agreement whereby the Father compacted with the Son to provide the salvation of some men and women through Christ's sacrifice. This sacrificial atonement for the sins of mankind made possible individual redemption through the Covenant of Grace, whereby the elect might receive saving grace through the aegis of the Spirit in return for their faith. (One aspect of Puritan theology that was not particularly well developed was their Christology. Having pointed to Christ's atonement as the condition that made the Covenant of Grace possible, they devoted most of their attention to the Spirit through whom saving grace was conveyed.)

The Puritans' extensive employment of covenant terminology led Perry Miller to christen their system "Federal Theology" (*foedus*: covenant) and to characterize that emphasis as one of the distinguishing marks of their thought. Certainly the Puritans were exceptional even in the Reformed tradition in their extensive utilization of contractual imagery. Not only their theology carried this hallmark. Their ecclesiology and social thought bore it as well; references to church covenants, social covenants, and national covenants abounded in their writings. But this should not obscure the fact that covenantal thought was not unique to the Puritans. They themselves looked to scriptural precedent—God's covenant with Abraham having an especially important place in their thought—and were influenced as well by the thought of other Reformed theologians. Covenant thought was present in Calvin's writings, but probably as influential in shaping Puritan views on the subject were the teachings of Zwingli and Bullinger. Similar ideas were elaborated by English and such Scottish theologians as William Tyndale, John Hooper, Robert Rollock, and John Knox decades before they were incorporated in the Puritan system by Cartwright, Perkins, Preston, and Ames.

The Puritan emphasis on the covenant arose out of the concern of ministers to explain the process of salvation to their congregations. The clergy gave special attention to the Covenant of Grace, since it described the process whereby salvation was effected. Through it God offered salvation to the elect, calling it return for true faith. But that faith involved more than mere intellectual consent to doctrine. It involved a total change in the believer's nature and behavior; it involved preparation for God's call and a commitment to lead a new life in the service of God.

PURITAN THEOLOGY:
PREPARATION AND CONVERSION

The Covenant of Grace explained how God provided for the salvation of the elect. But in their capacity as physicians of the soul the Puritan clergy were equally concerned with the way in which the divine decrees were effected in the lives of individual men and women. This resulted in a considerable literature dealing with the morphology of the conversion experience.

"I knew no more of that Work of Conversion," wrote Thomas Goodwin, "than these two general Heads, That a Man was troubled in Conscience for his Sins, and afterwards was comforted by the Favour of God manifested to him." Goodwin's description identifies the two essential elements of the process of salvation as man's conviction of sin and his experience of forgiveness. Most of the clergy in the Puritan brotherhood elaborated on this model, many of them describing five stages in man's progress toward God: election, vocation, justification, sanctification, and glorification. The first stage, election, referred to God's choice of those predestined for salvation, an action in which the individual was totally passive. The next stage, vocation, saw both the Spirit's offer to man of the grace that enables him to seek contrition and faith and also man's cooperation with the Spirit in turning towards God. This process culminated in the moment of justification, in which the choice of election was made effectual and the soul of man was redeemed. Sanctification was the term for the state in which the new saint lived after his justification. One of the elect would presumably reflect his new state by his actions. He would strive harder to abide by the standards of perfection, would show true repentance for his failings, and would lead a morally improved life. Still, he would have doubts as to the validity of his conversion, fearing lest it be a deceit of the devil to lead him into a sense of false assurance. Glorification, the last step in the process of salvation, was the removal of all such uncertainties regarding one's election. When this state of assurance would be reached was a matter of some dispute. William Ames and a few other clergymen believed that in some respects glorification could be attained in one's lifetime, but most of the ministers cautioned that doubt would cease only in the afterlife.

The extent to which men were able to discern their passage through these stages and the extent to which they were capable of cooperating with the Spirit in the process were other matters of dispute among the Puritans. Some believed that conversion involved a violent and memorable seizure of the soul by God's grace—something akin to St. Paul's experience on the road to Damascus; others argued that Christian nurture could bring a soul to sanctification without leaving an awareness of the actual moment of justification. As for man's role in his rapprochement with God, most clergy urged upon their congregations the need to prepare for justification. Others challenged that position as being a concession to the Arminian heresy of according man some responsibility for his salvation. In England these differences did not cause serious dissension until the 1640s because they were overshadowed by the greater differences separating Puritanism from the views of the hierarchy. In New England they became the sources of dissension from the first years of settlement.

Most Puritans believed that the Spirit worked through natural means and that man was called to attendance upon those means through which grace was conveyed. Foremost of these was the sermon, in which, according to Richard Baxter, it was the task of the preacher "to speak to Sinners with some Compassion, as a dying Man to dying

Men." Effectual sermons could waken men to their spiritual state, stirring the elect to review their consciences while conveying the grace that enabled them to do so. Regular readings of the Scriptures could likewise serve as spiritual stimuli and means of grace, as could prayer and regular examinations of one's spiritual state. Self-examination, if recorded in a diary, could in turn assist others to discover grace. If a man pursued such means diligently, and if they were in fact used by God to convey grace to that individual, he would eventually be brought to a realization of his evil ways (conviction of sin, in Thomas Shepard's schema) and to a spirit of repentance for them (compunction for sin). This state of contrition would be followed by one of humiliation, in which the individual would acknowledge his inability to reform without the aid of God. At that point the Spirit would have brought him to the moment of justification. These same means of grace, which served to prepare man for his conversion, would also serve—along with the sacrament of the Lord's Supper—to sustain the saint's faith after his justification.

PURITANISM AND THE MORAL LIFE

The theological content of his faith was important to the Puritan, but not as an end in itself which could alter his fate. True faith involved a delicate balance between reason and emotion. Knowledge was important in that it gave direction to piety—knowledge without emotional faith had no value. As Paul Baynes warned William Ames, "Beware of a strong head and a cold heart." Faith, as previously noted, was more than intellectual consent to dogma; it involved the believer in a commitment to act in the service of God. The sanctified man was a soldier of the Lord displaying, in the words of Richard Sibbes, "a holy violence in the performing of all duties."

William Ames's *Marrow of Theology*, one of the great works of Puritan systematic theology, opens with the admonition that "Theology is the doctrine or teaching of living to God," and his contemporaries more frequently commented on the Puritans' approach to the moral life than on the dissenters' doctrines. The Puritan had felt the work of God in his soul, and, despite his concern to rationally describe his conversion, it was the experience itself that set him apart from the nonelect. Many Puritans wished to deny participation in the Lord's Supper to those who lacked conversion. Without such a conversion one could not be a valid minister.

Those who had been justified looked upon that experience as a rebirth and felt called upon to demonstrate in their new lives a reformed character marked by sober, obedient godliness. They performed diligently in all of their secular roles, just as they were conscientious in the performance of their religious duties. They rejected the excesses in which so many of their fellow men indulged and imposed a rigid discipline upon themselves and their families. This did not mean that they were killjoys or prudish or in any other sense unwilling to use the fruits that God had placed in the world for them. They dressed as befitted their social class, they participated in lotteries, they drank alcoholic beverages, and they approached sex as more than a mere obligation. What is often dismissed today as "puritanical" is more appropriately attributable to the Victorians. This is not, however, to say that the Puritans were libertines, for they certainly were not. While they participated in the life of the world, they insisted upon moderation in all pursuits. As Richard Baxter put it, *"Overdoing* is the ordinary way of *Undoing."*

THE APPEAL OF PURITANISM

Puritanism in its unsteady but inexorable growth had to surmount formidable barriers. The Anglican establishment that the Puritans set out to change had the full backing of the state. Despite the presence of sympathetic individuals in the bureaucracies of civil and ecclesiastical government, the key positions in both of those spheres were generally in the hands of those who sought to destroy the movement. Elizabeth and her bishops, and James and his, had at their disposal the full machinery of church and state. They controlled the universities and censored the press. Aesthetically, the richness of Anglican church ornamentation, ecclesiastical music, and the liturgy attracted many to the state church. For the upper classes, support of the established church seemed part of their support of the social order from which they benefited. And in the reign of Elizabeth, the Church of England had the added benefit of being associated in the public mind with one of the most popular rulers in England's history. Yet there were needs that Puritanism spoke to more effectively than did Anglican orthodoxy. Because of its appropriateness to its age, Puritanism persevered despite all efforts to root it out.

Not the least of the advantages held by the Puritans was the unpopularity of the church itself. The dissenters' call for reforms struck a responsive chord in the hearts of many Englishmen, and the failure of the church to purify itself swung numerous men of piety into the ranks of the Puritan faction. One of the key abuses at which critics railed was the poor quality of the clergy. While the description of one such incumbent in Warwickshire—"an old priest and unsound in religion, he can neither preach nor read well, his chiefest trade is to cure hawks that are hurt or diseased"—was not typical, there is no doubt that the ministry was in sad need of repair in Tudor and Stuart England. The financial rewards were meagre and unlikely to attract worthwhile candidates; those who had talent frequently neglected their flocks as a result of having to take plural livings to sustain themselves. Educational preparation left much to be desired. Even the spiritual commitment of many ministers was suspect because of their willingness to accept all shifts of belief as they occurred, from Henry VIII to Elizabeth. The situation became worse in the seventeenth century because the rapidly rising educational level of the laity made clerical inadequacies even more obvious. In contrast to the typical beneficed clergyman, the Puritan minister must indeed have seemed literate, pious, and sensitive to the needs of believers.

The contrast between the Anglican "dumb-dog" pastors and the dissenting clergy was most obvious in the preaching of the Word. The sermon was an extraordinarily important institution in Elizabethan and Jacobean times. In lieu of newspapers, the pulpit served as the principal communicator of news. Sermons were a major means of adult continuing education, and they replaced the confessional as a tool of moral and socioeconomic guidance. And in an age with few opportunities for public entertainment, powerful preachers brought excitement to the illiterate masses. Over a thousand gathered regularly for the weekly St. Paul's Cross sermon in London, and of course the supplementing of sabbath sermons with weekly lectures was a response to the desires of the laity. Given the scope of this need, the Anglican record in meeting it was dismal. Elizabeth was suspicious of a preaching clergy, did nothing to improve the ability of her ministers, opposed the prophesyings, and sought the replacement of clerical sermons with Scripture reading and approved homilies. In 1622, James I ordered that exposition of the catechism replace Sunday afternoon sermons, and Charles I halted even these expositions.

While the authorities denied the need of preaching, the Puritans sought to meet it. In contrast to both the readings of the lesser clergy and the overly ornate, abstract, frequently dry sermons of the episcopal elite, the Puritan spiritual brotherhood cultivated a "plain style" of preaching in which they successfully applied the lessons of the Scriptures to the lives of individuals in a logical, direct form of presentation couched in a language appropriate to their audiences.

The religious persuasion of Englishmen from the pulpit was theirs virtually by default.

What particularly galled many Englishmen was the unwillingness of the church to remedy its clerical inadequacies while the princes of the church lived in a style resembling secular royalty. Puritan merchants and artisans raised money among themselves to supplement the incomes of pious preachers. But while the poverty of most pastors was a scandal in the church, Archbishop Whitgift was attended by about 1,000 servants, almost half of them gentlemen adorned in gold. Not only did such displays belie the hierarchy's claims of inability to relieve the financial plight of the lesser clergy, but the extravagances of the bishops' palaces formed an unfavorable contrast to the modest life style of the Puritan.

Still another abuse that detracted from the popularity of the church was the mismanagement of the ecclesiastical courts. The prosecution of godly preachers before the Court of High Commission gave the Puritans the aura of martyrs and aroused the anger of those congregations consequently deprived of their minister. But probably the greatest annoyance resulted from the numerous prosecutions of laymen for insignificant offences while more serious problems went untended. In the four and a half decades prior to 1625 there were an average of about three hundred prosecutions yearly in the court of the archdeacon of St. Albans, whose jurisdiction included approximately seven thousand communicants. Such petty aggravations often did more to change religious allegiance than did shifts in national policy.

Much more difficult to assess precisely in estimating Puritanism's appeal is the assurance it offered Englishmen in a time of tremendous instability and flux. The centuries that saw the rise and growth of Puritanism also saw the transformation of England from a feudal to a modern society, a fundamental change that implied innumerable smaller ones in the lives of individual Englishmen. The confiscation of the monasteries and other church properties by Henry VIII was one precipitant of change, initiating eight decades of unprecedented activity in the land market, with some families experiencing a meteoric rise of prosperity while many established families were all but destroyed. At the same time, in the years from 1520 to 1640, the population of the realm doubled. The landed class of England trebled in size. The middle class in town and country was gaining new importance—a sign of the changing economy and also one of the factors behind the burgeoning number of university graduates. In the countryside, village life lost much of its stability in these years, as thousands of Englishmen became rootless and mobile.

In this situation, Puritanism provided psychological certitude, which helped many to cope with and adapt to the changing circumstances of socioeconomic life. Anglicanism was incapable of doing so. From the time when the first Elizabethan bishops compromised their beliefs to accept church offices until the rise of the Arminian party of Neile and Laud, Anglicanism seemed to many to be a faith without a character, a compromise church based on the principle that the shape of most ecclesiastical matters was a matter of indifference. Puritanism, in contrast, generated in its members a sense of conviction. Not only was the Puritan convinced of the scriptural validity of his doctrinal system, but he had experienced the work of the Spirit in his heart and was sure of what God wanted of him. His faith offered a means by which he could explain the baffling changes that surrounded him. His self-discipline, generated by the dictates of faith, equipped him well to take advantage of the fluidity of the times. It justified his pursuits by relating them to a divine scheme. The certainty possessed by the Puritan intelligentsia must have been one of the most impressive aspects of their demeanor and undoubtedly attracted many of the confused and uncertain to their orbit. Ironically, in doing so, Puritanism made easier the transition to the modern world, the fear of which produced the uncertainty that was feeding the movement.

Other conditions of the time also fostered the growth and spread of Puritanism. For some Englishmen, such as the sailors of the West Country who fought under Drake and Hawkins against the Spanish, the most attractive facet of Puritanism was its militant anti-Catholicism. For others who were morally offended by the growing licentiousness of the court, the ethical standards of the dissenters were most appealing. And in locales where the dominant episcopal figure or local lord (or both) was a Puritan, the deferential nature of English society became an asset, rather than a liability.

By the 1620s these various elements had interacted to create a broad-based Puritan following. Geographically, the movement was strongest in London, East Anglia, Lincolnshire, the West Riding, the Midlands, and the Southwest. While its representatives could be found everywhere, those who showed the greatest tendency to accept Puritan teaching were of the middle class. This included owners of small firms, self-employed merchants, and artisans, such as clothworkers and shoemakers. Lawyers increasingly displayed a sympathy for Puritanism, partly because of the preachings of Richard Sibbes and other Puritans at the Inns of Court and partly because seventeenth-century political alliances pitted Puritans and lawyers together against the crown. As one might expect, Puritanism had greater appeal for the educated than for their less fortunate neighbors. And, while the upper classes were relatively less likely to ally themselves with the movement than was the middle class, the support of some influential peers—the Earl of Essex is a prime example—was politically and financially of the greatest importance.

3 | SOURCES OF THE GREAT MIGRATION

The strength that the Puritan movement had developed in the decades since the return of the Marian exiles rendered dangerous any attempts to disregard it or suppress it. That James I had tried the former, and his successor, Charles I, the latter, had to lead to major crises. Their policies toward the Puritans in fact produced two events of major significance—the Great Migration of the 1630s and the Puritan Revolution of the 1640s, the first leading to the creation of a New England on the shores of America, the second to a new England in the Old World.

PRELUDE TO THE GREAT MIGRATION

Historians seeking to trace the origins of the Great Migration begin with the failure of the Dorchester Company of Adventurers, a group of West Country investors who had sought to profit from the development of the coastal fisheries of North America. Formed in 1623, the Dorchester Company was a nonincorporated organization operating on a patent from the Council for New England, which had been created by royal charter in 1620. The council's leaders included Sir Ferdinando Gorges, Sir Francis Popham, and other members of the defunct Plymouth Company, sister group to the London Company that had initiated the settlement of Virginia. The council made little effort to settle its territories, preferring to subgrant to other groups such as the Dorchester Company.

Inspired by the Reverend John White, "the patriarch of Dorchester" and an active member of the Puritan brotherhood, the Dorchester investors hoped to establish settlements along the New England coast that would serve as permanent bases for supply of food and additional manpower for the company's fishing vessels. Most of the adventurers were Puritans, and they hoped that their outposts would contribute to the conversion of the Indians. But the central motivation of their enterprise was economic. Judged by that criterion it was a failure.

The company's first ships sailed for America in 1623. The land best suited for fishing stations was not conducive to agriculture, settlers did not appear in sufficient numbers, and the company's vessels were ill-managed. In 1625 a last effort was made to test the practicality of the venture. The company raised £1,000 and dispatched three ships, but this attempt also went awry. John White instructed Roger Conant to take charge of the remaining settlers and to hold them together pending White's efforts to revive the settlements.

The Dorchester Company collapsed in 1626. White and the company's treasurer, John Humphrey (son-in-law of the Earl of Lincoln), had begun to seek support from other figures in the Puritan movement. White in particular had come to look upon the struggling outposts as a potential refuge for Puritans from the growing oppression of the Anglican regime. It was this notion, together with more traditional hopes for profit, that began to attract members of the London Puritan community such as Matthew Craddock and Theophilus Eaton. In America, Robert Conant had moved his small party of settlers from their original outpost on Cape Ann to Naumkeag, a location further south along the coast.

John White's activities bore fruit in 1628 when the Council for New England granted to the New England Company the land from 3 miles north of the Merrimac River to 3 miles south of the Charles River and from sea to sea. This new group was a joint-stock company with capital of £3,000. Six of its members, including John Humphrey, were original patentees of the Dorchester Company, but with the new group the balance of power had shifted from the West Country to London.

Acting quickly, the new company in the same year dispatched the *Abigail* carrying forty colonists to reinforce Conant's band. Among the passengers setting forth from Weymouth was John Endecott of Devon, one of the leaders of the New England Company, who was to assume the governance of the Naumkeag settlement. The transfer from the Dorchester Company to the New England Company and from Conant's leadership to Endecott's was accomplished smoothly. Perhaps that is what prompted Endecott to rechristen the community Salem, after the Hebrew word for "peaceful"—an ironic choice, considering the community's later history.

Though the New England Company had been organized and

launched on its task, John White still sought further financial backing for the venture. His efforts were made more difficult by questions concerning the validity of the new company's grant. Primarily from ignorance of New World geography, some of the company's lands had also been granted by the Council for New England to other individuals. The resulting confusion was a cloud on the company's horizon and a discouragement to some potential supporters. Deciding not to seek a resolution of the difficulty from the council itself, the leaders of the New England Company sought a charter of incorporation from the king that would supersede the patent from the council and confirm the company's territorial and governmental rights.

Guided through the bureaucratic machinery by influential Puritans, the charter for the new Massachusetts Bay Company was issued under the royal seal on 4 March 1629. Later that month the company was formally organized under its new patent. Matthew Craddock was chosen governor of the company and Thomas Goffe lieutenant-governor. These two, with the organization's secretary and treasurer and eleven elected assistants, comprised the leadership of the company. The larger group, of all investors, met periodically. Effectively, Craddock was chairman of this new corporation's board of directors (the assistants), which governed the company's affairs subject to the meetings (General Court) of the stockholders (freemen). This English corporation had as its main goal the establishment and support of a New World colony. It gave John Endecott the title to go with his position, naming him governor of the colony and entrusting him with carrying out the decisions reached by the London-based organization. At the same time it dispatched more colonists to augment the population of Salem.

The dissolution of Parliament by King Charles in 1629 had added to the gravity of the Puritans' situation, eliminating hopes for parliamentary redress of their ecclesiastical and political grievances against the crown. The difficulties of their English situation, coupled with Endecott's favorable reports from Salem, stimulated growing interest among members of the Bay Company in viewing Massachusetts as a Puritan haven. As the company's membership expanded in 1629, the initiative in exploring this possibility centered on some of the new freemen from East Anglia, chief among them John Winthrop of Groton. In July of 1629, Winthrop and his brother-in-law Emmanuel Downing discussed migration with Isaac Johnson and Johnson's father-in-law, the Earl of Lincoln, and later they shared their conclusions with White, Humphrey, Craddock, and Sir Richard Saltonstall. Governor Craddock proposed facilitating emigration by transferring responsibility for governing the colony (not the company) to those who would be resident in Massachusetts. On 26 August 1629 twelve members of the company, including Winthrop, Humphrey, Saltonstall, and Thomas Dudley signed the so-called Cambridge Agreement, whereby they pledged themselves to emigrate to New England by the following year provided that the General Court approved transfer of the *company's* government and the charter itself to the colony. Three days later, in a session held at Goffe's home, the transfer was approved.

When Craddock had suggested transferring the government to the colony his expectation was that the company's government—and control of the business aspects of the venture—would remain in London. The Cambridge Agreement signified the determination of men in the process of deciding to emigrate to safeguard themselves as much as possible. If Massachusetts was to become a Puritan state it was imperative that the colony's future and that of the individuals settling there be safeguarded against any later change in the faction controlling the company. The decision to move the charter was a pragmatic one taken after the signatories' decision to migrate.

CAUSES OF THE GREAT MIGRATION

Why did John Winthrop and those who planned to follow him decide to leave their ancestral homes, separate themselves from relatives and friends, forsake—in many cases—the occupations for which they had laboriously prepared, and take up new homes and new vocations in the American wilderness? As with any decision reached by men and women, various influences worked on each individual; to attempt to identify a single cause—as some historians have attempted —is foolhardy. Yet it is possible to identify some of the attitudes and circumstances that were weighed by seventeenth-century Puritans as they considered whether to migrate to America.

Those who recorded their reasons for emigrating almost invariably mentioned their apprehension of England's future and their place in God's providential design. Most Englishmen of the seventeenth century accepted without question that their country was an "elect nation," chosen by God to play a great role in human destiny. The Puritans, however, were firmer adherents of this notion than most; it colored their view of domestic events and foreign affairs and was influential in determining Puritan views of the possibilities offered by New World settlement.

The Puritan view of England's mission rested heavily upon an interpretation found, among other places, in John Foxe's *Book of Martyrs.* In that catalogue of sufferings, Foxe had argued from his reading of the Book of Revelation that there were five distinct periods of church history. The first four had passed: that in which the church in all its purity was persecuted by heathen emperors; that in which the church was supported by the post-Constantine Roman state; that reaching from A.D. 600 to the Norman Conquest, during which time the church was retarded by the influence of the Roman primates; and the reign of Antichrist, inaugurated by the accession of Hildebrand to the papacy. The fifth period, initiated by the Reformation, was that in which Puritan Englishmen lived. It was a time when the forces of Christ and the forces of Antichrist did battle; the ultimate outcome would be the final triumph of the true reformed church. Foxe and those who shared such views believed that England's role was central. Referring to the preachings of the fifteenth-century English reformer John Wycliffe, William Bradford of Plymouth later claimed that "England was the first nation to which the Lord gave the light of the gospel after the darkness of popery." It was England's task to redeem Christendom, to restore the medieval unity of Europe by bringing all men under the Reformed Protestant banner. The Puritans tended in this fashion to be what would now be called postmillennialists: They believed in their God-aided sufficiency to usher in the millennium—the thousand-year rule of the saints foretold in Revelation.

Millenarian speculation of this sort was not limited to Puritans in Elizabethan and Stuart England, but it was certainly more prevalent in their ranks. The interpretation of history outlined above, and subscribed to in one variety or another by most Puritans, saw the basic division in the world as that between the forces of Christ and the forces of Antichrist. England's importance came from her election by God, and God's purposes were far more important than the secular government's economic or political concerns. In that the Puritan view of history tended to define national interests in terms of international reform, it was increasingly incompatible with the developing nationalism of the Anglican establishment, for it led to an indictment of the government for failure to advance reform at home and failure to champion Protestantism abroad.

This belief in their nation's mission increasingly alienated English Puritans from the government in the first decades of the seventeenth century. For while Elizabeth had stoutly resisted the influence of "Antichristian" Spain, James I and Charles I seemed ready to assist her attempts to restore popery throughout Europe. Such collaboration was suspected, for example, in the negotiations James carried on for a marriage of his son to a Spanish princess. Puritans greeted the failure of that match with relief, but the marriage of Charles to a French Catholic princess was almost as distressing.

Most damning in the view of the Puritans were James's policies toward the Netherlands and the German Palatinate. European Protestants viewed the sixteenth-century revolt of the Netherlands against Spanish rule as one of the great blows struck against Antichrist. Englishmen, particularly the Puritans, took great pride in the aid Elizabeth had extended to the Dutch. But the independence of the Netherlands was not assured. Fighting had ceased with the signing of a twelve-year truce in 1609, but Spain was fully intent upon recovering her former possession. As the renewal of hostilities drew closer, James I seemed increasingly reluctant to aid the Dutch. While the Puritans viewed the Calvinist Netherlands as a special sanctuary of the Lord, James was more impressed, and disturbed, by the growing commercial threat that an independent Dutch state posed to England's economic interests.

Even more decisive in alienating the Puritans from the crown was James's attitude toward English involvement in the Thirty Years War. What began in 1618 as a struggle between the Calvinist Elector of the Palatine and the Austrian Hapsburg Emperor Ferdinand over the throne of Bohemia gradually assumed the nature of a conflict to determine the religious future of the entire Germanic Holy Roman Empire. Dedicated Protestants and Catholics throughout Europe believed that the outcome of the struggle would go far toward deciding the final outcome of the continental religious struggle begun by Luther in 1517. In England the Puritans were well aware of the religious significance of the conflict, particularly as it broadened to involve the invasion of the Netherlands by the Spanish Hapsburgs. The situation demanded English action, particularly since the Elector of the Palatine was the husband of James's only daughter, Elizabeth. Here, in the eyes of the Puritans, was Armageddon, and England would be judged by the role she chose to play. Yet, as the imperial forces overran the Protestant states of Germany and defeated the Protestant armies of King Christian of Denmark, James I—and later Charles I—refused to aid the Protestant cause.

The Puritans forcefully protested the inaction of the government. John Preston criticized its foreign policy in sermons to Parliament in 1625 and at the royal court itself in 1627. Richard Sibbes, John Davenport, and many others delivered similar sermons to their congregations. Sibbes, Davenport, Hugh Peter, and others raised funds to support the German Protestants. Peter was one of a number of ministers who served as chaplains to English volunteers fighting on the continent.

Adding to the Puritan dismay was the influence on English policy of the Spanish ambassador. It was rumored that the execution of Sir Walter Raleigh in 1618 was at that envoy's insistence; English Catholics were going unpunished. Finally Charles I negotiated a treaty with Spain that included an Anglo-Spanish alliance against Sweden and the Netherlands and permission for Spanish bullion to be transported across England for the payment of Catholic troops fighting in Northern Europe. The cause of international Protestantism was on the decline, and, despite the promptings of the Puritan lay and clerical leaders, the Stuart monarchs refused to come to its aid. The Reformed Protestant cause continued to decline at home as well as abroad. The rise of the High Church party to power in the person of William Laud set the English church on a course that many believed would lead back to Catholicism. Laud had no such intent, but his authorization of books that reflected Catholic principles, the presence of a papal emissary amid the attendants of the Catholic queen, the relaxation of legal penalties against Catholics (while Puritans faced increased pressure to conform), the restoration of altars to the Catholic position, and the rise of ceremonialism—all these and the pro-Catholic foreign policy of Charles I fed Puritan suspicions that their government's true sympathies lay on the wrong side in the struggle between Christ and Antichrist.

During the rise of the High Church party, Puritan clergymen increasingly found themselves on the defensive. Ministers such as William Ames, Hugh Peter, and Thomas Hooker were but a few of those forced into exile. And the departure of men such as these from their pulpits threatened the bases of Puritan strength. Laud, of course, realized this and went beyond encouraging High Commission prosecutions and the ejection of individuals; in the late 1620s and early 1630s he struck at the chief mechanism developed by the Puritan faction for the spread of their influence—the Feoffees for Impropriations.

During the reigns of Elizabeth and James, Puritan lords and congregations had capitalized on opportunities to purchase rights of impropriation for scattered parishes throughout the realm, thereby adding piecemeal to the number of pulpits occupied by godly preachers who were not dependent on the bishops for their livings. In 1625, twelve Londoners of Puritan persuasion sought to bring some structure to this attempt to remodel the church from within and organized themselves into a committee known as the Feoffees for Impropriations.

They would raise funds from private sources and use those moneys to purchase available rights of impropriation; they would then appoint a Puritan clergyman to the living. Inspiration for this attempt had apparently come from John Preston. Members of the feofees included Richard Sibbes and John Davenport. To Laud, this enterprise was a "cunning way, under a glorious pretence, to overthrow the Church Government." Immediately following his elevation to the see of London in 1628, Laud began to gather information against the group. His efforts culminated in the trial and disbandment of the feofees in 1633.

Given their belief in their own destiny and in England's, the decline of the international Protestant cause and the reverses suffered by their party in England convinced numerous Puritans of the need for a new initiative. Some decided that preaching and writing were futile and that only by actually demonstrating the efficacy of their ideas could they hope to awaken their countrymen. Settlement of New England came to be seen as an errand into the wilderness; the creation of a model Puritan community would convert England—and through England the world—both by its example and by the prayers of its inhabitants.

This concept, best expressed by John Winthrop in a sermon to his fellow passengers as they journeyed to Massachusetts in 1630—"wee shall be as a City upon a Hill. The eies of all people are upon Us"— was offered by Perry Miller, in his essay "Errand into the Wilderness," as the central explanation of the Great Migration. It has been challenged by historians who have discounted the Puritans' hope of saving the world and by others who have sought to downplay the Puritan nature of the Great Migration. But dissent from the "Errand" interpretation is not altogether convincing. Certainly those Puritans who recorded their reasons for settling Massachusetts emphasized the redemptive function they hoped to perform. Edward Johnson, who was not one of the colony's leaders, wrote in his *Wonder-Working Providence of Sion's Saviour in New England* that the purpose of the colony was to "be set as lights upon a Hill more obvious than the highest mountain in the World." Clergyman John Norton spoke of New England as "holding forth a pregnant demonstration of the consistency of Civil-Government with a Congregational-Way."

But were not some settlers merely abandoning an England that they believed doomed to suffer God's wrath? Certainly the diary of Thomas Shepard reveals the profound relief with which he escaped the life of a fugitive forced on him by Laud's decrees. But it is equally obvious that had Shepard not believed his departure to be God's will he would not have left. Personal safety was not the chief determinative for men like Shepard and Winthrop. As John Norton later stated, their

flight was not like that of *Pliny's* mice, that forsook a house forseeing the ruine of it; or of Mercenaries, who flee from duty in time of danger; but Providence Divine shutting up the door of service in *England*, and on the other hand opening it in *New England*.

By emigrating to America they believed themselves to be assisting God's divine plan.

Of course not all Puritans came to such conclusions and departed England, and there is no doubt that many who did migrate possessed no special sense of mission. It is in trying to assess why certain individuals felt the call and others did not that economic and social factors came to the fore.

Few of the men who came to New England did so to escape economic deprivation. The cost of migrating limited the option to the middle class (while there were servants among the migrants, and they were of the lower orders, they did not migrate by their own free choice, nor were their numbers significant). Further, as historians Timothy Breen and Stephen Foster have demonstrated in their study of one year's migrants, for those who sought economic opportunity outside of England the Netherlands was a far more promising destination—and one where Calvinism was the state religion. Nevertheless, economics did play an important role in shaping the Great Migration. Dislocations caused by land enclosures in East Anglia and other regions, sluggishness in the textile industry due to the disruption of traditional markets and governmental blunders, the steadily mounting inflation— these were all considerations that John Winthrop described as God's ways of weaning his people from their native land. While most Englishmen affected by economic reverses did not emigrate, such difficulties increased the likelihood that an individual would respond to the urgings of his local minister or to the promotional literature of the Massachusetts Bay Company.

Social considerations were also influential. Some colonists came for reasons best explained as fellowship. The departure of friends and relatives was often a strong incentive for families to migrate. Even among the leadership group such ties were influential; strong familial and friendship ties bound the elite of the Puritan faction together. For instance, Thomas Shepard, noting the departure for America of Hooker, Cotton, and other clerical friends, was himself drawn closer to the same decision. When men of such stature led the way it was not surprising, given the deferential nature of English society and the

Puritan laity's spiritual need for preaching, that many followed. Tenants of John Winthrop joined him in his journey to America; large parts of Thomas Hooker's Chelmsford congregation accompanied him to Massachusetts and then again to Connecticut; likewise many members of St. Stephen's parish in London followed John Davenport to Boston and then to New Haven; Anne Hutchinson and her family sought John Cotton in Massachusetts when that divine's preaching and guidance were found to be irreplaceable in England.

These and other considerations played upon the minds and hearts of men and women in various shires of England, prompting some to make the journey to America while their neighbors stayed. The very region in which one lived could be a determining variable, in that it dictated the impact of various other pressures. Thus, one of the reasons for the greater migration from East Anglia than from the Midlands was the harsh treatment of dissenters in the former region by the bishops of Norwich, such as Matthew Wren, while, in the diocese of Lincoln, Puritans were protected by Bishop Williams.

For whatever individual reasons, some 21,000 Englishmen moved to the Puritan colonies in the decade of the 1630s. Most—judged by their stated reasons, by their choice of New England in preference to more economically desirable destinations, and by their conduct following their arrival—seem to have been motivated to some extent by religious concerns. Others, as John Cotton conceded, "came over hither not out of respect of spiritual ends, but out of respect to friends . . . but have here found that grace which they sought not for." Even in such cases, however, at least a latent sympathy for Puritanism probably shaped their choice. Some migrants, of course, were not in sympathy with Puritan ideals, or at least not with the way those ideals were to be institutionalized in New England. But the record of dissent in the region's early history indicates that group was small.

THE GREAT MIGRATION

The Massachusetts Company's transfer of power, necessitated by the General Court's acceptance of the Cambridge Agreement, was effected in October 1629 when the freemen chose John Winthrop governor and John Humphrey lieutenant governor to replace Matthew Craddock and Thomas Goffe. The new leaders at once undertook the gathering and supplying of a sizable fleet to carry themselves, their families, and hundreds of followers to the Bay Colony. With preparations completed in the spring of 1630, John Cotton traveled to Southampton to preach a departure sermon to the assembled voyagers. On 29 March 1630 the first seven vessels of the fleet, led by the flagship *Arbella*, set sail for the New World.

Arriving weeks later at Salem, Winthrop assumed control of the colony from Endecott. (With transfer of the government and charter of the company, the positions of company governor and colony governor had become one.) Salem was considered unsuitable to be the principal town of a large colony; a search was undertaken for a new site, and Boston harbor was the chosen location.

Thousands of Englishmen followed those who had come in the Winthrop fleet of 1630. The more populous Massachusetts became, the more it served to attract Puritan interest and migration—particularly when the Dutch, bowing to Stuart pressure after 1633, began to crack down on resident English Puritans. Stimulated by oral and written exhortations or touched more directly by Laud's persecution or by economic distress, groups of English Puritans chartered vessels or booked passage on ships sailing to Boston. Throughout the Great Migration of the 1630s, East Anglia remained foremost of the regions that gave their sons and daughters to populate New England, while relatively few came from the Midlands and from the West Country.

Insufficient data prohibit a full profile of the more than 21,000 who came in the migration, but the work of Breen and Foster has recently shed new light on those who emigrated in the year 1637. Their conclusions offer insights into the character of the Puritan exodus that are supported by demographic studies of selected New England communities. Migration in 1637 was evidently not a pursuit of the young. The cost of transporting a family to America prevented emigration by more than a few heads of household who were still in their twenties. Most were in their thirties. The typical unit of migration was the nuclear family of two parents, a few children, and in some cases a servant. Few single, unattached men traveled to the colonies, where bachelors were not really welcome. Farmers were the single largest vocational group of the migration, but most of those on the 1637 passenger lists were urban artisans who gave up their trades to try farming in America.

Clearly the emigrants to New England were not a band of adventurers. Rather they were sober rural and urban middle-class folk—the stock from which Puritanism drew its greatest support in Old England. From the status of a disaffected minority in their native land, these Puritan families became the foundation of the Bible Commonwealths.

PART TWO

THE EVOLUTION OF NEW ENGLAND

4 | PILGRIM PRELUDE, THE STORY OF PLYMOUTH

Once a year, in the autumn, Americans celebrate their heritage in a feast of Thanksgiving. It is a time when the "first thanksgiving" of the Pilgrim Fathers is fondly remembered. That event, the signing of the Mayflower Compact, the landing at Plymouth Rock, the story of Squanto, the romantic triangle of John Alden, Miles Standish, and Priscilla Mullin—all these Plymouth happenings form an important part of our national folklore. And yet, judged in terms of its actual political, economic, religious, and artistic contributions to the development of colonial society, Plymouth was probably one of the least important corners of British North America. The Pilgrim colony from its founding was small, poor, and culturally absorbed by Massachusetts long before political annexation to her northern neighbor finally came in 1692.

Why then is an examination of the colony's history valuable? Partly because of the mythic importance the Pilgrim story continues to have. Partly because understanding that history leads to a better understanding of the distinctiveness and significance of the Puritan achievement in the other New England colonies.

THE SEPARATIST TRADITION
AND THE SCROOBY CONGREGATION

The journey of the Pilgrims that ended on Cape Cod in November of 1620 began in the small Nottinghamshire village of Scrooby around the year 1606. It was then that a group of religious dissenters from

43

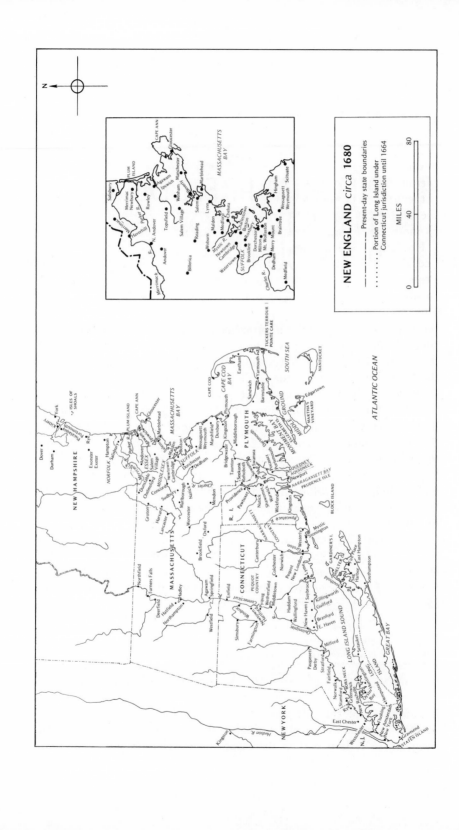

NEW ENGLAND *circa* 1680

– – – – Present-day state boundaries

⋯⋯⋯⋯ Portion of Long Island under
Connecticut jurisdiction until 1664

MILES

0   40   80

communities in northern Nottinghamshire gathered together to form a Separatist congregation. Unlike the Puritans, these men and women were convinced that the Church of England was too impure to be a true church. Rather than jeopardize their souls by remaining in it, they separated from the national church. Since their action was illegal it was not carried on with any public fanfare; hence the uncertainty surrounding the precise date when the congregation covenanted together. Soon, however, the group's existence did become known to the authorities. Its members were penalized, and they determined to move. Their first destination was the Netherlands.

Recent studies have emphasized that the Separatists themselves identified their churches as following in the tradition of the dissenting Protestants in Queen Mary's reign. During that monarch's attempt to restore Catholicism, the Marian exiles had in fact claimed to represent the true English church, though legally separated from the officially recognized church. More significant to later Separatists was the existence of an underground congregation in London, varying in size between forty and two hundred communicants, that governed itself and kept the cause of reform alive in England during the persecutions.

When Elizabeth's church proved less than satisfactory, some of the more radical dissenters followed the example of the Marian congregation in London and established their own church. By 1567, Anglican officials knew that such a Separatist group existed. A year later Bishop Grindal estimated that there were four or five ministers and over two hundred lay men and women in London who had withdrawn from their parish churches and who formed a more extreme faction in the Puritan movement. In the succeeding decades, spokesmen for the Separatist tradition began to emerge from their obscurity. In the 1580s, Robert Browne (after whom the Separatists were often called Brownists) published several treatises urging a reformation of the church "without tarrying" for the magistrate. Browne later retreated from the Separatist position, but in the 1580s he argued that the powers of a true church reside in a gathered congregation and that the ministry is subordinate to such a covenanted community. Henry Barrow and John Greenwood, who were arrested in 1587 and executed along with John Penry in 1593, were leaders of the Separatist movement in London; they had likewise publicly criticized the Anglican establishment and urged true Christians to withdraw from it. Their writings insisted that a true church could exist without a minister and without administration of the sacraments, which they believed could be dispensed only by a clergyman.

On most points of theology and church polity the Separatists were in full agreement with Cartwright, Perkins, Ames, and the other leaders of Puritan dissent. But there were issues over which the followers of Barrow and Greenwood parted company from the larger group of dissenters. Insignificant as those differences may have become later, in the decades preceding the settlement of New England they were sufficient to cause a recognizable split in nonconformist ranks. Primarily, the two bodies of dissenting thought differed as to the nature of the English church: the Puritans remained within the Anglican church because they believed it to be a true church, though corrupted; the Separatists denied that it was a true church and severed all relations with it and its members. Moreover, the Puritans were essentially internationalists who were interested in establishing a communion of reformed churches; the Separatists tended toward an isolationism in which they interacted as little with other Protestant churches as with the Church of England. Another difference was evident in questions of church polity. The Puritans, and not merely the presbyterian wing of the movement, placed a greater emphasis on the role and importance of the ministry than did the Separatists. These distinctions were most apparent in Elizabethan England but also influenced the comparative evolution of the Massachusetts Bay and Plymouth colonies and their mutual relationship.

The execution of Barrow and Greenwood in 1593 was but one sign of the mounting persecution of the Separatists in the closing years of the Elizabethan regime. Another Separatist leader, Francis Johnson, had been imprisoned in 1592. After his release he organized a plan, in cooperation with a group of merchants, for a Separatist colony in America. Receiving permission to leave England on condition that they not return, Johnson, his brother, and two other Separatists sailed on an exploratory voyage to the mouth of the St. Lawrence River in 1597. One of the ships was wrecked, the colonization effort of these "first Pilgrims" was abandoned, and Johnson, after a brief and illegal interlude in London, went into exile in the Netherlands as pastor of a refuge Separatist congregation in Amsterdam. Under his leadership, that church grew from a membership of about forty in 1597 to three hundred communicants twelve years later.

Francis Johnson's Amsterdam congregation was the model drawn upon in 1606 when the Nottinghamshire Separatists organized a congregation under the leadership of John Smyth and Richard Clifton. Shortly afterward the number of communicants and their dispersion made it more practicable to divide into two churches, with Smyth ministering to the congregation centered on Gainsborough, and Clifton to that of Scrooby. In the following year the congregation came to the attention of the authorities, but persecution was not severe—for the time being at least. Nevertheless, the prospect of more stringent action induced the congregations to emigrate, a decision strengthened by the imprisonment of one Scrooby member in November, 1607. The next month, four others were summoned to appear before the Court of High Commission. One was William Brewster, a gentleman who had attended the Elizabethan envoy William Davidson on missions to the Netherlands and who since 1590 had acted as master of the post in Scrooby. The whole congregation fled England before the scheduled date of the High Commission hearing.

FROM SCROOBY TO LEYDEN

The Scrooby congregation's first attempt to emigrate was unsuccessful. Leaving England without government consent was illegal, and consent was not readily available for Separatists. Betrayed by the captain of the ship engaged to carry them to the Netherlands, the refugees were apprehended and jailed for thirty days. Much of their property was seized. That effort in the autumn of 1607 was followed by a partially successful attempt the next spring; but not until that summer did all the members of the Scrooby church reach Amsterdam.

John Smyth's Gainsborough congregation had also emigrated but, in Amsterdam, remained distinct from Francis Johnson's church. Smyth, formerly a disciple of Johnson, began to advance new and radical views and to cast aspersions on the practice of the Amsterdam Separatists. Ultimately Smyth came to reject the validity of infant baptism and to insist that only adult converts be given the sacrament. His spiritual pilgrimage carried him into contact with the Mennonites, and after his death his followers affiliated with the Dutch Anabaptists. Francis Johnson, rejecting Smyth's radicalism, began to assert more forcefully than before the argument that power in the congregation resided primarily with the elders, not with the whole congregation. His insistence caused part of the Amsterdam congregation, under the leadership of the church's teacher, Henry Ainsworth, to secede.

Within a year of their arrival in the Netherlands, and before the actual split in the Amsterdam church, the Scrooby congregation, dismayed by dissension in the city's Separatist community, moved to Leyden. Richard Clifton, a strong supporter of Johnson, remained behind, and John Robinson was called as the group's new pastor. Robinson had been one of the early members of the congregation, and under his leadership the Scrooby Separatists maintained a tranquil existence in Leyden for nearly a decade.

Gradually, however, dissatisfaction with their situation began to grow. As Englishmen, they could not join the guilds. That exclusion, hand-in-hand with their agrarian backgrounds, reduced them to the status of unskilled urban laborers. Though their Dutch neighbors were hospitable, the Separatists found the culture of the Netherlands strange and Dutch observance of the Sabbath seemed lax. They feared especially for their children, who would grow up alienated from their English heritage and, as English Separatists in exile, alienated like their parents from full participation in the life of the Netherlands. A further cloud on their horizon was the approaching expiration of the Spanish-Dutch truce in March of 1621. The Separatists feared the effect that renewed hostilities might have on their future.

Troubled by these concerns, they began to discuss yet another move—to America. Their hope was not, as the Puritans' would be, to save the world. Rather they sought to establish a settlement where their religious freedom could be coupled with an English environment.

Having decided to uproot themselves once again, their primary task was to obtain financing. The congregation—with the exception of Brewster and a few others—was drawn from the struggling agrarian classes of the English countryside. What little they owned had largely been confiscated by the authorities in the course of their abortive attempts to emigrate. Economic opportunities in Leyden had not been such as to allow of any accumulation of capital. The Separatist group simply could not finance its own colony. The Dutch offered assistance if the Englishmen would settle in New Netherlands, but that was no solution for people intent upon retaining their English identity. Instead, they accepted the offer of London ironmonger Thomas Weston on behalf of a group of English investors. John Carver and Robert Cushman negotiated an agreement with the London group. A joint-stock company was formed with three classes of associates: merchant adventurers, English investors who backed the settlement financially but who had no intention of migrating; merchant planters who invested capital and who settled in the colony; and planters whose only investment was their commitment of personal energies to the colony. Each held specified amounts of shares in the company, and together they held common ownership for seven years of the total assets of the company, which would then be divided. This last provision meant a denial of private ownership of homes and garden lots. The congregation was critical of Cushman for having acceded to such all-encompassing demands, and the leaders of the emigrating group refused to sign the agreement, jeopardizing for a time the Pilgrims' departure. Thus relations between adventurers and planters got off to a bad start, and though the agreement was eventually signed and returned to England, ill feeling continued to mar the relationship between the investors at home and the colonists in New England.

PLYMOUTH PLANTATION: THE FIRST DECADE

Not all of the Leyden congregation was prepared to migrate in 1620. While an advance group of the church purchased the *Speedwell* and sailed for Southampton, the majority of the congregation, including pastor Robinson, remained in Leyden, intending to follow later. After two false starts from England in which *Speedwell* and her companion ship *Mayflower* had to put back to England because of the former's lack of seaworthiness, on 6 September 1620 *Mayflower*, now overcrowded with 102 passengers, set sail alone for the New World. Only thirty-five of the passengers were actually members of the Leyden congregation, and although many of the others were London and Southampton relatives and friends of the Separatists, the body of "saints" was significantly augmented by a party of "strangers" —non-Separatists engaged by the London adventurers to provide the colony with needed skills. The most famous of these were militia captain Miles Standish and cooper John Alden.

The *Mayflower*'s destination was the northern reaches of the territory granted to the Virginia Company of London, from whom Weston had received a patent for the Separatist settlement. But the *Mayflower* strayed, perhaps intentionally, from her intended course and touched North America at Cape Cod. An attempt to sail further south was thwarted by weather and sand bars, and the colonists— realizing the lateness of the season—decided to settle where they were. After exploring the coast they chose Plymouth harbor as the best site.

But the Pilgrims had no legal right to settle in New England, and consequently the colony's government lacked legitimacy. To remedy that deficiency the leaders drew up a political covenant that was signed by forty-one men, including all free adult male passengers. In this "Mayflower Compact" the signatories agreed to

covenant and Combine ourselves together into a Civil Body Politic, for our better ordering and preservation . . . ; and by virtue hereof to enact, constitute and frame such just and equal Laws, Ordinances, Acts, Constitutions and Offices, from time to time, as shall be thought most meet and convenient for the general good of the Colony, unto which we promise all due submission and obedience.

Having signed this document on 11 November 1620 the colonists reaffirmed the choice of John Carver as governor and prepared for their first winter in the New World.

The lateness of the season kept the settlers from extensive construction. Most of them lived on board the *Mayflower*, whose captain, Christopher Jones, had decided to winter in New England. In January the common storehouse, one of the few solid structures, burned, and some of the colony's needed supplies were destroyed. Only one passenger had died during the *Mayflower*'s voyage to America but the rigors of the journey had left many unable to resist the winter's cold. Almost half of the company perished before spring. Adding to the Pilgrims' difficulties was an abortive mutiny against Carver's authority. The promises of the Mayflower Compact were not unbreakable.

Spring brought relief. Homes were built, crops were planted. A fort was constructed for defense and was also able to serve as a meetinghouse. In March an English-speaking Indian named Samoset visited them. He had acquired their language from fishermen on the coast of Maine. Carver was able to establish relations with the regionally powerful Wampanoag tribe through the agency of Samoset and another English-speaking Indian, Squanto. The Plymouth governor and the Wampanoag chieftain Massasoit negotiated a treaty that brought the Pilgrims more than half a century of relief from Indian warfare and made possible the continued existence and growth of the plantation. Furthermore, Samoset and Squanto proved invaluable in assisting the colonists to adjust to the agricultural environment of the New World.

These blessings of the spring of 1621 were marred by the death of John Carver, who, weakened from the rigors of the winter, succumbed to sunstroke. Succeeding him as governor was William Bradford. Born in 1590 and raised as a farmer, Bradford by the age of twelve had become a frequent reader of the Geneva Bible and was one of the early members of a discussion group that met at William Brewster's house and that predated the formal organization of the Scrooby congregation. An inheritance received from his parents in 1611 had helped his economic adjustment in Leyden. He had bought a home, followed the trade of a weaver, and begun to accumulate a substantial library. Despite his comparative youth, he has been singled out for his abilities and was on the committee that worked out the practical details of the migration. When *Mayflower* arrived off Cape Cod he helped to explore the coast for a settlement site; in his absence his wife, Dorothy, fell overboard and drowned—a possible suicide.

Bradford assumed the governorship in 1621 and was reelected almost annually until his death in 1657. He was an active and energetic man, capable of confronting the London adventurers, of spearheading the development of the fur trade, of meeting challenges to the Pilgrim Way with determination and firmness. He was also a scholar: a man self-educated in many fields and languages, a still valued historian of the Separatist movement (his "Dialogues") and of his own colony (*Of Plymouth Plantation*). His love of his people and their land, his integrity and generally tolerant attitude are largely responsible for the attraction Plymouth history still holds for the twentieth century.

In his early years in office the young governor faced two major challenges: one as a result of the agreement with the adventurers, the other stemming from the introduction of new elements into the colony's population. The immediate difficulties between planters and adventurers were resolved in 1621. In June of that year Weston and his associates, apprised of the colony's location by the returning Captain Jones, procured a patent (in the name of John Pierce, one of their number) from the Council for New England. In turn the planters finally signed the distasteful financial agreement with the adventurers and dispatched it to England. But friction continued between the two groups, fed by the adventurers' lack of a return on their investment. Weston blamed the Pilgrims' lack of productivity on their contentiousness, a view not well received by Bradford. In fact, the physical rigors of the early years, the colonists' lack of familiarity with the soil and climate, the marginal quality of the soil, the Pilgrims' inexperience with fishing—all these precluded any major economic success. The famous "first thanksgiving" in the autumn of 1621 was the celebration of a harvest that meant much in Plymouth, but which brought little reward to the London adventurers.

Complicating the colonists' agricultural efforts was the system of enforced communism, whereby all of them worked company land and tended company livestock; surpluses were shipped across the Atlantic for the benefit of Weston and his associates. Further exacerbating the situation was the arrival of "particulars" among the reinforcements sent by the adventurers. These newcomers were not strictly members of the company; they were allowed to own and farm their own land because they had paid their own expenses. To ease the resulting tensions, Bradford in 1623 modified the communal system by assigning land to each family (based on family size) for its own use. Ownership of the land, however, was still held by the company.

During these early years the Pilgrims had no pastor. John Robinson and the remainder of the Leyden congregation still planned to emigrate, and the Plymouth settlers were content to await their arrival. A church was gathered and William Brewster read the Scriptures and preached. But the sacraments were not administered. As Separatists, the Pilgrims were confident that they formed a true church, despite lack of pastor and sacraments. The adventurers, being for the most part Church of England men, were not as satisfied with the situation, and in 1624 they sent the Reverend John Lyford to the colony. Lyford was an ordained Anglican clergyman, but on arrival he joined the Plymouth congregation and rejected all his ties to the Church of England. The congregation in turn allowed him to preach and consulted him on civil matters in recognition of his university training. But, still awaiting Robinson, the Pilgrims declined to ordain Lyford, and he thus could not administer the sacraments. Disappointed, he turned against Bradford and the Pilgrims and championed the disenfranchised and discontented elements in the colony, especially the particulars. Soon he organized a second church in the colony. Such diversity was not to be tolerated. Lyford was brought before the General Court of the colony and confronted with copies of complaints he had sent to the adventurers about the administration of Plymouth affairs. Lyford asked for and was granted forgiveness, but soon he began to criticize the colony again, this time for its Separatism. Called before the General Court once more, he was banished in 1625.

Lyford's complaints and the evidence of dissension in the colony added to the dissatisfaction of the adventurers. Finally they agreed to sell their interest in the colony to the planters for £1,800 (to be paid in annual installments of £200) and the colonists' assumption of £600 of the colony's debts. This decision allowed for a thorough reorganization of the colony in 1627. Bradford and eleven associates— thereafter referred to as "the undertakers"—assumed responsibility for making the annual payments in return for the colonists' agreement to grant them a six-year monopoly of the fur trade. More significantly, all assets were at last divided. Each adult male—a total of fifty-eight planters and particulars—was given one share for each of his dependents. All livestock, used land, and other assets were divided proportionally among the shareholders, the lots of land being distributed by lottery. Thus private property finally emerged in Plymouth. The old Pierce patent was canceled and the Council for New England issued a new one to Bradford and his associates. Such steps toward independence from the London creditors led to a final settlement of the colony's debts in 1642.

During the remainder of the first decade conditions in Plymouth stabilized, and the colony began its long period of slow and unspectacular growth. In the mid-1620s the establishment of a trading post at Mt. Wollaston (Merry Mount), slightly to the north of Plymouth, posed a minor danger to the colony when the leader of the venture, Thomas Morton, began to sell firearms and alcohol to the Indians. Miles Standish led a small expedition, which destroyed the outpost and sent Morton back to England. In 1629 about thirty members of the old Leyden congregation finally arrived, followed the next year by a second group. John Robinson, however, was not among the new arrivals: he had died in 1626.

In all, the Pilgrim achievement during their first decade was remarkable. Despite the obstacles posed by the lack of a charter, disagreements with their English backers, dissent within, and challenges from without, they had succeeded in establishing a colony that was politically and economically stable. But the settlement of Massachusetts Bay in the 1630s relegated Plymouth to the sidelines of New England history.

PLYMOUTH PLANTATION IN THE SEVENTEENTH CENTURY

The founding of Massachusetts had a dramatic impact on the Pilgrim colony—economically, politically, and in religion. Very rapidly the distinction between the Massachusetts Puritans and the Plymouth Separatists lost its meaning, and the story of Plymouth became in large part that of Puritan New England. And yet the smaller colony continued to hold on to much of its character and independence until late in the century.

Economically, seventeenth-century Plymouth was the poor sister of the Bible Commonwealths. Her soil was poor (a major reason for the gradual dispersion of settlement) and agriculture never rose above subsistence levels. In the 1630s the growing population of the Bay Colony did open an important market for Plymouth livestock, but the success of that venture declined when the Great Migration from England ended in the 1640s. Commerce, which played an important part in the evolution of Massachusetts, was limited in Plymouth by the absence of good ports of any size, the colonists' chronic shortage of investment capital, and the lack of the type of close personal contacts with London merchants that were to be so helpful to the merchants of Boston.

The principal profit-making enterprise of the Pilgrims was the fur trade. Starting in the 1620s, Bradford and his associates established trading contacts in Dutch New Netherland, in the Connecticut Valley, and on the Kennebec and Penobscot rivers in Maine. The returns from this activity financed the transportation of the other Separatists from Leyden and the payment of the colony's debts. Gradually, however, in the 1630s and 1640s, the fur trade too began to languish. The expansion of the white population and the movement of Indian tribes altered the nature of the trade, and competing merchants from Massachusetts and Connecticut brought greater resources to the trade and undercut Plymouth's brief monopoly. Some of the lost profits may have been offset by the modest growth of shipbuilding in the colony and the opening of a small ironworks at Taunton, but after midcentury there no longer existed a source of economic growth sufficient to sustain a steady increase in the colony's standard of living.

Plymouth's relative poverty contributed to its cultural backwardness, but other influences peculiar to the Separatists were at least as important. One was the absence of a pastor for most of the first decade. In 1629, Ralph Smith was ordained and the sacraments were administered for the first time. Smith and his immediate successors were not very satisfactory however, and their terms of tenure were for the most part brief. After 1654 the church was again without a pastor for almost fifteen years. By 1665 most communities in the colony were making do with lay preachers because they could not support qualified ministers. Compared to the other Bible Commonwealths, Plymouth stood out for the poor quality of her ministry, a situation fostered by the Pilgrims' insistence that a covenanted community need not have a minister to be a true church. That viewpoint set Plymouth somewhat apart from her Puritan neighbors.

In 1667 the Plymouth church called John Cotton the younger to preach and ordained him pastor in the following year, thus attracting for the first time a minister of religious distinction. Cotton's arrival was an important landmark, signifying new status for the colony and exemplifying the way in which the Pilgrim colony had begun to look northward for spiritual and intellectual leadership. Plymouth had no public schools during her first half century nor were children of the Pilgrims sent to Harvard. Unlike the Bay colony, with its numerous university graduates, Plymouth could boast only of William Brewster, who alone of the early Pilgrims had matriculated at a university, and he had not graduated. The Separatists believed in a university-trained clergy—Brewster's lack of a degree was probably the only reason he had not been called by the Plymouth church—but their failure to provide educational training for their children left them open to the religious influence of the Puritans.

None of this means that the Pilgrims were unconcerned about religion. Their commitment to their faith had led them to surmount numerous hardships in the odyssey from Scrooby to Plymouth, and once there they guarded their faith jealously. One has to look carefully to distinguish them from the Puritans. Even in Leyden they had begun to demonstrate a greater willingness than most Separatists to interact on some levels with non-Separatists. John Robinson himself had moved significantly in the direction of dialogue with the Puritan dissenters, and his followers had accepted his lead. In the New World such communication was even easier, for while the Puritans considered themselves still members of the Church of England, they had left its bishops and other unpalatable trappings an ocean away. There was little to distinguish the worship of Massachusetts from that of Plymouth—as Puritans and Pilgrims well knew. On most issues they acted in accord. Roger Williams was asked to move on when he came to Plymouth after his banishment from Massachusetts. In an action parallel to the Bay's, Bradford in 1645 refused to entertain a petition for religious toleration, and in 1649 the Plymouth authorities put an end to Baptist attempts to establish a church in Rehobeth. And when the Quakers came to New England, Plymouth joined with Massachusetts and Connecticut in passing legislation that was restrictive toward them.

Plymouth's political structure was also similar to the Bay's, with a few differences. As in early Massachusetts, the franchise was extremely broad in Plymouth's first years. Since all adult males were shareholders in the company, all had the right to vote. From 1623 to 1627 the particulars—who were not company members—were denied the franchise, but their inclusion in the land division of 1627 gave them full political rights. Those arriving in the colony thereafter do not seem to have been automatically granted the vote, but the criteria for freemanship were not spelled out until later. As late as 1658 the majority of adult males were freemen. And it should be remembered that many looked upon freemanship as a responsibility and were not eager to receive it—Plymouth communities had to impose the sanction of fines to guarantee attendance at town meetings.

Until 1638 all freemen were expected to gather in the town of Plymouth four times a year—March, June, October, and November—for meetings of the General Court. There they voted on laws, which might include regulation of wages and prices, granting monopolies, and Indian relations. Once a year they elected a governor and seven assistants. In point of fact these officials, particularly the governor, ruled the colony and the General Court bowed to their wishes. In 1638 the dispersion of population led to a system of representation whereby adult males (not just the freemen) of each community chose deputies to sit for them in the General Court.

In the last decades of Plymouth's independence the democratic aspects of the colony's political structure gradually altered. The threat from the Quakers after 1660 and the general climate of decline in New England contributed to a narrowing of the franchise.

During the years from 1620 to 1692 Plymouth expanded slowly and steadily. From the single town of Plymouth in 1620 the colony grew to eight towns by 1646 and twenty-one by 1691. But economically and culturally, ideologically and politically, the Bay gave the lead to the Pilgrim colony. When Plymouth was absorbed into Massachusetts in 1691, sixty-one years of preparation made the change welcome to many of the heirs of the *Mayflower* passengers.

5 | MASSACHUSETTS: THE ERECTION OF A CITY ON A HILL

The men and women who came to Massachusetts during the 1630s hoped to do more than merely escape from the threat of Laudian persecution: they wished to strike a blow for the true faith by the erection of a model Christian community. Like the Plymouth planters they too were to face and overcome foreign threats and domestic civil and religious dissent. But whereas the Separatists had already had experience in conducting their own religious and secular concerns, the Great Migration brought to Massachusetts few men with experience in regulating the affairs of a colony or in guiding the affairs of an independent congregation.

Coming to New England with great expectations, the Puritans gradually succeeded in shaping distinctive political and ecclesiastical institutions. The process of societal self-definition was largely completed by 1640, and it forms the key to understanding the events of that formative decade. As events unfolded, Puritanism was defined with more precision than ever before and figures like Roger Williams and Anne Hutchinson, who had been numbered among the faithful in England, found themselves outside of the bounds of the emerging New England orthodoxy.

EARLY TRIALS IN MASSACHUSETTS: 1628–1630

The initial task of governance in Massachusetts had fallen to John Endecott, and his two-year term of office foreshadowed a number of future events. Most significant were the governor's treatment of dissent and the formation of the Salem church.

From the very beginnings of the colony's history those who differed from the Puritan majority were encouraged to exercise their liberty to live elsewhere. Before Endecott's arrival the Pilgrims had taken action against Thomas Morton's outpost at Mt. Wollaston, Miles Standish having captured the self-styled "host of Merry Mount" and shipped him to England. Some of Morton's followers reunited after their chief's expulsion, and, when Endecott arrived in Massachusetts, Merry Mount was again functioning as a threat to the region's peace and moral tone. Since the community was closer to Salem than to Plymouth, Endecott led an expedition to Mt. Wollaston and completed the work that Standish had begun. The maypole was cut down and the inhabitants dispersed.

The new governor's promptness in dealing with Morton's followers was welcomed in Plymouth, and when the Salem colonists began to suffer from scurvy and other diseases in the winter of 1628–1629, the Pilgrim physician Samuel Fuller traveled north to lend his aid. Medical knowledge in the seventeenth century was far from extensive and it is questionable if his assistance was any great help. But Fuller was also a deacon in the Pilgrim church, and during his stay he conversed long and fruitfully with John Endecott and others in the community. In the process he dispelled many of the Puritans' misconceptions about Separatism (at least of the John Robinson variety).

Shortly after Fuller's visit, reinforcements arrived from England. Some of the newcomers lacked sympathy with the colony's purpose, and Endecott sent five such youths back to England, acting on the company's authorization to do so "rather than keep them to infect or to be an occasion of scandall unto others." Unable to accommodate all the newcomers in Salem, Endecott dispatched some to found a new community on the northern shore of Boston harbor, which community they named Charlestown.

Among the arrivals in 1629 were four ministers. One, Ralph Smith, was an avowed Separatist, who soon settled at Plymouth. The other three—Francis Higginson, Samuel Skelton, and Francis Bright—had been sent by the company to serve the spiritual needs of the settlers. Bright joined the Charlestown group, remaining for a year before returning to England. Higginson and Skelton stayed at Salem.

Members of the Salem community organized a congregation and chose Skelton as pastor and Higginson as teacher. Higginson then drew up a church covenant and a confession of faith. In August a date was set for the official formation of the church. Thirty Salem residents made their statement of faith and swore to the covenant— "We covenant with the Lord and with one another; and do bynd our selves in the presence of God, to walke together in all his waies, according to how he is pleased to reveale himself unto us in his Blessed word of truth." Following this, members of the congregation ordained the two clergymen. Representatives of the Plymouth church, including Bradford and Brewster, were delayed by adverse winds from participation in these rites but arrived later in the day and extended the right hand of fellowship to the new church.

The formation of the Salem congregation laid the basic ecclesiastical pattern that would be followed in New England throughout the seventeenth century and even later. The congregational selection and ordination of ministers and the subscription of members to a church covenant became hallmarks of the region's religious life. Other characteristics would be added later but without modifying the base (no testimony of having experienced saving grace was required for membership at Salem, though it would be in the future).

Not all members of the Salem community approved of their new church. The new congregation departed widely from the standard practices of the Church of England, not only in its organization but in its worship. The result was the first quarrel among the Massachusetts Puritans as to how far one had to depart from Anglican forms to achieve purity. John Browne, a lawyer, and his merchant brother, Samuel, believed that Skelton and Higginson had gone too far. They charged the clergymen with being Separatists who were well on the way to becoming Anabaptists. Their opposition to the ministers was significant, since John Browne was a member both of the company's board of assistants and of Governor Endecott's council. But when the Brownes went beyond criticism and began to hold their own meetings for readings from the Book of Common Prayer, the Governor's Council ordered them sent back to England. Arrived in London, the Brownes brought their complaints before the company's General Court. A committee of eight, which included John Winthrop and John Davenport, attempted to play down the significance of the dispute and found fault on both sides. The company's leaders sent Endecott a letter urging him to try to desist from any further actions that would reflect unfavorably on the colony. But the Brownes remained in England and the practices of the Salem church remained unaltered.

The circumstances surrounding the formation of the Salem congregation have been the center of a dispute since their occurrence, the principal issues being, first, whether or not the New Englanders had adopted Separatist practice and, second, whether or not their church practices were modeled on those of the Plymouth Pilgrims. Certainly,

English Puritans such as John Cotton were concerned that the Bay colonists had been unduly influenced by Separatists, and seventeenth-century enemies of the New England Congregational Puritans (such as the Presbyterian Robert Baillie) frequently stigmatized their foes by attempting to link them to the unpopular Separatists. But the Puritan colonists themselves vigorously rejected the appellation of Separatists and refused when called upon to deny their membership in the English church. While the general outlines of Congregationalism had been developed by Puritans in England, the details of polity and worship had not. The Salem colonists, forced to put theory into practice, undoubtedly did adopt some points of Pilgrim worship that went beyond what many of their English brethren believed advisable—lay preaching, for instance. But this did not mean that the immigrant Puritans had become Separatists, even of the Pilgrim variety. Their ability to develop close relations with the Pilgrims did not reflect their conversion but, rather, demonstrated the truth of John Robinson's earlier prophecy that in the New World differences between Separatists and nonseparating Puritans would fade in significance.

POLITICAL EVOLUTION AND CONFLICT:
1630–1645

The arrival of John Winthrop and his fellow voyagers in June of 1630 shifted the focus of Massachusetts affairs from Endecott and Salem to Charlestown, where Winthrop and the colony's other new leaders first settled. In July the new governor was one of a group that organized a congregation and called the Reverend John Wilson as pastor.

Though Governor Winthrop, Deputy Governor Thomas Dudley, and other officers of the company had been involved in estate management and county government in England, none had experience of the types of economic and political problems with which they would have to cope in the New World. In addition to making their personal adjustment to the wilderness they had virtually to create the institutions of a new society. Struggling to adapt the governing mechanisms of a commercial company to the needs of a civil colony, they gradually shaped a system that satisfied their own desire to control the colony as well as the wishes of the colonists to participate.

On 23 August 1630 the company's Board of Assistants held its first meeting in the New World. The charter vested control of the colony in the General Court, which was to meet four times a year. Governance between quarterly courts rested in the hands of the governor and his assistants who came as freemen to New England. Thus, those nine men were entitled to full rule and could have exercised absolute authority, meeting monthly as assistants and quarterly as the General Court.

One of the magistrates' first problems was the disruptive influence of Thomas Morton, who had returned to the scene of his former activities and resumed operations where he had left off. Once again he was seized and deported. (This time he remained in England and became one of the first of a growing number of detractors of the Bible Commonwealths.) In a far different vein, the assistants established wage and price controls. In Massachusetts, where land was readily available, the shortage of hired help was to place heavy inflationary pressures on wages throughout the seventeenth century, and in the early decades of settlement the magistrates frequently attempted to resist such pressures. Certainly some of the assistants must have been on familiar ground. Winthrop, for example, as a justice of the peace in England had undoubtedly sat in sessions for the assignment of wages for Suffolk workingmen. In August of 1630 maximum wages for carpenters, thatchers, sawyers, and other specified laborers were set at two shillings a day (eight pence more than the contemporary maximum in Suffolk), while commodity prices were set at four pence above the current English levels.

In September the assistants met twice. They forbade the sale of firearms to the Indians, put an embargo on corn shipments as a precaution against winter food shortages, and fined one of their number, Richard Saltonstall, for absence from the session. By the end of that month some of the new residents of Charlestown had begun to move: Despite the lateness of the season the scarcity of fresh water in the community led many to seek new shelter across the bay. The new settlement became the town of Boston.

In October the first General Court was held, the magistrates throwing the meeting open to all residents of the colony who cared to attend. They decided that in the future the assistants would be chosen annually by the freemen, and the governor by the assistants. At the same time they opened freemanship to all residents of the colony. That decision, dramatically broadening the franchise, was not required of the magistrates. In the seventeenth century the vote was not considered to be a right of Englishmen, nor even of propertied Englishmen. No provision of the charter mandated that the colony's leaders admit residents as freemen, though residents did hold the franchise in the Virginia and Plymouth colonies. The magistrates' decision was an act of faith in the quality of their fellow settlers. But at the same time that they decided to increase the number of freemen, they limited the powers that went with the title, placing all lawmaking and judicial power in the hands of the assistants, not—as the charter stipulated— in the General Court. It was the intention of the leaders to limit the freemen to the right to choose the assistants.

In May of 1631 there were 118 adult males, Puritans and non-Puritans, who presented themselves at the election meeting of the General Court to take the oath as freemen. At the same session the court placed a restriction on the franchise, requiring all freemen to be church members. This was a concession to the colony's mission, intended as a guarantee of godly government. Those nonmembers of the church who had earlier been enfranchised remained freemen, and since most adult males coming to the colony became church members this provision was not very restrictive at the time.

The colony's governmental system continued to evolve during 1632. In May the General Court decided that in the future the freemen, not the assistants, would elect the governor, though the choice had to be from among the assistants. In the same year the Boston church raised the issue of church-state relations, when it sought the advice of the Salem, Charlestown, and Plymouth congregations as to whether a person could hold office in both civil and ecclesiastical governments. The Puritans had suffered much in England from the combination of spiritual and secular power in one man and the decision was in the negative.

The exercise of power was also at issue in a dispute between the governor and the deputy governor. This clash between the judicious Winthrop and the arrogant Dudley was partly a conflict of personalities, partly an outcome of Dudley's rebuffed ambition dating from Winthrop's selection as governor. The deputy had frequently expressed annoyance at his superior's judicial laxity. Two issues in particular formed the basis for his complaints in 1632. The magistrates had earlier selected Newtown, down river from Boston, as capital for the colony and agreed to build their homes there. Dudley proceeded to do so and was irate when Winthrop and others finally decided to remain in Boston. More fundamental was Dudley's complaint that the governor was in violation of the charter in claiming greater power than his fellow assistants. In the summer, relations deteriorated to the point where a group of clergy and fellow magistrates had to bring the two together for reconciliation. Winthrop agreed to compensate Dudley for the latter's move to Newtown, and the primacy of the governor was established to Winthrop's satisfaction.

New problems continued to force adjustments in the political life of the colony. The Privy Council had responded to the Bay's critics in England by ordering an investigation of Massachusetts, and the magistrates had responded by levying taxes on all towns for the erection of fortifications at Newtown. The citizens of Watertown, led by the Reverend George Philip, refused to pay the amount levied on them, protesting their lack of involvement in the decision to levy the tax. Admonishing the Watertown dissidents for their action, Winthrop nevertheless suggested that a committee of representatives from the various towns be formed to advise the assistants on tax matters. The towns countered by demanding that the charter be shown to their representatives who, when shown the document, protested that they had systematically been denied the legislative rights of freemen. Winthrop argued that the broadening of the number of freemen had made their assemblage for legislating impractical. The townsmen insisted on their legislative rights, and a further modification of the colony government was introduced whereby the freemen of each town were empowered to choose up to three deputies to represent their interests in the General Court. Powers of legislation formerly reserved to the assistants thereafter were exercised by the entire court with the deputies and assistants sitting together.

Though deputies and assistants shared legislative power their relationship was imperfectly defined. While the deputies generally proved themselves as concerned with community mores as were the assistants, enacting legislation against tobacco, immodest fashions, and costly apparel, the two groups did occasionally disagree. An early instance of discord arose in 1634 over a petition of the citizens of Newtown seeking permission to remove from the Bay and settle in the fertile Connecticut Valley. The deputies voted approval of this request, but the assistants were opposed and asserted their right to veto any proposal before the court. Following a defense of this negative voice in a sermon preached by John Cotton, the deputies backed down for the time being.

The assistants had not been unanimous in insisting on the negative voice and in the winter of 1634–1635 one of their number, Israel Stoughton, prepared a manuscript in which he criticized the upper house's assumption of veto power and challenged the right of the magistrates to wield the broad powers they had assumed. Such a defection from their ranks pained the colony's civil leadership, the more so as the substance of Stoughton's arguments formed a repudiation of the political structure that most of the Bay's leaders viewed as having been ordained by God. Stoughton had, in fact, gone beyond the views of the deputies as well, and in March 1635 the General Court called Stoughton to defend his manuscript. Despite his willingness to be corrected, the court censured him and disabled him from holding office for three years.

Further refinements were made of the structure of the state in 1636. The General Court (presumably to entice more members of the English nobility to America) ordered that a number of magistrates be chosen for life terms on a new advisory council. They also ordered that quarter courts be kept, that citizens in remote towns be authorized to assign their votes to proxies for the annual court of elections, and that no church should be established in the Bay without the consent of the other churches and the magistrates. The court also authorized the establishment of a college. Though plans were delayed by the Antinomian Crisis, grants from the legislature and a bequest from John Harvard enabled the college to open its doors in 1638. The location of Harvard—in Newtown, renamed Cambridge—was a reward for that town's steadfastness to orthodoxy.

By 1639 the essential structure of state and church in Massachusetts was evident. The next few years saw further evolution, but more in the nature of adjustments than fundamental changes. In 1639 the life council was essentially scrapped; the General Court prohibited the towns from sending more than two deputies to the court; and there was a flurry of complaints against the merchants for their excessive prices, focusing especially upon Robert Keayne.

A lengthy discussion of a legal code, begun in 1635, was revived in 1641. In that year Nathaniel Ward prepared a document that was adopted by the General Court and published as the "Body of Liberties," a statement that was less a legal code than a bill of rights that would serve to protect the rights of citizens until a comprehensive code was ready. Finally, in 1648 the court adopted the *Book of Laws and Liberties Concerning the Inhabitants of Massachusetts.* The code had been drafted by a committee that included John Winthrop, Nathaniel Ward, Richard Bellingham, John Cotton, Thomas Shepard, and Richard Mather, with Ward primarily responsible for the final product. *The Laws and Liberties* was not a code in the sense of a systematic arrangement of the law, but rather an alphabetical collation of various legal rules. It reflected the Puritans' desire for a knowable and precise law that the citizens could easily understand and follow.

In 1642 the court began hearings on a complaint against Robert Keayne for having illegally acquired one of Goodwife Sherman's sows. For two years the deputies and assistants quarreled over the merits of the case until their inability to agree led to the physical separation of the two groups in 1644. Though the right of the assistants to a negative voice was again questioned, Winthrop successfully defended it.

RELIGIOUS CONTENTION:
ROGER WILLIAMS AND ANNE HUTCHINSON

The crablike progress toward consensus that marked the Bay's political evolution can be seen in the religious history of the 1630s as well. Just as the Puritans had no blueprint for civil government, so too their concepts of church order were but vaguely defined. For those who could not reconcile themselves to the emerging consensus the cost of defeat was banishment.

The year 1631 brought the first cloud on the religious horizon. In February of that year Roger Williams arrived in the colony. Born in about the year 1603, the son of a shopkeeper, Williams had been educated at Charterhouse and at Cambridge University through the patronage of Sir Edward Coke. He was a man of brilliant intellect and he was initially welcomed by the colonists, including John Winthrop (who had had contacts with Williams in England). The Boston congregation —the original Charlestown church relocated—tried to persuade Williams to accept a call as teacher, especially since John Wilson was planning a lengthy trip to England to collect his family. Williams, however, had strong Separatist leanings and refused to consider the appointment unless the Bostonians would repudiate their ties with the Church of England. When the congregation refused, he moved to Salem. Francis Higginson had died, and when that church called Williams as teacher he seemed willing to consider. Since the young clergyman had made clear his Separatist tendencies, Salem's interest in securing his services prompted a pointed inquiry from the General Court. The congregation withdrew its offer and Williams and his wife moved, for the time being, to Plymouth.

Finding Plymouth's Pilgrims insufficiently Separatist, Williams once again appeared in Salem in 1633. Taking advantage of the practice of lay sermonizing, he began to serve as an unofficial assistant to pastor Skelton. Soon the two united in criticizing the practices of their clerical colleagues. The clergy had begun the practice of gathering together regularly to consult with one another, and Williams and Skelton saw in this the threat of an emergent presbyterianism. Their complaint was denied and the clergy continued to consult. Far more serious was Williams's charge that the king had no right to grant Massachusetts to the Puritans because the land belonged to the Indians. Williams had set forth his arguments in a treatise that he had earlier shown to Bradford of Plymouth, and he intended to communicate his views to the king. The General Court censured Williams in 1633. Daunted by this rebuke, he dropped his plans and appeared before the next court penitent.

During the same spring Skelton died and the Salem church called Roger Williams as its pastor. An appealing person in many respects, Williams's insistence on a thorough and literal working out of the implications of his theology had always been a matter of concern to the clergy and magistrates of the Bay. Like other Puritan clergy, Williams used typology—the demonstration of New Testament occurrences as fulfillments of Old Testament premonitions—as a tool of scriptural analysis. But whereas most Puritans who employed this device emphasized the analogous relationship between ancient and modern events—seeing, for instance, Israel as a model for New England— Williams emphasized the radical difference the incarnation had effected. He specifically came to deny that Israel was a "type" for anything thereafter and denied that the civil magistrate in modern times had any right or obligation to become involved in spiritual affairs. Fearing the contamination of God's ordinances by the secular state, he denied the magistrates' authority to punish breaches of the first table of the ten commandments (which effectively denied the Puritan state's right to protect the true faith) and argued that a magistrate ought not tender oaths to unregenerated men (which would have abolished all civil oaths). In addition to these criticisms of the civil practices of Massachusetts, Williams's concern for the purity of worship led him to argue that the elect should not join with unregenerate men in prayer or worship—even those unregenerates who were in their own family.

In April of 1635 the governor and assistants summoned Williams to discuss his views on oaths. Some of the clergy who were present delivered the opposing view, which was naturally more convincing to the magistrates. But Williams was not swayed, and he was brought before the entire General Court in July.

Massachusetts was not designed to be a pluralistic state, and Roger Williams had consistently proffered views that were not only heretical in the eyes of the clergy and magistrates, but which if acted upon would have proved subversive to the leadership's envisioned "city on a hill." Forced to act by Williams's intransigence, the General Court warned the Salem congregation against installing the dissident in an official position. Lest the recommendation not carry enough weight, the court deferred action on a Salem petition seeking enlargement of the community. Ominously, the court also declared that those who persisted in maintaining the views expressed by Williams might have to be removed from the colony.

Despite his later reputation as a conciliator, Williams's reaction to the court's decisions was far from conciliatory. He informed the Salem church that he could not in conscience communicate with the other churches of the Bay and that he would not maintain communion with the Salem congregation unless it joined him in renouncing ties with the other churches. Faced with the threats of the General Court and Williams's own intransigence, the Salem congregation began to back away from its fiery member and ultimately repudiated his views. In October, Williams was again called before the General Court, where Thomas Hooker sought for the last time to win him to New England's orthodoxy. This effort failed, and the court sentenced Williams to depart from the Bay within six weeks. The sentenced man's health was weak, however, and the season late. Sentence was deferred until spring on condition that Williams not seek to spread his condemned opinions. But this he was unable to do, and in January of 1636 the assistants issued orders for his immediate transportation to England. Winthrop, disagreeing with Williams but not wishing to see him dispatched to the England of William Laud, warned him of the magistrates' edict and Williams was able to escape south to the Providence territory. In Salem the last signs of his influence were gradually stamped out by Hugh Peter, who became the congregation's next pastor.

In 1634, while the magistrates' controversy with Roger Williams was still in its early stages, William Hutchinson and his family arrived in Boston, where he soon established himself as an important figure in the mercantile life of the colony and a respected member of the church. Possessed of a strong personality, William's wife Anne had been primarily responsible for the family's remove from England. A disciple of John Cotton, she had found no spiritual mentor capable of providing the same solace when Cotton left his living in Lincolnshire to become John Wilson's colleague in the Boston church. Like so many other Puritans, the Hutchinsons followed their pastor to America.

While William was making a mark in the commercial affairs of the town, Anne was achieving her own place in its spiritual life. In the spring and summer of 1635 she began to hold weekday meetings at which she gave oral resumes of the preceding Sabbath's sermons for the benefit of women who had been unable to attend. The privacy of her home created an atmosphere of informality and encouraged her listeners to seek clarification of difficult points from Mrs. Hutchinson.

Anne Hutchinson was a remarkably astute and intelligent woman—particularly in a time when women were not encouraged to develop their talents. Her meetings grew in popularity. Soon men as well as women, Sabbath keepers as well as absentees, sought out her home, and the numbers necessitated a second weekly session.

None of this was necessarily dangerous. Laymen were still encouraged to seek God's will on their own in the Bay—Winthrop himself, though not a clergyman, had preached on occasion and was certainly ready at all times to voice his views on theological issues. The year 1635, with uncertainty created by a Privy Council examination of the Massachusetts charter and by the Roger Williams controversy, was a natural time for the elect to seek all the guidance they could find. But the return of John Wilson in October 1635 caused a change in Mrs. Hutchinson's meetings.

John Wilson's sermons as pastor of the Boston church began to disturb Mrs. Hutchinson almost immediately. Wilson, like most of the clergy of the Bay, placed a strong emphasis on human actions as a means of preparation for God's grant of saving grace and as evidence of sanctification. But such a thrust had been absent from the pulpit of the Boston church during Wilson's journey to England. The congregation had listened primarily to John Cotton, who resembled the English Puritan Richard Sibbes in de-emphasizing preparation in favor of stressing the inevitability of God's will. These two positions were matters of different emphasis only; neither Wilson nor Cotton believed that works could help to *save* man. In all likelihood most members of the Boston congregation saw no difference at all in the sermons of the two men. But to Mrs. Hutchinson—theologically astute and long an adherent of Cotton—there was a difference, and she soon began to make adverse comments on Wilson in her private meetings.

Mrs. Hutchinson's shift from expositor to critic was initially masked from the colonial officials because of growing concern over the actions of the Pequot Indians in southern New England. The Pequots had murdered nine Englishmen in 1634, but the disreputable character of the victims had cast doubt as to who bore the responsibility for the incident. The Massachusetts authorities entered into a treaty with the tribe in the hope of preventing further bloodshed. The Pequots failed to live up to the agreement, however, and in July 1636 they murdered trader John Oldham. The Massachusetts authorities dispatched John Endecott and ninety volunteers to retaliate. Endecott found few Pequots, and his destruction of Indian property only served to inflame the tribe. During the winter of 1636–1637 the Pequots held the garrison of Saybrook under a virtual siege. Though the Indian menace was soon laid to rest with the success of Massachusetts and Connecticut forces in surrounding and killing over five hundred of the tribe at Mystic, while it continued the war posed a serious threat to the colonies that added to the atmosphere of crisis in which the Hutchinsonian faction would emerge and be judged.

By the summer of 1636 the meetings in the Hutchinson household were attracting individuals of considerable status, including such wealthy and powerful citizens as William Aspinwall, William Coddington, and John Coggeshall—all three of whom had served as Boston deputies to the General Court. Henry Vane had also become one of Mrs. Hutchinson's disciples. The young Puritan son of the Comptroller of the King's Household, Vane had arrived in the Bay in 1635 and was chosen governor in 1636. The group's significance was further heightened by the popular notion that John Cotton was their mentor and by the definite clerical support of the Reverend John Wheelwright—Anne's brother-in-law—who arrived from England in June of 1636.

Mrs. Hutchinson had begun to broaden her attack. Having visited other churches of the Bay she began to argue that not only John Wilson in Boston, but all of the clergy of Massachusetts save Cotton and Wheelwright were preaching not the Covenant of Grace, but a Covenant of Works. They were, in her eyes, placing so great an emphasis on the individual's good conduct as to imply that such conduct was indispensable to salvation. Anne Hutchinson herself denied this, maintaining that assurance of salvation was conveyed not by action but by an essentially mystical experience of grace—an inward conviction of the coming of the Spirit to the individual that bore no relationship to outward conduct.

Despite the attempts of some past historians to envision the Hutchinsonian dispute as involving a clash between forces of liberty and repression, the argument between the orthodox and the Hutchinsonians was truly over theology and public order. In the opinion of the orthodox Mrs. Hutchinson was an antinomian, looking inward for assurance and guidance rather than toward the institutions of church and state. Her views, all the more dangerous because they represented a further development of, rather than a break with, orthodoxy, were a threat to order in both realms. To Anne Hutchinson, the clergy and the magistrates were no better than Arminians.

Mrs. Hutchinson's views, in divorcing questions of conduct from evaluations of one's spiritual state, were of the sort that would have offered spiritual and psychological solace to those mercantile elements in Boston who were troubled and doubt-ridden by the community's criticism of their business practices. Her supporters in the city comprised a majority of the church and in October of 1636 they moved to reform the congregation by moving that John Wheelwright be called as a second teacher. Winthrop, who by then was aware of and opposed to the views of the Hutchinsonians, forcefully opposed the appointment and was able to prevent the necessary consensus from developing. Rebuffed at Boston, Wheelwright was called to minister to a new church at Mt. Wollaston, where many of the Bostonians owned property.

What concerned the orthodox clergy as much as Mrs. Hutchinson's errors was the authority lent to those views by her association with Wheelwright and Cotton. In fact, neither of those ministers was probably aware of the full system of her thought and both would have found much in it to reject. Wheelwright, however, by virtue of his family relationship and his arrival after the lines of battle were drawn, quickly became a Hutchinsonian partisan. Cotton was a different story. His position was more ambiguously stated, and his stature in Old and New England required that an attempt be made to save him for the orthodox camp. In December of 1636 his fellow clergy visited Cotton in his home to question him about his attitude toward the Hutchinsonians. If they were less than fully satisfied with his answers, they were even more disturbed by their confrontation with Anne Hutchinson, whom they had summoned to the meeting. As some of them later recollected, she cast doubt on whether the ministers were themselves justified.

This confrontation only served to harden the lines of division. In January 1637 the Boston church was barely restrained from censuring pastor Wilson. In the months that followed Mrs. Hutchinson and her more dedicated followers left the meetinghouse whenever Wilson rose to preach. The General Court ordered a colony-wide day of fast and prayer for the calming of the disturbances in the churches. But John Wheelwright used the occasion to preach a sermon that further inflamed the controversy.

A majority of the Boston church protected Mrs. Hutchinson from her congregation's censure, and government intervention was prevented by Governor Vane's support of the faction. Thus the general elections of 1637 assumed a great significance, and the transfer of the court of elections to Newtown—away from the center of antinomianism—was a shrewd tactical success for the orthodox. John Winthrop was the choice of the orthodox for governor, and suddenly freemanship had a new importance. Some men from Newbury traveled 40 miles to Newtown to be made freemen and cast their votes for Winthrop. The election was no real contest. Winthrop was chosen governor with Dudley deputy governor. Endecott was chosen to the life council. Vane was not even chosen to be among the assistants. Spurred by rumors that additional sectaries were planning to migrate to the colony, the court proceeded to adopt an aliens act forbidding any new arrival from purchasing a home in the Bay or from remaining in any town for more than three weeks without authorization from one of the life council or two of the magistrates. The court charged John Wheelwright with sedition for remarks in his fast-day sermon. He was questioned and found guilty, sentence being deferred until the next session.

The rise of Anne Hutchinson seemed to indicate that the doctrinal structure of Puritanism was too loose, that it allowed too much freedom to untrained minds, which might easily fall into error. To remedy that deficiency in their "city on a hill," a synod was called, which assembled at Newtown on 30 August 1637. The clergy of the Bay were in attendance as were John Davenport (recently arrived from England), as well as Samuel Stone and Thomas Hooker from Connecticut. Hooker and Peter Bulkeley of Concord were chosen moderators and the assembled ministers proceeded to discuss, define, and confute eighty-two errors that were to be guarded against by the faithful—many of them opinions that had been attributed to the antinomians. On the last day of the synod the clergy also concluded that private religious meetings such as those that had taken place in the Hutchinson home should be discouraged and that the critical questioning of the clergy should be forbidden.

The errors of the dissidents having been demonstrated, the judicial proceedings against the Hutchinsonians continued. Henry Vane had left the Bay just prior to the opening of the synod. In November of 1637 the General Court passed sentence on John Wheelwright, disenfranchising and banishing him. Two of the lay members of the faction were next dealt with. John Coggeshall was disenfranchised and William Aspinwall was banished. The court then called Mrs. Hutchinson. The magistrates proceeded according to standards that do not satisfy modern legal ethics, but which were no worse and in some respects superior to those employed in England at that time. Though she defended herself ably, Mrs. Hutchinson's claim to have received direct personal revelations from God aroused her judges and contributed significantly to her conviction and sentencing to banishment. Other supporters were then disenfranchised and members of the faction were ordered to admit their errors or suffer being forbidden to bear arms. John Cotton, whose views could have enabled him to move in either direction, was himself in a dangerous situation, but he bowed to the wisdom of his clerical colleagues. He had tried to understand and help

Anne Hutchinson but had never embraced her more controversial views. After her sentencing, he made his peace with his ministerial brethren and accepted their definition of orthodoxy.

By the end of November 1637 the Hutchinsonian threat was at an end, though the loose ends remained to be tied up. Coddington, Coggeshall, and others received permission to leave the colony and made preparations to settle in Rhode Island. John Wheelwright declined to join them; perhaps he had discovered at last the extent of his differences with his sister-in-law. He journeyed north instead, into the New Hampshire territory. The Boston church, though stricken by the action against its members, entertained a motion to censure John Winthrop for his part in the proceedings against the Hutchinsonians. That effort had no chance of succeeding, but Winthrop used the occasion to delineate another rule of the Bay, maintaining that the church had no authority to censure a public official for action undertaken in a public capacity. In March of 1638 the Boston church tried and excommunicated Mrs. Hutchinson and she departed for Rhode Island.

EXTERNAL THREATS

John Winthrop's dream of a "city on a hill" must have seemed ephemeral during the 1630s. The evolution of political and ecclesiastical institutions precipitated numerous disputes, any one of which could have permanently split the colony. The Pequot War posed a different but no less serious threat. And the world outside New England continued to impinge upon the colonists. Occasionally news from Europe was heartening. The Protestant forces of Gustavus Adolphus had swept to a series of triumphs in the German struggle. Believing that their prayers had been in part responsible for that reversal of the tide the citizens of the Bay gathered in their churches to offer thanks to God for his blessings on the Protestant cause. But for most of the decade foreign news was more threatening than reassuring.

Sir Ferdinando Gorges, one of the principal figures in the Council for New England, had been ignorant of the Bay Company's royal charter. Apprised of it in 1632, Gorges sought to restore the colony to the council's control. He was able to use his influence at court to bring the question of Massachusetts before the Privy Council. Enemies of the Bay, such as Thomas Morton, came forward to testify to the colonists' denigration of the Anglican church and the royal will. A committee comprised of twelve members of the Privy Council and two principal secretaries of state investigated the complaints lodged against the colony. In January of 1633 the committee submitted to the king a report favorable to the colony, in which it cited the potential usefulness of Massachusetts as a provider of naval stores. But the report ignored the colony's legal status—which Gorges had called into question. In May the committee began to address the legal issues under its new chairman, the recently appointed archbishop of Canterbury, William Laud.

In April of 1634 the Privy Council's investigatory committee was enlarged and reconstituted as the Commission for Regulating Plantations. Still under Laud's chairmanship, the new body was empowered to govern and legislate for all English colonies, to safeguard the Anglican church overseas, and to hear complaints against and remove colonial officials. Massachusetts had already begun to erect fortifications in Boston harbor, and when news of the Laud commission's activities was received the General Court ordered further fortifications, organized armed militia bands and compulsory military drill, and appointed a military council that included Winthrop and Endecott.

With the hostile eyes of William Laud upon them the magistrates must have been shocked when John Endecott chose that delicate time in the colony's relations with the mother country to deface the English flag. Endecott, having discussed the matter with Roger Williams, concluded that the red cross in the English ensign was a papist ornament, since its use had been granted to the English monarchy by the papacy. Acting on this belief he cut the cross out of the flag at Salem. This could easily have been construed as an act of rebellion, and one of the members of the General Court lodged a complaint against Endecott. But while the former governor's action was thought to be ill-timed, there was noticeable support for the act itself. The General Court was initially unable to agree on any punishment, and their eventual decision to censure the Salem magistrate and disable him from holding office for one year was no more than a slap on the wrist.

Meanwhile, in England, King Charles instructed the attorney general, Sir John Banks, to call in the charter of the Bay colony by instituting quo warranto proceedings. Informed of this, the Massachusetts clergy urged the magistrates to defend their lawful possessions should a governor-general be sent from England, and the magistrates continued with their preparations to offer such resistance. For a while in 1635 it appeared that there might be fighting in Boston harbor. The king, assuming that quo warranto proceedings would bring the desired result, gave Gorges and Sir John Mason a commission to govern the region in his name. They had ordered the construction of a large vessel to carry them and troops to New England. But—through God's agency as the colonists saw it—the vessel broke up upon launching and the immediate threat to the colony was deferred. In June the magistrates of the Bay received notification that the Court of King's Bench had vacated the charter. In July, Charles I announced his assumption of the government of the colony and appointed Gorges governor. But the king, himself in severe financial straits, had no funds to give Gorges, and the new governor had already exhausted his resources. While the Massachusetts leaders prepared to defend themselves should it prove necessary, the attention of the English court was increasingly drawn to a threat closer to home. Charles I's attempt to impose the Book of Common Prayer on Scotland had led to the signing of the National Covenant by the Presbyterians of the northern kingdom and the outbreak of the Bishops War. The king found himself incapable of supporting his army in the field. He had, as Winthrop soon concluded, "neither heart nor leisure to look after the affairs of New England." Fortunately—providentially the colonists would have said—English developments were thereafter to occupy the king until his death and thus to assure the continued life of the Bible Commonwealths.

Through conflict with the English government and among themselves the colonists had come to define what they meant by a godly society in church and state and guarded their "city on a hill" against external and internal threats. The very survival of the colony as a Puritan state was frequently in jeopardy, but the settlers had succeeded not only in surviving but in erecting a civilization that could serve as a model for seventeenth-century England and for later generations of New Englanders.

6 | VARIATIONS ON A THEME: CONNECTICUT, NEW HAVEN, RHODE ISLAND, AND THE EASTERN FRONTIER

During the formative decade of Massachusetts history, while Winthrop, Cotton, and others were putting their ideals of religious and political perfection into practice, three other colonies were established in New England and the settlement of the northern frontier was advanced. Two of the new colonies—Connecticut and New Haven—were true sister colonies to the Bay and Plymouth. Their leaders were animated by the same desire for reform as possessed the guiding spirits of Massachusetts, and they set about erecting new societies in the same fashion. The third new colony, Rhode Island, was peopled largely by exiles from the Bay—men and women like Roger Williams and Anne Hutchinson who could not live with the Puritans of Massachusetts and who, in learning to live with each other, advanced the cause of religious freedom in the Western world.

CONNECTICUT

In 1634, with the controversy between the magistrates and Roger Williams building toward its eventual climax, the preaching of John

Cotton producing a religious revival that would alter the membership requirements of the Massachusetts churches, and the gravity of the Privy Council's hearings becoming more evident, the settlers of Newtown, Massachusetts, began their plans to migrate to the Connecticut River valley. Though they cited as reason their need for more land, there was more involved in their decision.

Newtown had been selected as a site for settlement in December of 1630. The magistrates had chosen the community to be the colony's capital and ordered fortifications to be erected. Thomas Dudley settled there, as did John Haynes, another of the assistants. In 1632 the town's population was augmented by the arrival of immigrants from Chelmsford, Colchester, and Braintree in England. The newcomers organized a church that was presided over by its lay elders until the following year, when Thomas Hooker and Samuel Stone arrived and were ordained pastor and teacher. Within a few months discontent in Newtown and other towns gave promise of a large secession from the Bay. The citizens of Newtown complained that their land was arid and sandy, and that there was not enough of it. Watertown and Dorchester inhabitants had similar complaints. They contrasted their situations with the reported fertility of the Connecticut River valley and sought permission to leave the Bay.

The General Court in September 1634 denied the Newtown petition, but within a year it became obvious to the court that the migration was inevitable and authorization was grudgingly granted. Citizens from Watertown, Dorchester, and Newtown became the founders respectively of the Connecticut towns of Wethersfield, Windsor, and Hartford.

Land hunger was very likely a central concern of the migrants, just as they had claimed. But the precariousness of Massachusetts' situation was probably an added incentive for the removal, just as it was likely to have contributed to the assistants' reluctance to let them go. The sense of kinship in a common cause that had motivated many of the early colonists had been partially destroyed by the charges of Roger Williams, the dispute between Winthrop and Dudley (particularly poignant in Newtown), and the Watertown protest over tax levies. More serious was the threat that the English courts might vacate the charter. The shaky start that the colony had gotten off to must have encouraged many to think of starting anew.

Also contributing to the colonization of Connecticut were a number of jealousies that divided the elite of the Bay, most significantly that between John Cotton and Thomas Hooker. Both had been prominent clergymen in England, but Hooker was probably the more celebrated in their homeland. In New England the magistrates initially singled out Hooker by frequently seeking his advice and selecting him to publicly debate Roger Williams. But Cotton gradually began to eclipse the Newtown clergyman in importance. This was partly the result of the eclipse of Newtown by Boston. Had the river town in fact become the colony's capital Hooker's preeminence would have been assured. Winthrop's remaining in Boston put Cotton closest to the magistrates and guaranteed his recognition as the colony's foremost clergyman (a position jeopardized by the antinomian controversy but soon thereafter recovered). This must have been galling to Hooker on a personal level, but it was of greater significance in that he did not see eye to eye with Cotton on a number of theological points, the most important being church membership. While Cotton was downplaying preparation yet insisting on compelling evidence of saving grace from candidates, Hooker was a strong preparationist who believed that prospective members should be accepted at the slightest sign of the stirring of grace in their souls. Cotton's strategic location seemed likely to assure the success of his views and to make the Massachusetts way less satisfying to Thomas Hooker.

Such friction probably contributed to the wanderlust of the Newtown leaders. But it should not be exaggerated. Once Hooker and Haynes were established in Connecticut it did not take long for relations with Massachusetts to be regularized.

Having decided to leave Massachusetts, the leaders of the secession met frequently during the winter of 1635–1636 to determine the best means of advancing the new settlement. The land along the Connecticut River had been claimed by Plymouth, which had established a trading post near the site of Windsor. Furthermore, in 1630 the Council for New England had granted a large expanse of territory—including the Connecticut River region—to the Earl of Warwick, who had shortly thereafter transferred the title to the Puritan-dominated Providence Company, whose members included Lord Say and Sele, Lord Brooke, Sir Richard Saltonstall, John Pym, and John Hampden. In 1635 the officers of the Providence Company commissioned John Winthrop, Jr., to secure their title and erect a fort at the mouth of the Connecticut River, which Winthrop established and named Saybrook. When the Hooker group began to lay their plans the leaders of the migration met with the younger Winthrop and some of the Massachusetts magistrates. As a result of those deliberations the General Court of Massachusetts and Winthrop junior (as agent of the Warwick patentees) jointly appointed eight commissioners to govern the new settlements for the twelve months from March 1636 to March 1637.

While the agreement seemed to recognize the territorial claims of both Massachusetts and the Warwick patentees, in fact Connecticut was an independent commonwealth from the first meeting of the commission. Roger Ludlow, deputy governor of the new plantation, presided over those meetings in the absence of the younger Winthrop, who, though technically governor, never attended the commission's sessions.

By the end of 1636 at least eight hundred men, women, and children had struggled overland from Massachusetts with their livestock and other possessions to take up residence in Hartford, Windsor, and Wethersfield. After the expiration of the Bay's commission, the towns of Connecticut elected representatives to their own General Court, their assumption of governmental rights probably precipitated by the need for direction in the Pequot War, which conflict dominated the agenda of the first four sessions of the court. That menace ended, the Connecticut magistrates directed their attention to the regularization of government in the colony. The need for some form of constitution had possibly been felt by the colonists during the Pequot War, and the colony's desire for confederation with the other New England colonies made independent organization even more desirable.

Thomas Hooker preached a sermon to the General Court in May of 1638 setting forth his views on civil government, most of which were subsequently incorporated into the colony's constitution. The chief difference between Hooker's ideas and the political principles of the Bay's leaders lay in the clergyman's description of the rights of the people. Applying Congregational religious theory more directly to the political process than was usual, he contended that "the foundation of authority is laid in the free consent of the people." He pointed out that if the magistrates were chosen by the free consent of the people the subjects would be more likely to submit to authority. At the same time, Hooker expressed the belief that the electorate had the right to set the bounds for the power of those whom they elected. Spurred on by Hooker, the General Court set out to draft an instrument of government. John Haynes and Edward Hopkins shared in the drafting, but Roger Ludlow was primarily responsible for the final document, the Fundamental Orders of Connecticut, which was adopted by the General Court on 14 January 1639 and gave the new colony essentially the same forms of government as the Bay.

During its early history the river colony's growth was steady, though not spectacular. The population of eight hundred in 1636 increased to two thousand by 1642 and thirty-two hundred in 1654. The inhabitants derived their livings almost exclusively from agricultural pursuits; Connecticut in its early history spawned no commercial rival to Boston. Socially this resulted in a land of few extremes, the colony being noted for neither poverty nor riches. Politically the colony was engaged in frequent boundary disputes with Massachusetts, Rhode Island, New Haven, and—most serious—the Dutch in New Netherland. But there were no internal divisions such as had riven Massachusetts in the 1630s, attributable perhaps to the relative tolerance of Connecticut.

NEW HAVEN

New Haven is now a secondary city in Connecticut noted primarily for the presence of Yale University. But in the mid-seventeenth century it was the seat of government of the most territorially ambitious of the Puritan colonies and the one most dedicated to the ideal of the "city on a hill." In that very dedication lay the seeds of the colony's eventual demise.

The story of the New Haven colony begins in England with the members of St. Stephen's Church, on Colman Street in London, who provided many of the original settlers of the colony and its two most important leaders—John Davenport and Theophilus Eaton. Davenport was a twenty-seven-year-old vicar, a dropout from Oxford, when called to be pastor of St. Stephen's in 1624. Suspected of Puritan sympathies from the start of his ministry, in the early stages of his career he vigorously denied such charges. At his new parish he quickly acquired a considerable reputation as an effective preacher. Encouraged by his success he returned to participate in the Oxford disputations of 1625 and received his degree. Drawn into the circle of preachers concerned with the poor livings of the church, he became a member of the Feofees for Impropriations. In 1627 he joined Richard Sibbes in organizing the drive to raise funds for the German Protestants. Davenport was also interested in overseas colonial outlets for Puritan energies. He was one of the original group that took over from the Dorchester Company of Adventurers and then developed into the Massachusetts Bay Company.

When William Laud became bishop of London, Davenport's difficulties began in earnest. The feofees' activities were stopped, and Davenport was criticized by the court for his actions on behalf of the Germans. By the early 1630s any doubts as to the Puritan sympathies of the pastor of St. Stephen's had long since been dispelled. When Laud became archbishop of Canterbury, Davenport left the country and took up residence in the Netherlands. He served briefly as a chaplain to the émigré queen of Bohemia, entered into a dispute over church government with John Paget of the English church in Amsterdam, and shared ministerial duties to the English congregation in Rotterdam with Hugh Peter. But during these years the Dutch were responding to Laud's pressure by making things more difficult for the Puritans in exile. In 1635 Davenport returned secretly to England.

Davenport found many of his former parishioners disillusioned by the rise of Laud and the policies of the English government. Together with his boyhood friend and parishioner of St. Stephen's, Theophilus Eaton, he organized a group willing to emigrate to New England. After a delay in their originally scheduled departure the aspiring colonists sailed from England and arrived in Boston in June of 1637.

The Davenport-Eaton group remained in Boston for almost a year. During that time Davenport became involved in the Hutchinsonian controversy. His prestige and the wealth of many of the other members of his party spurred numerous efforts from towns in the Bay to persuade the newcomers to settle in their jurisdictions. But many of the former members of St. Stephen's were London merchants who wished to found their own mercantile center, since they recognized they would be at a disadvantage in the Bay competing with the established merchants of Boston. Then, too, the precariousness of the situation in Massachusetts, which had been one of the causes of the migration to Connecticut, might also have influenced them. The Pequot War had stimulated interest in a move to the northern shore of Long Island Sound; Eaton led a group that explored the coast and selected a site.

In March of 1638 the Davenport-Eaton group left Boston, having added to their number many citizens of Massachusetts who desired to throw in their lot with the new enterprise. In April they arrived at Quinnipiac, as the new settlement was called until the name was changed to New Haven in 1640. The colonists purchased land from the Indians but possessed no legal title in the eyes of English law. The original settlement encompassed only the town that was to be named New Haven, and, though the government and laws of the settlement spoke of a magistrate and four deputy magistrates, the actual government was essentially that of a town meeting. As in Massachusetts, only church members were eligible for the franchise. Davenport had lived with John Cotton during his stay in Boston and the two shared similar ideas on civil government. Cotton had provided Davenport with a copy of his *Discourse about Civil Government in a New Plantation Whose Design is Religion*, in which the Boston clergyman set forth the case for limiting civil office and freemanship to church members. Cotton also sent to New Haven a copy of his proposed legal code, *Moses His Judicials*, which was drawn largely from the Bible. The code was rejected by the Massachusetts General Court, but due to Davenport's influence it received a more sympathetic reception from the New Haven lawmakers.

The five years following the settlement at Quinnipiac saw the transformation of New Haven from a town with great aspirations to an actual colony. Nine months before Connecticut adopted the Fundamental Orders, the colonists at New Haven adopted a similar, if more conservative, Plantation Covenant. In 1641 a church dispute in Wethersfield, Connecticut, led a faction from that community to secede and settle on land claimed from New Haven, the new town of Stamford becoming the second community in the colony. At about the same time the colony also expanded to the southern shore of Long Island Sound, the town of Southold accepting New Haven's control. In 1643 the New England Confederation was organized and, by virtue of her jurisdiction over Stamford and Southold, New Haven was invited to membership with Massachusetts, Connecticut, and Plymouth. At that point the towns of Milford and Guilford, both of which had been founded independently at an earlier date, surrendered their independence and joined the growing New Haven colony. In the seventeenth century, transportation by water was, when available, faster and cheaper than transportation by land routes. The real spine of the New Haven colony was Long Island Sound, and the colony's leaders saw their future as being based on commercial control of the territories bounded by the sound. At its furthest extent the colony was concentrated in the region of the present state of Connecticut, bounded by Guilford on the east and Milford in the west, with settlement extending not much more than 15 miles inland. To the west of the coastal possessions of the colony of Connecticut, New Haven claimed jurisdiction over Stamford and (after 1650) Greenwich. A third region of control lay across the sound and included the Long Island towns of Southold, Southampton, East Hampton, Oyster Bay, and Huntington. At various times the colony also maintained a settlement on the Delaware River.

As the various towns were added to the New Haven jurisdiction, adjustments were made in the colony's governance to provide the new settlers with representation. Following the addition of Milford and Guilford in 1643, a new frame of government was adopted. The New Haven Fundamental Agreement of October 1643 represented the limitation of the right to vote and hold office to "free burgesses," who had to be church members. The General Court was composed of the governor, deputy governor, magistrates, and two deputies from each town, and possessed both legislative and judicial authority. Sessions were semiannual until 1648, when annual sessions were instituted. Trial by jury was abolished in the colony, apparently because in the smaller towns it would have been impossible, after eliminating interested parties, to raise a jury of twelve church members. Theophilus Eaton, governor of New Haven from its founding until his death in 1658, was the leading force behind this substitution of magisterial for jury decisions.

Like Connecticut, New Haven was chronically involved in disputes over her boundaries, the most serious of which was with the Dutch. In 1640 a number of merchants and citizens of the town of New Haven, including Davenport, had formed the Delaware Company for the purpose of exploring the Delaware River basin for its potential as a location for trade and settlement. At the time the region was claimed by both the Dutch and the Swedes. The company received permission from the Swedes to settle on the east side of the river, at Salem Creek, and the New Havenites acquired land on the west bank by purchasing it from the Indians. But the Dutch soon intervened; they destroyed the trading post and jailed the leaders of the expedition. New Haven still claimed the region, but the Dutch refused to acknowledge their rights and successfully prevented any permanent settlement.

This failure on the Delaware was only one of the blows struck at the economic dreams of the New Havenites. Considerable effort was put into inducing John Winthrop, Jr., to initiate an ironworks in the colony, but his departure after the project had been started doomed the plan to failure. An attempt was made to engage in shipbuilding on a large scale, and an 80-ton vessel was constructed in New Haven for the purpose of opening a direct trade with England, but the ship, carrying substantial exports, was lost on its maiden voyage. Business transactions were hampered by a shortage of currency, most of the merchants having exhausted their resources in the original journey to New England, the year's stay in Boston, the struggle to establish the new colony, and unsuccessful ventures such as the ironworks. The settlement on the Delaware was a last hope for commercial salvation, but it failed. Despite the ambitions of the founders, New Haven remained primarily an agricultural colony during its independent existence.

While the colony did not establish a commercial empire it did become noted for religious zeal. The churches of New Haven closely regulated the lives of their members. Indeed, during the history of the colony the list of those censured and excommunicated from the church for moral shortcomings included one of the seven pillars of the church, the wife of Governor Eaton, and the colony's first schoolmaster, Ezekiel Cheever. When the majority of New England's clergy began to advocate a change in the ecclesiastical system by an extension of baptism, it was Davenport who led the opposition and who was instrumental in the Cambridge Synod's rejection of Richard Mather's liberalizing proposals. In the 1640s and 1650s no New England colony exceeded New Haven in its zealous support of the English Puritan revolution.

RHODE ISLAND

If Connecticut and New Haven were true sister colonies to Massachusetts, the former slightly more liberal and the latter more conservative, Rhode Island had considerably less in common with the Bay and was regarded with suspicion and fear by her neighbors. Populated largely by exiles from Massachusetts, the colony provided a test of what would develop if certain elements in the Puritan system were pushed further than the orthodox would allow. Out of such attempts came the first stirrings in America of the Baptist church and the Society of Friends.

When Roger Williams left Salem in January of 1636 he traveled south into land claimed by Plymouth and then, warned off by the Plymouth authorities, to one of the estuaries of Narragansett Bay, where he purchased land from the Indians and laid the foundation of what became Providence. Gradually other settlers joined him and the town grew, almost all of the inhabitants pursuing farming on a small scale. Originally the heads of the various resident families met as a governing body. Later, single men were also admitted, and Williams drew up a covenant whereby all pledged themselves to abide by the decisions of the majority in secular affairs. From the start there was no claim for government control over matters of religion.

Two years after the settlement of Providence, the population of the Rhode Island territory was further augmented by the arrival of a new group of exiles from the Bay. William Coddington, assisted by Williams, purchased from the Indians the large island of Aquidneck lying between Narragansett Bay and the Sakonnet River. His party of "antinomians" included John Clarke, John Coggeshall, William Aspinwall, William Dyer, and Anne Hutchinson. They laid out a town at the island's northern end, which later was named Portsmouth.

Coddington, a wealthy, respected merchant, became the community's chief magistrate. But the spirit of cooperation that had bound the group together in Massachusetts and in the founding of Portsmouth was soon shattered. Anne Hutchinson, against Coddington's wishes, welcomed Samuel Gorton to the settlement. Gorton soon demonstrated that his religious eccentricities were matched by political ambitions that were anathema to Coddington. When Coddington was absent from the town in April of 1639 a union of Hutchinson and Gorton followers ousted the chief magistrate and replaced him with William Hutchinson.

Coddington and his supporters seceded from the community and founded the town of Newport on the southern end of the island. When Mrs. Hutchinson and Gorton fell out in 1640, Coddington engineered the union of Newport and Portsmouth, creating a separate colony with himself as governor and individuals drawn from both towns as assistants. In 1641 the Aquidneck colony proclaimed itself a democracy with religious freedom for all. (Mrs. Hutchinson remained in Portsmouth until her husband's death in 1642, whereupon she moved to Long Island and then to Eastchester, in New Netherland, where she and her entire household, save for one daughter, were massacred by Indians in the summer of 1643.)

Samuel Gorton had opposed the union of Portsmouth and Newport and challenged the constitutional authority of the new colony's magistrates. He was imprisoned and then banished. Denied freeman's status in Williams's Providence, he and his followers moved on to Pawtucket. The proprietors there—Benedict and William Arnold— wished to merge with Massachusetts, and so Gorton's party purchased land slightly to the south, founding the town later named Warwick. With the connivance of the Arnolds, the local Indians repudiated their sale of land to Gorton, and the Massachusetts authorities seized him and briefly jailed him. After his release he journeyed to England and returned with the home government's permission to settle at Warwick, which he did.

With the founding of Warwick, Rhode Island contained five towns —Providence, Portsmouth, Newport, Pawtucket, and Warwick—all of which, except for the united towns on Aquidneck, were autonomous settlements. Each acknowledged the sovereignty of the English government and each was suspicious of its neighbors. The Arnolds at Pawtucket and Coddington at Aquidneck developed close ties with the Bay and even considered merger with Massachusetts, which would have been anathema to Williams at Providence and Gorton at Warwick. All were democratically governed, with basically all landowners eligible to vote, and all practiced religious toleration. Out of their divisions Roger Williams gradually shaped a single colony.

Williams had continued to develop his ideas following his exile from the Bay. In March of 1639 he had taken part in the organization of what is regarded as the first Baptist church in America, being baptised by immersion by his former Salem parishioner Ezekiel Holliman and himself in turn baptizing Holliman and ten others. But within about four months he had left that congregation, having become convinced that its organization was invalid since a church could only be true if it traced its origin to the apostles. He became a seeker until he concluded after a few years that there were no legitimate churches, the true church having lost its authority during the corruptions of the Middle Ages. Restoration could only come through the direct intervention of Christ. Churches until that time could only be imperfect replicas of the true church. This reinforced his typological arguments for denying the state any authority in religious matters. Ultimately, like his Rhode Island neighbors, Williams worked for the establishment of a total separation of church and state so as to safeguard religion from the influence of secular rulers.

In his writings on secular affairs Williams expressed his belief that the state was a purely civil institution. Individuals who had covenanted together in a community had the right to choose their magistrates, and the magistrates derived all of their authority from the people (not from God). Magistrates were retained in office by popular will and could be removed by the people. In joining a political community, however, the individual did bind himself to accept the will of the majority, and Williams was emphatic about the right of the magistrate to maintain order in secular affairs even if disruptive elements claimed that their consciences dictated opposition to the common will.

In 1643, Williams became convinced that the various settlements in the region had to be united if they were to succeed in resisting the territorial ambitions of the neighboring colonies. He traveled to England and, with the help of Sir Henry Vane (then over his embarrassments in the Hutchinsonian controversy and one of the leading figures in Parliament), obtained from Parliament a legal patent authorizing the political union of Providence and the Aquidneck settlements as "Providence Plantations." After Williams's return, an assembly of freemen from Providence, Portsmouth, Newport, and Warwick met and established a federal commonwealth. Initially all freemen could meet in the legislative assembly, a quorum of ten from each town being necessary to conduct business, but after 1650 it became a representative body. The assembly met four times a year, once in each town. The officers of the colony, including a president and four assistants, were elected annually. The spirit of the colony was expressed in the preamble to the instrument of government, which explained that "the form of government established in Providence Plantations is DEMOCRATICAL, that is to say, a government held by the free and voluntary consent of all, or the greater part of the free inhabitants." Nevertheless, the towns retained a strong degree of autonomy, and undesirable laws could be recalled by popular vote.

Williams's actions in bringing the settlements together were not greeted with universal applause. Coddington in particular launched a number of efforts in the colony and in England to circumvent the patent and reestablish his own small empire. It took another trip to England by Williams and John Clarke and Williams's own assumption of the colony's presidency, from 1654 to 1657, before Coddington finally accepted the union.

THE EASTERN FRONTIER

As with Rhode Island, the growth of settlement in northeastern New England was more the result of individual initiative than of any organized plan. Some of the towns were founded by men expelled from the Bay. But whereas Providence Plantations went its own independent way, many of the northeastern settlements were soon absorbed into the jurisdiction of Massachusetts.

In 1622 the Council for New England had granted Sir Ferdinando Gorges and Captain John Mason all the territory between the Merrimack and Kennebec rivers from the coast to the sources of the rivers. A year later Gorges and Mason sent a party to settle at Strawberry Bank at the mouth of the Piscataqua River near Dover, a small independent settlement that had been established a short time earlier. In 1629 the two proprietors divided their territory along the Piscataqua, Gorges getting the eastern portion, which became Maine, while Mason received the future New Hampshire, including the two small settlements on the river. In 1635 Mason died, and his heirs allowed their rights to fall into neglect.

In 1637, John Wheelwright, having been expelled from the Bay, traveled north with a following of about twenty families, among them that of William Wentworth (whose descendants would become the dominant political figures in eighteenth-century New Hampshire). Spending the winter at the Strawberry Bank settlement (later Portsmouth), in the spring they moved to the falls on the Squanscot River, where they founded the town of Exeter. They organized a church with Wheelwright as pastor, and the thirty-five male church members of the new community signed a civil compact binding themselves to majority rule.

While Exeter was being settled by Wheelwright, another group of exiles from Massachusetts took up residence at Dover. Chief among the newcomers was Captain John Underhill, another supporter of Anne Hutchinson. Underhill helped to organize a church at Dover and served briefly as the settlement's governor. The new congregation called as its minister Hansard Knollys, who had earlier lived in Boston but who was also a suspected antinomian. In 1640 a former Anglican clergyman, Thomas Larkham, who had been admitted to the Dover church, succeeded in supplanting Knollys as pastor. The revelation of Larkham's scandalous private life led to Knollys's reinstatement, but the night after Larkham had been excommunicated for moral misconduct Knollys was himself discovered in the bed of his maid. The disorder that surrounded these events included riots and threat of worse, and the situation ultimately required intervention from both the governor of Strawberry Bank and a commission from Massachusetts.

In 1638 the General Court of Massachusetts had trespassed on the Mason patent by authorizing a group of Bay colonists to move from Newbury across the Merrimack River to settle at Winnecunnet, later Hampton. Rather than allow the residents to divide the land as usual, the court placed control of the land in the hands of three Massachusetts residents who remained in the Bay, establishing a precedent that would be followed a century later when Massachusetts set out to repopulate Maine towns abandoned in the Indian wars. In 1641 Massachusetts accepted jurisdiction over the Piscataqua River settlements of Strawberry Bank and Dover. Though there remains some confusion as to the sequence of events, it seems that the annexation was precipitated by the residents of Dover. Many of that town's inhabitants were Puritans who had been disturbed by the poor state of the ministry in their community and hoped to achieve some stability in church affairs by the annexation. The inhabitants of Mason's old post at Strawberry Bank were not known for any Puritan sympathies, but they had prospered over the years and probably sought the protection that the Bay could offer them against internal unrest and foreign threats. Those already resident in the newly acquired territory were allowed to retain their voting rights regardless of their church status. In 1643, Exeter petitioned for annexation. When that action was completed all New Hampshire settlements had been brought under the jurisdiction of Massachusetts. John Wheelwright's banishment from the Bay was revoked in 1644, and three years later he accepted a call to be pastor at Hampton.

For forty years the Bay colony was to administer New Hampshire as a part of Massachusetts. During that period the settlements originally founded for economic reasons or by exiles from Massachusetts were transformed into images of the Bay towns. Churches and schools were forced upon the eastern frontier and that wilderness was civilized by the forces of American Puritanism.

Recent historians have been critical of those who in describing Massachusetts have called it New England. Certainly it would be misleading to ignore the differences in the various colonies of the region. And yet, as a group, the seventeenth-century English colonies had much in common with each other. Connecticut and New Haven were, with Massachusetts and Plymouth, true Bible Commonwealths—sister colonies that did not differ sharply in purpose but diverged slightly in the intensity and fashion in which each pursued their common goals. The eastern frontier, founded for different ends, soon came to share in the goals of the American Puritans. Only Rhode Island, where Puritanism burst its bounds, qualifies as a colony with a different view of the role of the state and the mission of its people.

7 | ORTHODOXY IN NEW ENGLAND: THE STATE

Within a decade and a half the citizens of the Bible Commonwealths had structured a society unique in the English-speaking world. They had hoped to create a model society, and their political and ecclesiastical institutions were in fact studied in the 1640s and 1650s by English Puritans engaged in restructuring their own society. While the various forms of colonial civil and ecclesiastical government differed slightly, the institutions of the region—always excepting Rhode Island—reflected common assumptions and beliefs that enable us to speak of a New England Way. That system of beliefs which emerged from the labor of the founders served as the framework within which future generations of colonists sought to solve the problems of their own times. When, in later decades, individuals such as Increase Mather bemoaned the decline of Puritanism, they were registering their sense of loss at the erosion of the values represented in the institutions of church and state bequeathed to them by their ancestors.

SECULAR ORTHODOXY:
THE PURITAN CONCEPT OF SOCIETY

The governmental systems that the colonists established in their separate corners of New England were not quite identical. The franchise, limited to church members in Massachusetts and New Haven, was broader in Connecticut, where "admitted inhabitants" who took an oath of loyalty could vote in town elections, and the right to participate in colony-wide politics was extended to whomsoever the General Court thought worthy, regardless of their church status. Relations between magistrates and deputies also differed—Connecticut magistrates did not possess the negative voice of their counterparts in Massachusetts and New Haven—as did the frequency of legislative meetings (annually rather than quarterly in New Haven). The distribution of authority between town and colony governments also varied slightly. But such instances of colonial individuality were more than balanced by the essential similarity of the Bible Commonwealths. Drawn from common backgrounds, motivated by a similar vision, the Puritans— always excepting the Rhode Islanders—shared similar views on the nature of society and politics and demonstrated those common bonds in their history.

The world view on which all the Puritans based their political structure was predominantly medieval, a reflection of their English heritage, and not at all distinctive of the Puritans. But as with so much else, what the Puritans touched they modified. While the basic communitarian theme in their thought was not original, their use of the concepts of calling and the covenant to bolster it did produce a new variant to the theme.

John Winthrop said to his fellow passengers on the *Arbella*,

Wee must be knitt together in this worke as one man, wee must entertaine each other in brotherly Affecion, wee must be willing to abridge ourselves of our superfluities, for the supply of others necessities, wee must uphold a familiar Commerce together in all meekenes, gentleness, patience and liberality, wee must delight in eache other, make others Condicions our owne, rejoyce together, mourne together, allwayes haveing before our eyes our Commission and Community in the worke, our Community as members of the same body.

In these lines and in the remainder of his lay sermon, "A Model of Christian Charity," are to be found most of the key elements of the Puritans' view of society—their awareness of community and individual interdependence, their awareness of the various callings of men, and their sense of mission.

The Puritans believed that man, depraved by the effects of original sin, would naturally sin. While grace restored some of man's ability to pursue right, the controls of human society were necessary to curb the sinful impulses of the individual. Consequently, they emphasized man's duty to work with his fellows in pursuit of common goals. Each individual was under an obligation to use his gifts for the public welfare and not his own advancement.

Society had, in the view of the Puritans, been ordained by God but required the cooperation of its members if progress was to be achieved. Members of a state were mutually dependent, each possessing certain

God-given gifts upon which his neighbors relied. In elaborating on this point the Puritans spoke of each man having a particular calling. In the pre-Reformation Christian tradition the concept of calling had referred to the sense of vocation felt by those who entered the religious life as priests or nuns. While medieval philosophers and theologians believed that each man was placed in his particular station in life by God, it was not until the Reformation that the concept of calling was extended by the reformers—particularly Calvinists—to spiritualize the honorable secular activities of ordinary men and women. In Puritan parlance, "calling" referred to an individual's occupation, and also to the other roles in which he performed—as father or son, husband or wife, subject or ruler, and so forth. After due consideration of the clues offered by God, a man was expected to choose and settle into those roles for which God had suited him. Having discerned his calling, it was his duty to work at it to the best of his ability.

Socially, the doctrine of the calling was extremely conservative. As Winthrop expressed it in his "A Model of Christian Charity," "in all times some must be rich, some poor; some high and eminent in power and dignity, others mean and in subjection." While changing one's calling was possible when private necessity and the public good so dictated, such occasions were rare, and the individual was discouraged from aspiring to a higher place than that for which God had suited him. The Puritans did attempt to moderate the harsh effects that are often bred by this type of rigid stratification, suggesting that there was a spiritual equality among all vocations. In the eyes of God, wrote William Perkins, all callings were equal, "though it be but to sweep the house or keep sheep." Each individual is called to make a unique and necessary contribution to the public welfare—society, in fact, was a community of specialists united by their need for one another. The man of high rank who used his status to abuse those who served less glamorously was forgetting the mutual dependence of the broad society on the contributions of all members.

Politically, the doctrine of the calling was also conservative, in that it mitigated against democratic impulses that Puritanism itself generated through religious emphasis on the priesthood of all believers and the perseverance of the saints. Political society for most Puritans was seen as being divided between those whom God had suited for the role of rulers and those whom God had called to be ruled. The necessity of having different men serving these distinct functions was the basis for John Cotton's objection to democracy—"If the people be governors, who shall be governed?" If the people were rulers and ruled themselves, then the functions of magistrate and subject were confused. One man could not have both callings simultaneously. Furthermore, the concept of calling meant that God had especially fitted certain men to serve in positions of authority, to be magistrates. Such men were chosen by God, vested with God's authority, and were to be trusted and obeyed.

The basis of all societies was a social covenant that implicitly or explicitly bound citizens together in quest of common goals. In Plymouth the Mayflower Compact was just such a covenant, as were Connecticut's Fundamental Orders and New Haven's Fundamental Agreement. In Massachusetts the colonists similarly viewed the charter as serving as a social contract that they explicitly ratified each year through their participation in the electoral process. Under the terms of such a covenant it was the responsibility of the eligible voters to carefully weigh the qualifications of the prominent men in the community, seeking to determine whom God had suited for the role of magistrate and choosing those individuals for office. Once elected, the magistrates were to be obeyed, even if a demonstrated lack of ability or judgment displayed the error of the people's choice. Only in the case of an evil ruler were the people justified in opposition, and even rebellion. In all other cases opposition to the magistrate was opposition to God, from whom all rulers derived their authority. The magistrates in turn had a responsibility to exercise their authority in such a way as to promote the common weal.

In New England the proper ordering of the state was even more essential than elsewhere because, whereas all societies were bound together by covenants requiring members to bear certain responsibilities to each other, the American Puritans saw themselves as also being engaged in a national covenant with God. They had been chosen by God to assist him in the redemption of the world by their complete obedience to his will. If they adhered to that covenant, Winthrop told his fellow migrants,

the Lord will be our God and delight to dwell among us, as his owne people and will command a blessing upon us in all our wayes, soe that wee shall see much more of his wisdome power goodness and truthe then formerly wee have beene acquainted with, . . . for wee must Consider that wee shall be as a City upon a Hill, the eies of all people are uppon us; soe that if wee shall deale falsely with our god in this worke wee have undertaken and soe cause him to withdrawe his present help from us, wee shall be made a story and a by-word through the world.

The colonists' resulting determination to adhere strictly to the terms of their national covenant with God definitely colored their concept of the proper scope of governmental activity.

The American Puritans believed in a strong and active government. It was the responsibility of the state to oversee the conduct of the citizens, seeing to it that they adhered to the path of righteousness or were punished for wandering from it. If the government failed to maintain proper standards, God would punish the whole people. The magistrates and legislatures established wage and price controls so that no individual could seek his own enrichment at the expense of the common good. They provided for school systems to provide future generations of leaders. Local government by town meetings and boards of selectmen prevented the admission to communities of undesirable newcomers. The town selectmen assumed responsibility for disadvantaged members of their towns (victims of Indian attacks, survivors of disease, and so on) by aiding them in their rehabilitation. Town meetings also regulated the personal conduct of community inhabitants with a sharp eye and a heavy hand.

SECULAR ORTHODOXY: CHURCH AND STATE

Of all the areas of governmental concern perhaps the most important for the Puritans, and yet the one they were most ambivalent about, was the safeguarding of the faith. The assumption by numerous historians that the Bible Commonwealths were theocracies still clouds our understanding. The fact is, of course, that the men who founded Massachusetts Bay and her sister colonies (Rhode Island excepted) believed that there was one true faith, one true way to worship according to God's wishes, and that it was possible to determine what that path of truth was. As a result, they felt it to be the duty of the magistrates to punish open expressions of heresy. Paradoxically, the Puritans arrived at this view as a result of their belief in the separate spheres of church and state. Drawing heavily upon the Bible, the colonists contended that the visible church, representing Christ's kingdom on earth, was a spiritual organization dealing with matters of the spirit and limited in its authority to spiritual powers. Thus, in dealing with those who held erroneous views in matters of faith, the church was and should be limited to attempting to persuade the individual of his error, to warn him of the dangers he faced if he publicly persisted in it, and—as a last resort—to expel him from the spiritual society by excommunication. The state, however, was an institution of the world and thus empowered to use secular weapons: corporal punishment, banishment, execution. Like the church, the state had a responsibility to uphold the true religion lest the public heretic prove to be a threat to the stability and purity of the commonwealth. The Puritans were not exceptional in this—all European governments believed in their responsibility to do likewise. In fact, though rarely given credit for it, the Puritans were less rigorous than many governments of their time in that they did not search out the secret thoughts of men but contented themselves with taking action against public expressions of heresy.

If, however, it was the duty of the state to support the true faith, who was to determine what the true faith was? Despite their unpleasant experiences in England the Puritans were willing to leave the determination of the state religion to civil authorities. The only alternative would have been for the clergy to dictate religious policy to the government and that would have blurred the distinction, which New Englanders wished to maintain, between church and state. They believed that in England there had been an insufficient separation of the two spheres. The king was head of church and state, bishops sat in Parliament and on the Privy Council, and at the parish level church officials were burdened with numerous secular tasks. In New England such combinations of authority were avoided. There were no church courts, and all matters of a secular nature were dealt with exclusively by civil authorities. Though some colonies limited the franchise to church members, that restriction was viewed as a means of keeping heretics and evildoers out of office; and loss of church membership by excommunication did not entail loss of freemanship. Those who held office in the church were prohibited from holding office in the state. By these and other means the colonists succeeded in achieving a greater separation of church and state than existed anywhere in Europe.

Nevertheless, though separate, the two spheres cooperated closely in the Bible Commonwealths. The magistrates frequently consulted the clergy, for the latter were not only skilled interpreters of the Bible but also the intelligentsia of early New England. The goal of the state was a godly society and legislation was designed to support that goal. While the clergy did not rule, and while their advice was occasionally rejected, magistrates such as Winthrop and Eaton were dedicated Puritan laymen equally committed to the establishment of God's way in the North American wilderness. Their administrative actions differed little from what might have been expected if a Cotton or a Davenport had sat in the governor's chair.

THE FRANCHISE IN NEW ENGLAND

If historians have not always agreed on whether or not Massachusetts was a theocracy, they have had similar difficulty in determining the extent to which the Puritan colonies were democratic. During the pre-Miller era of Puritan studies, historians frequently drew a picture of seventeenth-century New England in which the narrow forces of theocracy struggled in vain to suppress the gradually triumphant forces of democracy. That version of the past has been universally rejected. In the first place it is evident that the magistrates on most issues did represent the will of the freemen—and of the vast majority of non-freemen as well. Furthermore, if democracy is to be gauged by the percentage of adult colonists who were freemen, the earliest years of the Bay were the most "democratic." Historians are now much more careful about imputing twentieth-century concepts of democracy to sevententh-century society.

New Englanders of the colonial period rejected the concept of demo-cratic government. While they believed in popular participation in the electoral process, they denied the legitimacy of popular rule. John Cotton expressed the prevalent view when he described the govern-ment of the Bay as a "mixt aristocracie," by which he meant that the people's role in elections was to choose a ruling class. In fact, the broad franchise was instituted more for the purpose of binding the people to their government than to encourage the expression of popular views. God, the Puritans believed, had chosen a few to lead the many.

Viewed in this light, the size of the franchise has a different signifi-cance from that which we attach to it in the twentieth century, par-ticularly at the local level. The emphasis that the Puritans placed on order and unity led them to develop a system of town governance, in which popular participation was designed to promote consensus rather than ensure pluralism. Taught that their responsibility was to select those men chosen by God for leadership, the electorate—in some com-munities 70 percent of the adult males—used their votes to elect and repeatedly return to office a relatively small number of leaders.

Those chosen as town selectmen were generally drawn from the wealthier, better-educated segment of the population. They were, par-ticularly in the early decades of settlement, entrusted with virtually absolute authority. Their recommendations to the town were rarely rejected, their decisions hardly ever questioned. Nevertheless, the town meeting carried out an important function. In the absence in the New England wilderness of many of the traditional institutions of social control, the Puritan settlers depended on the authority of the town meeting to provide social coherence. Communal agreements were reached by informal compromise and then presented to the electorate for legitimization.

The key to the broad franchise rested in the role of the town meeting in legitimizing decisions. If that function were to be effectively served it was vital that as many adult males as possible be included in the process. The more men involved in ratifying policies, the greater the social pressure to abide by those policies. Thus, in many towns, adult males who were not colony freemen were allowed to vote in the town meeting. Informally encouraged in Massachusetts, Plymouth, and New Haven, the broader franchise for town voting was incorporated into Connecticut's legal code.

Voter participation at the colony level was based on similar assumptions. Freemen were expected to exercise the vote as a means of confirming their adherence to the social covenant and ratifying the right of the Winthrops, Eatons, and Bradfords to rule. As at the local level, the hallmark of colonial government was stability. The same men were chosen for high office with monotonous regularity. No parties developed to challenge the political homogeneity of Massachusetts, Connecticut, New Haven, or Plymouth. Far from offering the voters a cherished opportunity to choose between conflicting views of where the colony should go, the franchise was a responsibility that also made one eligible for the obligations of jury service and office holding. It is not surprising, therefore, that while about 48 percent of the adult males were Massachusetts freemen in 1647, a substantial number of those who were eligible had declined to seek freemanship.

The forms of government in the Bible Commonwealths provided for popular participation without determining its nature. The Puritan concept of calling and the concern for consensus dictated the shape that participation would take. For as long as those values were dominant the freemen of New England would work in concert with the magistrates to preserve the society they had helped to found in the 1630s.

8 | ORTHODOXY IN NEW ENGLAND: THE CHURCH

The marrow of Puritan theology, as developed in England, was carried to America and ably defended by the early settlers. But if they continued to adhere to the faith as set forth by Ames and Perkins, they nevertheless developed religious emphases of their own—particularly in the area of polity—which were significant enough to attract the attention of their English contemporaries and of later historians.

RELIGIOUS ORTHODOXY: CHURCHES OF VISIBLE SAINTS

Perhaps the most notable contribution New Englanders made to the Puritan movement was the restriction they placed on church membership. During the long development of Puritanism numerous English physicians of the soul had contributed to the production of a sizable amount of distinctively Puritan writings on the morphology of conversion. Those works were exercises in practical divinity, intended to assist tortured souls in their progress toward God by offering them a map by which they could gauge their experience against the norm. In New England the Puritan clergy applied their knowledge of the conversion process to the development of new standards for admission to the church. To the normal criteria for membership in any religious group—knowledge of and belief in the doctrines of the faith, and an upright life—New Englanders added the insistence that the candidate offer proof of his election.

English Puritans had long argued that faith was an indispensable mark of the true church. They justified remaining within the Church of England primarily because they believed that God used the national church as a means of bringing saving faith to the elect. In many parishes Puritan preachers took the position that the Lord's Supper was the seal of the covenant for transmitting sustaining grace, rather than a vehicle for God to work the conversion of the chosen. They concluded that admission to the communion table should be limited to those with saving faith. But lacking the disciplinary powers to test communicants and exclude the unworthy, one's worthiness to receive the sacrament was a matter for each individual's judgment.

What occurred in New England was not a radical shift in belief, but rather, the extension of that line of thought in new circumstances. The new requirement was probably first imposed in the Boston church during the absence of pastor Wilson. Shortly after John Cotton's assumption of the post of teacher his evangelical preaching stimulated a religious revival whereby, according to Winthrop, "more were converted and added to that church, than to all the other churches in the bay." Such revivals were not unknown to English Puritans, and they would occur periodically in New England throughout the Puritan era, but the effect of the Boston awakening of 1634 was especially important. The new converts, prior to their admission into the church evidently took advantage of the then current practice of lay sermonizing (prophesying) to relate to the congregation the path whereby they came to believe in their election. What started as an edifying exercise very soon came to be recognized as an essential step in one's admission to the church. The following year, when a new group of settlers moved into Newtown to replace the Connecticut-bound Hooker congregation, they sought the advice of the magistrates and clergy on organizing a church and were informed that candidates for membership should not only make a confession of their faith, but also "declare what work of grace the Lord had wrought in them." In 1636 another embryo church, in Dorchester, was prevented from forming because its members were not able properly to describe their saving experience (though the church soon remedied this and was properly organized). By 1640 the new requirement was firmly entrenched throughout Massachusetts and New Haven, and was also imposed in Connecticut, though not so rigidly.

By the end of the 1630s, however, the requirement had become more sophisticated than John Cotton had probably envisioned, because to Cotton's insistence on evidence of saving faith had been added a rigid prescription of how that faith be demonstrated. For ministers like Thomas Shepard, evidence of faith should include a description of one's preconversion preparation for grace. Here Shepard was in the tradition of those English Puritans, such as Richard Greenham, Richard

Rogers, and John Preston, who had written at length on the way in which prevenient grace enables the elect to prepare themselves for justification. But, whereas those English authors had described the process so as to provide a guide for the individual conscience, to Shepard—as historian Norman Petit has demonstrated—"it would appear that man must be limited in his range of preconversion experience, with preparatory 'rules' imposed 'to satisfy the conscience of other men.'" The dramatic, unprepared-for seizure of man by God that Puritans such as Sibbes and Cotton (and Anne Hutchinson) had emphasized was downplayed in New England. Those who sought membership in the churches had to show, in effect, not only a conversion experience but also a preparation for it if they were to satisfy the congregation. As Petit has observed, "when the ministers demanded preparatory experiences of an extensive nature while at the same time holding to Cotton's strict admissions policy, they erected a formidable barrier to the communion table." Richard Baxter, the English Presbyterian, criticized the practice as "taking a very few that can talk more than the rest, and making them the Church." But in the early history of New England the dangers were not foreseen—perhaps because a majority of most communities proved eligible for membership.

By erecting such a barrier, the Puritans believed that they had come closer than any prior religious group to closing the gap that had always existed between the members of the visible church and those numbered among the invisible communion of the saints. Not that they believed that they had closed the gap. New Englanders always acknowledged that hypocrites might deceive a congregation and be admitted into its midst. But they had enough confidence in their understanding of the working of grace to believe that they could generally detect whether or not a conversion narrative was feigned.

RELIGIOUS ORTHODOXY:
CHURCH POLITY AND PRACTICE

While the requirement of saving faith for church membership was the most significant ecclesiastical innovation of the New England Puritans, their congregational church organization also differed from Anglican practice and even from that of the earlier classis movement of Elizabethan Puritanism. Even in its initial organization a New England church was on its own, with no supervision from an ecclesiastical hierarchy.

The founding of a congregation typically began with the selection of a group referred to as "pillars of the church"—usually seven men, occasionally more. Candidates volunteered themselves for this distinction, believing themselves worthy by virtue of their belief, election, and upright lives. The candidates then questioned each other in order to satisfy themselves that all were of the necessary caliber; those who failed to satisfy their peers were eliminated from further consideration (without jeopardy to their chances for church membership). Those who emerged from these private conferences then volunteered for similar scrutiny from the other members of the community. Those eliminated were replaced by other candidates, and the process was repeated. It usually took a few months for the "pillars" to be selected. When the community was comprised of old neighbors from England or from elsewhere in New England the process could be much quicker; but in some instances it dragged on for over a year.

Once chosen, the pillars of the church agreed to a church covenant. They then examined the other members of the community who sought membership, accepting those who met the requirements. Next, all members voted in the election of the congregation's officers, after which the selected pastor and teacher (if there was more than one minister) were ordained. The congregation invited representatives from neighboring churches to attend the ordination, one of the visiting clergymen traditionally preaching an ordination sermon after which the congregation's lay elders would ordain their chosen ministers by imposition of hands.

The number of officers that a congregation would elect depended on its inclination, its wealth, and the availability of candidates. The Cambridge Platform—the official statement of the New England Way—recognized five different positions. The pastor, often the only clergyman in a church, was empowered by his ordination to administer the sacraments and to preach. In preaching his duty was "to attend to exhortation: and therein to administer a word of Wisdom." In some of the larger congregations two ministers were employed; the second, termed the teacher, shared the ministerial duties of preaching and administering the sacraments. The Cambridge Platform set his particular preaching responsibility as "to attend to Doctrine, and therein to administer a word of knowledge." The distinction between the two was thus in reference to their prime preaching orientations, the pastor's proper subject being the Christian life and how to lead it, while the teacher's was the exposition of doctrines.

Whether a congregation ordained one or two clergymen, they sought individuals who were prepared for the ministry by virtue of an exemplary spiritual life but also as a result of university training. The first generation of colonial clergy had been educated in English universities. It was largely to insure a supply of competent candidates for future generations that the magistrates of the Bay founded Harvard in 1636.

The ruling elders were elected laymen who shared the government of the congregation with the ministers but who had no share in preaching or the administration of the sacraments. Their specific functions were to preside over admission of new members; to call the congregation together when there was occasion for a meeting and to dismiss them at its conclusion; to prepare an agenda for business meetings so that affairs might be handled expeditiously; to see that no member of the church lived inordinately out of rank or place, was without a job, or worked lazily; to prevent or, that failing, to heal disputes or differences that threatened the harmony of the congregation; to visit and pray over the sick—and to attend to anything else that needed attending. The tasks were many and the rewards slight. Despite ministerial emphasis on the need for ruling elders and scriptural justification for their election, the office was soon abandoned in many congregations.

The one lay office that was generally maintained was that of the deacon. It was the deacon's task as financial officer to receive the offerings of the faithful, to maintain the treasury of the church, and to provide for the disbursement of funds to the ministers and to the needy of the parish. The fifth church office—that of ancient widow—was an honorific title given to elderly women who were exemplary for the aid and comfort they brought to the sick and others in need.

These officers in an individual church, together with the remainder of the congregation, were the judges as to the acceptability of an individual for membership in the church, and they were free to adopt whatever criteria for entry they desired. Most, however, followed a similar procedure. An applicant for church membership would initiate his candidacy by informing the elders of the congregation of his desire to join. The elders (including the ministers) would examine the candidate in private to ascertain his knowledge and his religious experience. If they were satisfied they would then present the applicant to the full congregation and ask the members to report any transgressions of which the applicant was guilty. After the candidate had made a public confession of these sins, testimony was given as to the candidate's good character. At this point it was customary for a male candidate to narrate to the congregation the way in which he had been brought to God. In many churches female applicants were allowed to relate their conversion experience in a private session to the elders; the pastor would then read it to the congregation. The narrative could be followed by questions. Then the candidate was asked to make a profession of faith and the congregation voted. If approved, the candidate swore to the covenant and was admitted to the congregation.

Once in the church, a member was still subjected to the congregation's scrutiny. If he wished to move he needed permission from his church, and to be admitted to another congregation he had to have a good reference from the church he was leaving. Members of the church were subject to admonition, censure, and excommunication for failure to behave in a manner appropriate to the elect. While Anne Hutchinson was excommunicated by the Boston church for theological error, Robert Keayne was censured by the same congregation for sharp business practices. The covenant one swore to in joining a congregation made each member his brother's keeper.

Nonmembers as well as members—all residents in a Puritan community—were required to attend religious services, and most did so willingly, the members to reinforce their souls in grace, while the nonmembers hoped that the services might be the means chosen by God to effect his call on their souls. As reported by Thomas Lechford in the 1640s, the typical morning service in the Boston church on the Sabbath began with the pastor delivering "a solemn prayer continuing about a quarter of an hour. The teacher then readeth and expoundeth a chapter, then a psalm is sung. . . . After that the pastor preacheth a sermon, and sometimes *ex tempore* exhorts. Then the teacher concludes with prayer and a blessing." After noon the congregation would return for another, similar service of prayer, psalms, and sermon.

The Puritans maintained a belief in only two sacraments, the Lord's Supper and baptism. Both were generally administered on the Sabbath. The Lord's Supper was celebrated with a memorial service one Sabbath morning a month, only members being permitted to partake in the bread and wine. Baptism was administered by one of the ministers at the conclusion of afternoon Sabbath services, with a short sermon preached on the occasion. Though the Puritans believed that only adult believers could become members of the church they did not, like the Baptists, restrict the sacrament of baptism to adults. Any child, one of whose parents was a member of the church, could be baptized, on the assumption that the covenant promise between God and the elect extended—as did the covenant between God and Abraham—to the seed of the saints as well, and that upon reaching maturity the children of the chosen would fulfill the requirements and be admitted into full church status. When large numbers of baptized children matured and failed to qualify for membership, it would precipitate a major crisis for the New England Way.

RELIGIOUS ORTHODOXY: CONGREGATIONAL GOVERNANCE AND CHURCH RELATIONS

To say that each congregation of believers was autonomous, free to determine its own officers, membership, and practices is accurate—but only to a degree. The theoretical independence of the church members was in practice limited by the forcefulness of their pastor and the influence of neighboring churches. Yet no individual or group could exert force on a congregation, and a determined congregation could persevere in a controversial course. Many congregations rejected their ministers' advice in the debate in the 1650s over the Half-Way Covenant. The Newbury parish of Thomas Parker and James Noyes maintained an anomalous presbyterianism in the face of pressure from neighboring churches and the magistrates.

The most variable governmental relationship in New England church life was that between a pastor and his congregation. As Professor David Hall has recently demonstrated,

On paper, at least, the model of mixed government struck the proper balance between liberty and order. But a paper model it remained, and one that was curiously vague in its specifications: it could be "variously interpreted by a dictatorial pastor, a determined eldership, a vigorous *classis*, or a rebellious congregation."

While each church's history was in some certain respects unique, it is possible to detect a general pattern in seventeenth-century relations between pastors and their flocks. The early clergy—the generation of Cotton and Shepard, of Hooker and Davenport—was a generation of charismatic, evangelical preachers, who in theory were totally dependent on their congregations but in practice were rarely questioned by the faithful. Gradually, however, largely as a result of changes in New England society, the authority of the ministers began to decline. Congregations began to reject the advice of the clergy, became niggardly in salary negotiations, and showed a willingness to release their pastors. Unable to maintain their power by force of personality, the clergy in the latter half of the century began to stress the sacerdotal source of their authority, as opposed to the congregational sources, arguing that the ministry was in fact a sacred order deriving its powers from Christ. But even at a time when the faithful were generally most forceful in asserting congregational authority over their shepherds, there were notable exceptions. Democratic forms notwithstanding, men like John Wise, Increase Mather, and Solomon

Stoddard were virtual dictators in their churches as the seventeenth century drew to a close.

It is somewhat easier to generalize about the relations between churches. Congregationalism inferred the independence of the individual church for all superior authority. But if churches were autonomous, the similarity of practice in them certainly indicates a form of cooperation and interrelation between them. Such contacts took a number of forms in the seventeenth century, all of them serving to substantiate the New Englanders' claim that Congregationalism served as a "middle way" between Presbyterianism (which vested synods with authority over congregations) and radical Independency (which denied the desirability of any relations between churches).

All congregations in New England were expected to preserve "church-communion" with one another and with the other reformed churches of Christendom. The Cambridge Platform set forth a number of ways in which such church communion could be maintained, all of which were common practice in the Bible Commonwealths: (1) by caring for each other's welfare; (2) by consultation when one church could contribute to the discussion of a point at issue in another; (3) by admonishing neighboring congregations for any visible offense in their teaching or practice; (4) by members of one church visiting another and participating in the Lord's Supper; (5) by recommending members to the church in the community to which they move; and (6) by aiding neighboring churches in their time of need. In addition to these contacts, the churches were also brought together through advisory meetings of the clergy and in representative synods.

During the early 1630s the clergy of the Bay took it upon themselves to meet regularly to discuss their common problems, as they sought to implement their ideas in a new environment. Roger Williams and Samuel Skelton had protested these sessions as incipient presbyterianism; but the participating clergy pointed to the writings of Ames and of Henry Jacob, and to necessity, to justify their practice. Their actions in these sessions ranged over a wide field. They discussed such issues as the significance of church covenants, the authenticity of episcopal ordination, congregational membership requirements, and standards of clerical excellence. In none of these were their decisions binding on the churches, but they were usually successfully introduced into congregations by the individual clergy. The consociated ministers also authorized a number of official clerical responses to treatises by English ministers. They advised the General Court when asked. Eventually they came to assume certain administrative functions, such as supervising the Indian missions, calling synods, and preparing catechisms. They frequently arbitrated in cases of disputes between congregations.

In the mid-1640s the rise of Presbyterianism in Civil War England raised a concern among many laymen, and clergymen as well, about the growing powers of these exclusively clerical consociations. The Cambridge Assembly, the first representative synod of ministers and laymen in New England, therefore curbed the powers of such gatherings. Nevertheless, if synods became more frequent after 1648, clerical conferences continued because they were in fact essential to the New England Way. As long as synods were merely advisory and not authoritative, the best means of insuring orthodoxy was through clerical agreement and cooperation. When the vast majority of the ministers were in agreement, their united voice was capable of curbing most congregational dissent. Later, when the unanimity of the clergy shattered, the uniformity of New England soon eroded.

9 | NEW ENGLAND AND PURITAN ENGLAND

The first American revolution against the British crown did not begin in the 1770s, but in New England in the 1640s. Colonial Puritans watched with anticipation the unfolding of the English Civil Wars and cast their support to the rebel Parliament and the emergent regime of Oliver Cromwell. Having come to New England to change the Old, the American Puritans felt themselves key participants in the English struggle, and their reaction to the unfolding of that event provided much of the structure to the colonies' history in the 1640s and 1650s.

CIVIL WAR IN ENGLAND

John Winthrop had come to America in 1630. Another country squire from East Anglia considered emigration on at least two occasions, but decided against it. So too did many Puritans, laymen and clergy alike. Some were members of the social elite and immune from serious harassment. Others were shielded from hierarchical surveillance by their obscurity. Some, clergy especially, were forced to live the lives of fugitives. The call of the New World was not strong enough, God's intention not clear enough to bring them to emigrate. But they followed events in the Bible Commonwealths and drew highly unfavorable contrasts between the decline of godliness in England and its advance in America.

The 1630s was a decade of growing friction between Charles I and his English Puritan subjects. Having disbanded Parliament in 1628, the king launched the nation on a decade of rule by monarchical fiat. The imposition of legally questionable taxes and forced loans, the prosecution of John Hampden and others, and continuing foreign friendships with Catholic powers were matched in the ecclesiastical realm by the disbanding of the Feofees for Impropriations, the increased persecution and deprivation of Puritan clergy, the growing ceremonialism of Anglican worship, and an attempt to impose the Prayer Book on Scotland. This last offense against the sensibilities of his oldest subjects brought opposition to Charles to the breaking point. The Scots signed a national covenant to fight for their faith, and the king was forced to call a Parliament to finance a military expedition against the northern kingdom. But the "Short Parliament" (1639) refused to approve taxes without a royal pledge to initiate reforms. Charles suspended it and once more resorted to forced loans—unsuccessfully.

By 1640, when a truce brought an end to the second season of campaigning, the Scots were in possession of northern England, and Charles was forced to put his cause at the mercy of a new Parliament. The "Long Parliament" assembled in November of 1640. Under the leadership of John Pym, John Hampden, the Earl of Warwick, and others, the legislature forced the king to acquiesce in the imprisonment and trial of key counselors (including Archbishop Laud) and the reversal of the toleration of Catholics, and to promise the frequent convening of Parliament and the initiation of ecclesiastical reform. Reacting to the mounting criticism of his conduct of the realm's political and religious affairs, the king made an attempt in January 1642 to seize the leaders of the Parliamentary party. Failing in that ill-advised venture, he left London and declared Parliament in rebellion, thus initiating the English Civil Wars.

From 1642 to 1649 the kingdom was torn by military conflict. The royal forces won an early strategic triumph at the battle of Edgehill and occupied Oxford, but they failed to take full advantage of their position. In 1643 the royalists won victories in the north and west, after which Parliament entered into a formal alliance with the Presbyterian Scots. The following year saw a Parliamentary triumph at Marston Moor; but overall inefficiency in the operation of their military affairs caused them to restructure their forces in 1645 with the creation of a New Model Army under the command of Sir Thomas Fairfax. The New Model's victory at Naseby (1645) precipitated the king's surrender to the Scots. But after two years of fruitless negotiations for a constitutional settlement, Charles agreed in 1648 to a treaty with the Scots, who pledged themselves to restore him to the throne in return for the establishment of a Presbyterian church. The New Model's victory over the Scots at the battle of Preston (1648) was followed by an Army purge of the moderate Parliamentarians and the trial and execution of the king by the remaining legislators.

Religious reform had been one of the key concerns of Parliament in the years leading up to the outbreak of the Civil Wars, and in 1643 an assembly of divines was convened in Westminster to advise the lawmakers on ecclesiastical change. Agreement on religious reformation was difficult to achieve. Most Puritans had had little need to consider issues of church government and were prone to accept the Presbyterian polity of neighboring Scotland, in which thinking they were encouraged by representatives of the Scottish kirk. A few Erastians wished state control of all church affairs. A handful of clergymen, returned from exile in the Netherlands, advocated a Congregational system, of which they had had experience and which they claimed had also been proven effective by the New England Puritans. The religious scene was even more confused outside of the Westminster Assembly, for the breakdown of ecclesiastical discipline occasioned by the Civil War allowed the proliferation of numerous sects, which advocated the independence of individual congregations and doctrinally advanced such heresies as Anabaptism and antinomianism. The demand of England's Scottish allies that a Presbyterian structure be adopted, the obstruction of the Congregational minority in the Presbyterian Assembly, and the "Independent" alliance in Parliament of Erastians, Congregationalists, and the sects all created an uncertainty as to the religious future of the Puritan state that was still unresolved when Charles I met his death.

NEW ENGLAND AND THE
PURITAN REVOLUTION

When John Winthrop received word late in 1640 of "the Scots entering into England, and the calling of a Parliament, and the hope of a thorough reformation," he had more than one cause for rejoicing. At the very least, evidence of Charles's preoccupation with domestic affairs gave promise to the Bay colonists of the safety of their charter. More important, it appeared that the settlers' purpose in coming to America might finally be served. As news from England in 1641 continued in the same vein—of Laud's imprisonment, the Earl of Stafford's execution, the enforcement of the laws against Catholics— New Englanders redoubled their prayers and entered into two decades of determined support of the Parliamentary cause and the resulting Puritan regime.

Almost from the start, with the holding of a day of thanksgiving in 1642 for the "good success" of Parliament, New Englanders viewed the unfolding of English events as (to quote Thomas Shepard) a "blessed worke of a publique Reformation," and they claimed paternity.

Woburn's Edward Johnson described the Civil Wars as "Things thus concurring as an immediate answer of the Lord to his people's prayers and endeavors," while Taunton's minister William Hooke claimed that "Wee have done enough and enough to overwhelm old England with the wrath of God." Their example was being followed, their prayers had been worthwhile.

In continuing their efforts on behalf of English reform, the colonists turned most frequently to prayer. Believing that God would answer the petitions of his saints, the Puritan believed that "Churches of praying believers are terrible as so many Armies with Banners, as so thundering Legions." Just as in the 1630s they had assembled to beseech divine aid for the Protestant cause in Germany, so in the 1640s the colonists gathered in their churches on specially appointed days of fast and in weekly Sabbath services to call down God's wrath on the royalist forces. It was, preached William Hooke, the duty of the American Puritans to "lye in wait in the wilderness, to come upon the backs of God's enemies with deadly Fasting and Prayer, murtherers that will kill point blanke from one end of the world to the other." There were twelve special fast days observed in Massachusetts by 1644 alone; Connecticut and New Haven both decreed a monthly day of fast and prayer in support of the Parliament.

Prayer was a weapon available to all of the colonists. But the clergy, with special qualifications, had special responsibilities. Having been architects of the New England Way, the colonial ministers offered to their English brethren the lessons learned in America during the 1630s. "Great pity were it," explained John Cotton, "that they should want any light which might possibly be afforded them." The colonists took a stand supportive of Puritan reform and wrote treatises for English publication that ably defended the Puritan position. In the debate between Englishmen over the varieties of Puritan reform, New Englanders generally supported the Congregational cause. The leaders of that party were the friends and disciples of the colonial clergy, and the latter—particularly Cotton, Davenport, Hooker, and Mather— provided their English brethren with the period's most forceful and effective defenses of Congregational polity.

For many colonists it was not sufficient to support the cause of reform from distant New England. No matter how convinced they were of the efficacy of prayer and the power of the written word, they nevertheless sought direct participation in the struggle. Many reached positions of importance: ten rose to the rank of major or above in the Parliamentary army; others sat in Parliament; many accepted clerical positions in the new English church.

The clash between Puritans and Anglicans in their native land not only forced individual colonists to express their sympathies but also posed the political problem of how the colonial governments should act in light of the growing rift between king and parliament. Urged by sympathetic Englishmen to send agents to England who could represent the colonies' interest in the changing political situation, the Massachusetts magistrates chose the Reverend Hugh Peter of Salem and the Reverend Thomas Welde of Roxbury to serve as a delegation to the mother country. In England the two agents successfully sought from Parliament a relaxation of the customs duties payable by the colonies. They raised funds for the support of Harvard and for the advance of a colonial ironworks. As instructed, they contributed to the cause of English reformation by their promulgation of the New England Way and their participation in the religious debates of the decade. And by their very presence they demonstrated the support of the American Puritans for their English brethren. When their official mission ended, both stayed on in England to contribute as individuals to the same cause.

Even more dramatic evidence of the Bay's new posture was revealed in May of 1643 when the General Court struck the king's name from the oath of allegiance tendered to the freemen. The following year, when Captain Jennyson of Watertown questioned the authority of Parliament he was brought before the General Court and persuaded of the error of his views. In 1644 when, according to Winthrop, "some malignant spirits began to stir, and declare themselves for the king," the General Court passed an order prohibiting any demonstration of support for the royalist cause by action, word, or writing.

Without any apparent need for lengthy debate, Massachusetts had effectively acknowledged Parliament's supremacy at a time when the outcome of the English struggle still remained in doubt. Her sister colonies were just as prompt in taking a stand. Rhode Island and New Haven, content to be charterless in the 1630s, sought recognition from the new home government. Roger Williams succeeded in winning a patent for the Providence Plantations. New Haven's General Court voted in 1644 to "putt forth their best endeavour to procure a Pattent from the Parliament, . . . judging it a fit season now for that end." The colony's envoy was lost at sea and the search for a charter abandoned, but in 1648 New Haven did receive recognition from a joint committee of the two Houses of Parliament. Such signs of colonial efforts to achieve a closer relation with the Puritan regime in England continued throughout the 1650s and were in marked contrast to the policy adopted by other British colonies, such as Virginia.

THE ENDECOTT ERA IN NEW ENGLAND

In 1649—on 30 January—Charles I was executed for crimes against the English people. In New England, John Winthrop died on 26 March 1649. The guiding spirit of the Great Migration and the most compelling expositor of the Puritan errand into the wilderness, Winthrop is often seen as the epitome of the Bay colony's early history. But no less important was the man whom he succeeded in 1630 and who was chosen governor in 1649. John Endecott sat in the Massachusetts governor's chair for more years than any other individual from 1628 to the present. The scourge of Thomas Morton's Merry Mount, the military chieftain who led the first punitive expedition against the Pequots, the iconoclast who cut the cross from the king's ensign—Endecott was the American Puritan counterpart of Oliver Cromwell, and he presided over Massachusetts affairs for most of the decade of Cromwell's English rule. In his earlier career he was subject to outbursts of religious fervor in which he showed little or poor judgment. But his dedication was never questioned, and when entrusted with the authority of the governorship he was to prove far more judicious than his earlier reputation might have led one to suspect.

The most significant development in Anglo-American Puritanism during Endecott's tenure in office was Oliver Cromwell's dominance of the English interregnum. Cromwell had been viewed as a friend of New England and of the English Congregationalists during the period of the Civil Wars, and the colonists had close relationships with him. Salem's Hugh Peter had served as a chaplain in the Ironsides. Guilford township's Samuel Desborough had a brother (John) who was married to Cromwell's sister. Jane Hooke, the wife of the Reverend William Hooke (Davenport's colleague at New Haven after he left Taunton), was Cromwell's cousin; her brother, Edward Whalley, and her nephew, William Goffe, were two of the Lord Protector's most trusted lieutenants. Upon his migration to England, William Hooke was appointed Cromwell's family chaplain.

Personal contacts with the Protector gave the colonists confidence in England's future and a sympathetic ear in the highest councils of government; but more important in securing the colonists' loyalty to the new regime was Cromwell's patronage of the English Congregationalists and his expressions of concern for the New Englanders. While Cromwell's recognition of the political impracticality of immediately enforcing religious conformity on the English people has led to his classification as a disciple of religious toleration, such a conclusion is at least a little misleading and it was far from that reached by the American Puritans. The Lord Protector's closest religious advisers were Thomas Goodwin and John Owen, both Congregationalist disciples of John Cotton. Hugh Peter and William Hooke were also members of his inner circle, and both were former New Englanders. It was to Congregationalists such as these and to moderate Presbyterians that Cromwell entrusted the approval of new ministers and the ejection of unfit clergymen. As Lord Protector his government took firm steps against some of the extreme sectaries of the time, such as the Fifth Monarchy men, Unitarians, and Quakers. And it would appear that the Savoy Declaration of 1658—an English Congregational version of the New England Cambridge Platform of church order—was intended for adoption as the new orthodoxy of the realm. Certainly New Englanders saw Cromwell as a friend and disciple and rejoiced in his reign as ushering in the new Congregational English Church.

Equally appreciated by the American Puritans was the Lord Protector's solicitude for their secular needs. Following his victory over the Scots in the battle of Dunbar, Cromwell sent many of the captured Scots to New England as indentured servants to alleviate the American labor shortage. He offered the colonists a chance to settle in Ireland after his pacification of that nation. Following the conquest of Jamaica (an undertaking launched upon by Cromwell after soliciting John Cotton's advice and one in which a number of New Englanders participated) he wrote to colonial leaders—especially New Haven's Governor Eaton—offering the American Puritans a chance to move to that warmer clime. But most indicative of the new relationship was the positive response Cromwell gave to the colonists' request for military aid against their Dutch neighbors.

The Bible Commonwealths, particularly New Haven and Connecticut, had been troubled almost from their founding by the Dutch presence to the west. A Dutch trading post—Fort Good Hope—was located in Hartford. The boundary between the Dutch and the New Havenites was constantly in dispute, and the two rival colonies also clashed over their rights to lands along the Delaware. In 1638 the concerns raised by these conflicts had led some New Englanders to propose a political union of the Bible Commonwealths, and in the following year John Haynes and Thomas Hooker had traveled to Boston to lobby for such a plan. These efforts finally bore fruit in 1643, when commissioners from Massachusetts, Connecticut, New Haven, and Plymouth gathered in Boston and concluded articles of confederation creating the United Colonies of New England. This New England Confederation was "a league of friendship and amity for offense and defence, mutual advice and succor, upon all just occasions, both for preserving and propagating the truths and liberties of the gospel, and for their own safety and welfare." Each colony appointed two commissioners to the meetings, which were held successively in the capital towns of the member colonies. A vote of six of the eight commissioners was binding on the united colonies.

The New England confederates maintained a constant pressure on the New Netherland authorities to reach an accommodation. Finally, in 1650, Peter Stuyvesant, the Dutch director-general, journeyed to Hartford to meet with the commissioners. Both sides hoped that the resulting Hartford Treaty would bring peace to the rival colonies, but Stuyvesant's seizure in 1651 of New Havenites bound for the Delaware reopened hostilities.

In 1652 news from Europe revealed that England and the Netherlands were at war, the Council of State having reacted, over Cromwell's objection, to the commercial threat posed by the Dutch. Stuyvesant formally renounced all concessions he had made at Hartford. Rumors and reports from friendly Indians and from Englishmen living in New Netherland indicated that Stuyvesant was stirring up the Mohawk tribe to fall upon the English. New Haven and Connecticut, as the most exposed colonies, pressed their fellow confederates to unite in launching an attack on the Dutch.

Massachusetts was reluctant to go to war, so New Haven and Connecticut appealed for aid to the English government. Connecticut appointed Captain John Astwood to journey to England to present the colony's case in cooperation with Governor Hopkins, who was already in London. New Haven also entrusted petitions to Astwood. In addition William Leete wrote to his former neighbor Samuel Desborough asking the latter to intercede with Cromwell, and William Hooke wrote directly to Cromwell outlining the situation and requesting aid.

In February of 1654 orders were received from Parliament confirming that the Dutch should be treated as enemies of England. In Connecticut the Puritan authorities immediately seized Fort Good Hope from the Dutch. Meanwhile, in England, Cromwell—now Lord Protector—commissioned Major Robert Sedgwick and Captain John Leverett (both natives of Massachusetts) to head an expedition comprised of four vessels and a handful of English troops to aid the colonists in the capture of New Netherland. The force reached New England in the late spring, and all of the confederate colonies joined in the preparations, New Haven and Connecticut making the greatest efforts. A combined English and colonial force of some nine hundred infantry and a troop of cavalry were poised to strike early in July, when word was received of the conclusion of a European peace.

Thwarted from action against New Netherland, Sedgwick and Leverett diverted their force to French Canada. They captured St. John and Port Royal, the province of Acadia being added to the British Empire and rechristened Nova Scotia. But the most important aspect of the Sedgwick-Leverett expedition was the evidence it gave the colonists of Cromwell's concern for their future.

The economic fortunes of the region during the 1650s also gave cause for confidence. Earlier, the outbreak of the revolution had brought an end to the Great Migration and caused the colonies' economies to falter. The dwindling of immigration reversed the status of New England's balance of payments and precipitated a severe currency shortage. "Merchants would sell no wares but for ready money," Winthrop had written; "men could not pay their debts though they had enough, prices of land and cattle fell soon to the one-half, yea to a third, and after one-fourth part." In 1644, Welde and Peter had successfully petitioned Parliament for an exemption of the Bible Commonwealths from the payment of all import and export duties. That advantage over the other English colonies became more valuable with the growth of the West Indian sugar colonies. Gradually capturing the West Indian trade, New England began to recover from the depression of the 1640s, so that by the late 1650s foreign trade had reached considerable proportions and New England once again enjoyed prosperity.

10 | THE NEW ENGLAND WAY IN AN AGE OF RELIGIOUS FERMENT

The English struggle and the Puritan triumph stimulated the confidence and aggressiveness of the New Englanders. They lent their energies to support of God's cause and developed a closer relationship with the English government than would have been conceivable in the 1630s. At the same time they were aware of the danger that the fragmentation of the English Puritan movement could pose to the New England Way. The possible triumph of Presbyterianism in Old England could lead to attempts to impose that discipline on the Bible Commonwealths; the seductive ideas of English sectaries threatened to spread to America if not zealously guarded against. So, while the colonists broadened their involvement in "foreign" affairs during the period of the Puritan Revolution and the interregnum, they were also forced to meet new internal challenges to the stability of their social and religious experiment.

DEFENDING CONGREGATIONALISM

When the Westminster Assembly convened in England in 1643 three New England clergymen were invited to take seats in it. John Cotton, John Davenport, and Thomas Hooker were interested, but declined. It had become obvious from English reports that the assembly would be dominated by Presbyterians, with few supporters of the New England (Congregational) Way in attendance. Hooker particularly felt that he and his colleagues could best aid the reform cause by their writings and by perfecting the model of their churches—and by defending those churches against Presbyterians in their own midst. For

115

the Presbyterian minority in New England, which had been of little significance in the 1630s, assumed new importance as Presbyterians rose to power in England.

Thomas Parker and James Noyse were cousins. The former was the pastor of the Newbury, Massachusetts, congregation and the latter was teacher. They administered their congregation not as a gathering of saints but as a reformed parish. They opened baptism and the Lord's Supper to all but notorious sinners. Their practices represented a significant deviation from the polity of the New England churches as commonly practiced and was far closer to the ecclesiastical system advocated by Presbyterians and practiced in Scotland. In September of 1643, Parker and Noyse were asked to discuss their viewpoint at a meeting with their clerical brethren at Cambridge.

John Cotton and Thomas Hooker jointly presided over the Cambridge Assembly of 1643. Clergymen from the various colonies were entertained in the new buildings of Harvard College. Both sides presented their arguments, and the majority expressed disapproval of some of the Newbury church's practices. Parker and Noyse agreed to consider the points made by their colleagues but were unconvinced. Noyse prepared a treatise expressing his dissent and dispatched it to England for publication. Parker wrote to a friend sitting in the Westminster Assembly, setting forth his belief that the churches of New England "have a great need of help in the way of Discipline, and we hope that we shall receive much light from you." Parker's English correspondent published the letter in an attempt to undercut the arguments of English Congregationalists. When copies were received in New England it caused considerable alarm to the majority of the American Puritans, who were apprehensive of just such "help" from a Presbyterian England.

It soon became apparent that Newbury was not the only congregation with a pastor eager to exercise the autocratic authority identifiable with Presbyterianism. Peter Hobart, pastor of Hingham, was another. By 1645, Hobart had become accustomed to denying his congregation any significant voice in church affairs. When he and his family began to exercise undue power in civil affairs as well, it became a matter for the intervention of the magistrates.

Most of the inhabitants of the Massachusetts community—including the Hobart family—were immigrants from Hingham, England. Anthony Eames was a member of a minority of settlers from the West Country of England. Nevertheless, his neighbors had chosen Eames to be commander of Hingham's militia band. When the band was raised to the status of a company in 1645, its members chose Eames captain and submitted his name to the colony magistrates for approval. But Eames was not allied with the Hobart faction. His independence worried the pastor's family and they used their influence to secure the company's reversal of its original nomination. Urged on by the Hobarts, the company then chose Bozoan Allen as captain.

The magistrates—with Deputy Governor Winthrop playing a key role—heard both sides and refused to ratify the change, confirming Eames in the post. But the incident became more serious. The militia company refused to obey Eames's orders. The Reverend Hobart accused Eames of untruthfulness in his testimony before the magistrates and demanded his excommunication from the Hingham church. The accused captain appealed for assistance to the magistrates, who asked the Bay clergy to attempt to delay the excommunication. At the same time they demanded that five of the leaders in the community's resistance post bond for later trial before the General Court. Three of the five thus singled out were pastor Hobart's brothers.

The situation reached a climax with the jailing of the Hinghamites who refused to post bond. Eighty-one residents of the town signed a petition to the General Court criticizing the magistrates' conduct. Charges were leveled at Winthrop in particular. Stepping down from his position of eminence in the court, Winthrop ably defended himself. He was exonerated; the court found the Hingham militia guilty of having mutinied against their rightful commander; the leaders of the Hobart-Allen faction were fined.

The court having handed down its verdicts, John Winthrop delivered a lecture to the deputies—and through them to the freemen—on the nature of liberty. He stressed that when a leader was elected to a post he received authority from God to carry out his tasks. While the people had the right to remove an evil ruler, they must guard against mistaking an officeholder's human frailties for crimes. Continuing to stress the need for dutiful submission to legitimate authority, Winthrop distinguished between natural and civil liberty. Natural liberty involved a freedom for man (who was by nature corrupt) to follow his inclinations to do evil as well as good. It was incompatible with civil liberty, which was freedom to do good and the preservation of which was the proper end of government.

Presbyterianism and politics were intertwined in the Hingham dispute, the issue ultimately becoming more political than religious in nature. A similar mix of Presbyterianism and politics occurred in the controversy over the Remonstrance of 1646. Citizens of Massachusetts, even those who were godly men in their external behavior, were not allowed membership in the churches without proof of regeneration. Many of those thus excluded felt themselves unfairly denied, particularly as they would have been welcomed into the Presbyterian parishes of Puritan England. Some were further troubled by their exclusion from freemanship. In May of 1646, Robert Child, Thomas Fowler, Samuel Maverick, Thomas Burton, John Smith, David Yale, and John Dand presented a petition for redress of grievances to the General Court. The remonstrance's tone was aggressive. The petitioners complained of the lack of a printed body of laws (which was in preparation but not yet published), the exercise of the negative voice by the assistants, and the disenfranchisement of taxpayers who were upstanding citizens but not church members. The remonstrants demanded the adoption of a Presbyterian parish-type concept of church membership. They made it clear to the magistrates that should the General Court not grant their demands the petitioners would appeal to England. The court delayed action until its fall session.

In the ensuing months, clergymen in most communities spoke out against the remonstrants in their weekly sermons. There had never been any evidence of significant popular support for Child and his fellow petitioners. After the clergy's offensive, any possibility of such support was gone. In October 1646, John Winthrop, Thomas Dudley, Richard Bellingham, and Nathaniel Duncan were instructed to prepare the court's answer to the remonstrants. Recognizing that their cause was lost in the colony, Child and Fowler made preparations to depart for England and appeal the expected decision of the court.

The General Court assembled on 4 November and the assistants and deputies called Child and Fowler before them. Accused of planning to appeal illegally to Parliament, all of the remonstrants were asked to post bond for future appearance. Two refused and were jailed. The following day Fowler forfeited his bond and sailed for England, accompanied by William Vassall. (A Plymouth resident and thus not one of the signers, Vassall was a determined enemy of the Bay; he had advised the Hingham dissidents and the Child petitioners and had himself unsuccessfully petitioned the Plymouth magistrates for similar changes.) In Boston, the General Court found the remonstrants guilty of "blameworthy action" and fined them. Child prepared another petition, this one aimed at Parliament and requesting a governor-general for New England. He was seized and detained under guard while awaiting trial for having failed to pay his earlier fine. It was June of 1647 before Robert Child could leave the Bay, and by then the English authorities had rejected the appeal of Fowler and Vassall and made clear their disinclination to consider future appeals over the heads of the Bay authorities.

Paralleling the danger to orthodoxy posed by the interaction of domestic and English Presbyterianism, the mid-1640s also saw the rise of a sectarian threat. In England the dismantling of the Anglican church, the breakdown of authority during the Civil Wars, and the dissension between Presbyterians and Congregationalists were but three of the factors behind the rise and spread in the 1640s of numerous religious viewpoints judged heretical by the Puritan leadership. Anabaptists, Fifth Monarchy Men, Familists, Quakers, Traskites, Ranters, Adamites, Grindletonians, and others posed a threat to the religious stability of England and their ideas crossed the Atlantic to threaten New England orthodoxy as well.

As early as 1644 concern about the potential spread of Baptist views had led the General Court to legislate against the dissemination of any arguments challenging the validity of infant baptism. Further legislation was passed two years later. Outside of Massachusetts, in the Rhode Island settlements, Baptist views spread without fear of government suppression. In 1639, Ezekiel Holliman and Roger Williams had formed the first Baptist church in America, at Providence. Five years later Dr. John Clarke founded a Baptist congregation in Newport. More extreme than their former neighbors (they would have put it that they were more logical), these Baptist exiles from the Bay insisted that only the regenerate believer should be baptised and they denied the value of the sacrament as a means of assisting men to prepare for God's call. In effect, the Baptists accepted most of the views of the Congregationalists, advancing the logic of Congregationalism one step farther. It was precisely their roots in orthodox Puritanism that made the Baptists a threat to the orthodox and brought the wrath of the Bay magistrates down upon them.

In the 1640s Baptist tracts from England reached Massachusetts and four of the colony's divines prepared refutations of them. George Philips, John Cotton, Thomas Cobbett, and Thomas Shepard all took up their pens, both to warn England of error and to point out the Baptists' mistakes to their fellow colonists.

ASSERTING CONGREGATIONALISM: THE CAMBRIDGE PLATFORM

Faced with such challenges from both the Presbyterian and sectarian wings of the Puritan movement, the General Court—in the same session that it received the Child petition—issued a call for a synod of representatives of the various New England churches. The summons expressed a desire for an authoritative settlement of ecclesiastical practices that would answer English requests for some such document and which would also serve to encourage a uniformity of practice among the region's churches. Of particular concern to the magistrates was a treatment of issues that had arisen in reference to church membership. The magistrates also wanted the Bible Commonwealths on record in favor of Congregationalism, in an effort to forestall any English plans to impose Presbyterian practices on the colonies.

Not all of the churches were eager to participate. When the synod was called to order in September of 1646 at Cambridge, four Massachusetts congregations had no representation. Concord's absence was accidental, and Hingham's pastor Hobart was disinclined to support the assembly; but the Boston and Salem churches had expressed serious doubts about the synod's legitimacy. The polemical struggle between Presbyterians and Congregationalists and the writings of various English Independents had made many in those congregations overly sensitive about anything that could conceivably be seen as a threat to congregational autonomy. Soon, however, the opposition to the synod was overcome in both congregations and the colony's two oldest towns belatedly sent representatives.

In its first session the Cambridge Synod adopted a report declaring itself to be an advisory rather than a governing or judicial body and named John Cotton, Richard Mather, and Ralph Partridge to prepare a model of church government. When the synod reassembled Mather presented a draft that included his own plan for extending baptism to the children of all baptized church members, rather than continuing to restrict the sacrament to offspring of the converted. The proposal was a response to the failure of baptized children to have conversion experiences, the subsequent question as to the eligibility of their children for the sacrament, and the beginning of a decline in the percentage of the population numbered as church members in full standing. It would also have been a conciliatory step in the direction of the type of parish system advocated by Parker and Noyse and might have thus been acceptable to a Presbyterian Parliament. For that reason alone it attracted considerable support from those who wished to forestall any English tampering with the colonial system.

But the political situation in England was changing. Whereas the Presbyterians had held the ascendancy in Parliament as well as in the Westminster Assembly during the early years of the Civil War, their position had steadily eroded as the decade wore on. Congregationalists began to garner the invitations to preach in Parliament that had previously gone to Presbyterians. Though the Presbyterian church system had been adopted by Parliament in 1645, with the shift in power it was not enforced.

With the rise to power of their English allies, the New England Congregationalists were correspondingly less concerned with the threat of English action against the colonial church system. What had been a minority against innovation, led by John Davenport, became a majority. Richard Mather's suggested plan was rejected. The decision having been made to retain the requirements for church membership, the synod proceeded to adopt a statement of faith and polity that reflected the New Englanders' continued desire to serve as a model for international reform. In their preface to the Cambridge Platform the representatives expressed the hope that the document that followed would serve the dual purpose of maintaining the integrity of the faith practiced in New England and that "the example of such poor outcasts as ourselves, might prevaile if not with all . . . yet with some other of our brethren in England." In matters of faith, the New Englanders

having perused the publick confession of faith, agreed upon by the Reverend Assembly of Divines at Westminster, and finding the summ and substance thereof (in matters of doctrine) to express not their own judgements only, but ours also, . . . wee thought good to present . . . our professed and hearty assent and attestation to the whole confession of faith (for substance of doctrine) which the Reverend assembly presented to the Religious and Honourable Parliament of England.

Having thus asserted their maintenance of "the same Doctrine of the truth of the Gospel, which generally is received in all the reformed Churches of Christ in Europe," the New Englanders set forth in subsequent sections of the Cambridge Platform their system of church government. Containing nothing that could not be found in earlier works by Cotton, Hooker, Davenport, and others, the document set forth the central elements of the New England Way and an explanation of the ways in which the civil magistrates and the fellowship of the congregation could work officially and unofficially to maintain an orthodox consensus. The document was sent to the General Court of Massachusetts, which commended it to the churches for their consideration and eventually endorsed it. It proved equally acceptable in Plymouth, Connecticut, and New Haven and became the established explanation of New England Puritanism.

THE BAPTIST CHALLENGE RENEWED

Despite the widespread acceptance of the Cambridge Platform, tensions in the religious life of the colonies remained. Presbyterians such as Parker and Noyse were unconvinced by the Congregationalist apologia and continued in their distinctive church practices. Regardless of official vigilance, Baptist views likewise remained a threat.

William Witter, originally a member of the Salem congregation, had begun to express questions about infant baptism as early as 1644. Like other isolated dissenters in the colony during that decade, he was occasionally brought into court to answer for his views but suffered no harsh penalties. Sometime between 1646 and 1651 he was rebaptised and joined John Clarke's Newport congregation, though he continued to live in Lynn, just outside Salem. In 1651 his rebaptism was discovered and the Salem church excommunicated him. Witter had interested some of his neighbors in his views and he requested the Newport church to send some emissaries to carry on the work of conversion. In July 1651, John Clarke, Obadiah Holmes, and John Crandall arrived in Lynn.

The three Rhode Islanders led religious services in Witter's home and baptized two or three converts. Discovered and arrested, they were brought to Boston and presented before Governor Endecott for trial. All three were found guilty and fined, with provision that they be whipped if they refused to pay. A well-wisher paid Clarke's fine, and Crandall was released on bail; but Holmes refused to pay and was kept in jail until September, when he was whipped. The three left Massachusetts (Crandall forfeiting his bail). John Clarke later publicized the incident in his *Ill-Newes from New England*, hoping by that volume to persuade the English authorities to impose toleration on Massachusetts. That effort failed, but Baptist influence persisted in the Bay.

Far more serious than the Lynn incident was the conversion to Baptist views of Henry Dunster, the president of Harvard College. When Dunster in 1654 failed to present his newest child to be baptized in the Cambridge church, the congregation's young pastor, Jonathan Mitchell, met with him and tried to persuade him of the validity of infant baptism. But it was the Harvard president who was best prepared to debate the point. Next the General Court instructed nine ministers and two lay elders to confer with Dunster. This too was fruitless. Dunster could have kept his views to himself, conformed outwardly, and maintained his position. Some urged him to do so. Instead, he resigned the presidency of the Puritan college and retired to Scituate in the Plymouth colony, where he died four years later. The same year that Dunster departed, Thomas Goold of Charlestown became convinced of the error of infant baptism. Though the magistrates had no suspicion of it at the time, within ten years Goold would succeed in founding the first Baptist church of Boston.

Dunster's removal brought an end to the last major Baptist challenge of the 1650s. But the second half of that decade saw a new threat in the arrival of members of the Society of Friends. As with the Baptists, the roots of the Quaker movement are to be found in Puritanism. In their emphasis upon the immediacy of religious experience they resembled such Puritans as Richard Sibbes and John Cotton and bore an even closer resemblance to Anne Hutchinson. The Quaker point of departure from the Puritan tradition came in their insistence on individual obedience to the inner light of Christ within each of the saints. They de-emphasized the Scriptures as a rule of life and in their religious practice abandoned a structured liturgy, a separate ministry, and the sacraments. Their thought was theologically threatening to the orthodox Puritans and the social implications of their beliefs was as potentially subversive as had been the views of Roger Williams and Anne Hutchinson.

In July of 1656 the first of the Quakers arrived in Massachusetts. Mary Fisher and Anne Austin traveled to Boston from the Barbados Islands. They were detained by the magistrates, and the books they carried with them were seized. After five weeks they were sent back to Barbados, but a few days after their banishment eight more Friends arrived. They received the same treatment. In October the General Court took notice of this new threat and passed legislation making shipmasters who brought Quakers to the colony liable to fines, and Quakers themselves subject to whipping, imprisonment, and banishment.

Despite the new laws Massachusetts gained no relief from the Quakers, and they began to trouble other colonies as well. In 1657, missionary Friends arrived in Newport, where they found that since as early as 1641 some of the former followers of Anne Hutchinson had in fact been Quakers in all but name. These former "antinomians" were readily drawn into the fellowship of the Friends, making Rhode Island the center of American Quakerism for decades to come. The harvest reaped by the Friends in Rhode Island only reinforced the antipathy felt toward the new sect by the orthodox clergy of New England. Some had already noted with foreboding the similarity between the viewpoints of the old Hutchinsonians and the Quakers. In his *The Heart of New England Rent at the Blasphemies of the Present Generation*, the Reverend John Norton conceded the attractiveness that Quaker views would hold for many, but emphasized that the very lure of those views was another reason for vigilance on the part of the magistrates. In 1658 the commissioners of the United Colonies recommended that the member colonies of the confederation legalize the use of the death penalty for Quakers whose fanaticism caused them to return to the colonies after banishment.

The decades of the revolution and the rule of Oliver Cromwell in England were by no means untroubled years for the American Puritans. The fragmentation of English Puritanism into Congregationalists, Presbyterians, Baptists, Quakers, and a multiplicity of other sects posed threats to the Congregational way of New England and highlighted areas where the orthodox consensus was fragile. But whatever their trials, the 1640s and 1650s were decades of confidence in New England. The example of their "city on a hill" was being followed. The colonists had accomplished the errand on which they had been sent into the wilderness. The charter of Massachusetts and the future of her sister colonies seemed safe, with Archbishop Laud executed and their coreligionists in power. The American Puritans were given commercial concessions that became the foundation for future prosperity. Rather than fearing the arrival of English troops to be used against them, they could count upon being able to call English troops to their aid. With such signs of God's favor, none could doubt that the colonists would be able to overcome whatever troubles might appear on their horizon.

11 | CHANGES IN RESTORATION NEW ENGLAND

Between 1660 and 1665 the course of New England history took an abrupt turn, as a new regime came to power in England. Each of the Bible Commonwealths wrestled in turn with the problem of adjusting to that reality. Massachusetts proved divided in its response, revealing divisions that laid the basis for the later loss of the colony's charter. New Haven was eliminated from the map, a victim of the startling expansion of Connecticut, the colony which under the skilled leadership of John Winthrop, Jr., managed actually to profit from the troubled and fluid nature of the times. Equal in importance to the political effects of the Restoration was the blow to the colonists' sense of mission. Their vision of a "city on a hill" evidently a mirage, the unity of the American Puritans began to disintegrate amid the rise of economic self-seeking, challenges from other faiths, and disputes over a redefined purpose for the colonies.

THE DECLINE AND FALL
OF THE ENGLISH PURITAN STATE

In October 1658 the Lord Protector, Oliver Cromwell, died. He had named his son Richard to succeed him, but Oliver's death was the signal for the factions he had precariously held in control to make a new bid for power. Ill suited to control the turbulent forces around him, Richard Cromwell soon resigned his office and retired to private life. The collapse of the Protectorate ushered in a struggle between the Parliamentary republicans and the leaders of the army. In the confusion, citizens refused to pay taxes, there were a number of unsuccessful royalist uprisings, and the City of London refused to cooperate with the generals. In the winter of 1659–1660, General George Monck, commander of the English occupation troops in Scotland, marched south at the head of his troops to restore order. With surprising ease he brushed away the opposition and entered London. Monck restored to power the survivors of the old Long Parliament, and that legislature organized new elections. Assembling in April 1660, the new Convention Parliament was dominated by Presbyterians and royalists. It tendered to the exiled son of Charles I an invitation to return to England and assume the throne. On 25 May 1660 Charles Stuart landed at Dover.

The Restoration (of the monarchy) meant the restoration of Anglicanism as well. Thomas Goodwin, John Owen, and the other leaders of English Congregationalism lost their positions of prominence in the government and universities. Presbyterians, Baptists, Congregationalists, and other non-Anglicans were deprived of their livings. Many looked to New England as a refuge. John Leverett, Francis Willoughby, and Increase Mather were but a few of those who gradually migrated to the colonies to resume interrupted careers. Others, like William Hooke, remained in England and went underground—forced to move from place to place to avoid the authorities. Some were even less fortunate. Hugh Peter and others branded as regicides were beheaded.

In civil affairs the new king surrounded himself with advisers such as Edward Hyde, earl of Clarendon, who were advocates of imperial centralization. Commonwealth and Protectorate legislation pertaining to the colonies was invalidated, though often replaced with similar regulations. The Navigation Act of 1651 had required the products of Asia, Africa, and America headed for English possessions to be carried in English ships. European goods shipped to English markets had to be carried either in English ships or in ships of the country where the product originated. In 1660 the new regime passed its own Navigation Act, which differed from the Cromwellian statute in that only English vessels were permitted to transport goods to the English colonies and in enumerating a list of colonial products (including sugar, cotton, indigo, and tobacco) that could be exported only to the mother country.

In the year of his accession, Charles II appointed a Council of Trade and a Council for Foreign Plantations. Both new groups had membership drawn from the ranks of "civilian" experts as well as from the Privy Council. Of the two, the Council for Foreign Plantations was the more important to the colonies. It was instructed to improve communications between the home government and the colonies, to investigate charges of colonial evasions of the Navigation Act and similar laws, and to recommend imperial policy to the Privy Council. Its creation was yet another sign of the growing trend toward centralized government.

THE RESTORATION AND MASSACHUSETTS

The Restoration placed the New Englanders in a precarious position. They had sided with the Parliament and expended considerable effort on behalf of the rebel cause. Convinced that their coreligionists were destined by divine providence to succeed, they had denied their allegiance to Charles I, tacitly acquiesced in his execution, and recognized the legitimacy of the Commonwealth and Protectorate. Moreover, Massachusetts had been in the monarchy's disfavor prior to the Civil War, while the other Puritan colonies either lacked charters or had questionable claims to legitimacy. In 1660 the very survival of the Bible Commonwealths was in doubt.

Adding to the difficulty of the task of adjustment before them, the American Puritans entered into this troubled period deprived of some of their most tested leaders. John Winthrop had passed away in 1649. Thomas Dudley died in 1653. John Haynes, who had served one term as governor of Massachusetts and seven terms as governor of Connecticut, died in 1654. Edward Hopkins, seven times governor of Connecticut, died in 1657. Theophilus Eaton, governor of New Haven from 1639 to 1657, passed away in 1658. Francis Newman, Eaton's successor, died in office in 1660. Plymouth's two outstanding magistrates were both deceased at the time of the Restoration—Edward Winslow died participating in the English assault on Jamaica in 1655 and William Bradford passed away two years later. In their churches, too, New Englanders entered the 1660s bereft of experienced guides: Thomas Hooker had passed away as early as 1647; Thomas Shepard died in 1649, John Cotton in 1652, Nathaniel Rogers in 1655, Ralph Partridge in 1658, and Peter Bulkeley in 1659. Many of lesser eminence were gone also, to their maker or to England. It was largely a new and inexperienced guard that faced the problems of the Restoration.

In Massachusetts the attempts of the king and his ministers to regulate the empire stimulated the rise of three factions. One group consisted of blatant royalists, such as Thomas Breedon and Thomas Deane; few in number, they were essentially merchants who had little sympathy for or loyalty to the colony's goals and leadership. At the other political extreme was a commonwealth faction led by Governor John Endecott, Deputy Governor Richard Bellingham, and magistrates Daniel Gookin and Thomas Danforth. They held to the belief that the colony's charter had been a contract between the English crown and the Massachusetts Bay Company whereby the colony became a virtually autonomous commonwealth. Recognizing the superior force of England, these Puritan stalwarts nevertheless sought to preserve as much independence for the Bay as was possible, and they were supported by a broad spectrum of the population, including most artisans, farmers, clergymen, and some merchants. Poised between royalists and commonwealthmen was an alignment of moderates who wished to see the colony left to pursue its own ends but who believed that the chief cause of royal interference in those pursuits was the colony's assertion of its independence. These moderates rivaled the commonwealth faction in their pedigrees; led by magistrates Simon Bradstreet and Daniel Dennison, they numbered among their ranks such influential men as deputy Edward Johnson, ministers John Norton and John Wilson, and merchants John Hull and Joshua Scotow. They maintained a sentimental attachment to the land of their birth and looked upon New England's history as demonstration that an acknowledgment of English sovereignty was not incompatible with the pursuit of the colony's interests.

Immediately upon receipt of the news of the Restoration the commonwealthmen and moderates came into conflict in the General Court. With each faction almost equal in strength the colony seemed incapable of settling upon a single approach, as first one and then the other faction gained an advantage. Initially Endecott adopted a stance of ignoring the wishes of the new king. Edward Whalley, William Goffe, and John Dixwell—three of the signers of Charles I's death warrant who had been exempted from royal pardon—fled to the Bay and were cordially welcomed by the governor and other leading citizens. In October the Reverend John Norton and other moderates urged the magistrates to adopt a conciliatory policy to the new regime by acknowledging the king. Their advice was neglected.

Soon troubled by news that their enemies in England were demanding revocation of the Bay's charter, the magistrates called a special session of the General Court to prepare an official address to Charles II. Even then their petition was less a humble acknowledgment of royal authority than a defense of the Bay and a request for the new monarch's favor. Declaring the colony's right to "our liberty to walk in the faith of the gospel" as they saw it, the legislators beseeched the king to spurn the advice of the colony's enemies and specifically defended the treatment they had meted out to the Quakers.

This was not the type of humble submission that was being tendered to the king by other colonies, and it received a cool reception in Whitehall. The Bay's moderates gained further strength as the threat of English intervention grew, and the magistrates grudgingly took additional steps toward regularizing relations with England. The regicides had already left Massachusetts, but Governor Endecott went through the motions of trying to apprehend them, commissioning two young royalists—Thomas Kirke and Thomas Kellond—to seek out and seize the fugitives. Also, in May 1661, the General Court censured John Eliot for the antimonarchical views expressed in his book *The Christian Commonwealth*.

Finally, on 7 August 1661, the General Court proclaimed the king in the fashion desired by Whitehall. The moderates wielded enough strength to have John Norton and Simon Bradstreet chosen as agents to carry the letter to England and represent the colony there. But their instructions were prepared by commonwealthmen and severely limited their freedom of action on behalf of the Bay government. The king's advisers drafted a response in which Charles thanked the colonists for their expressions of loyalty and agreed to a confirmation of the charter. In his letter the king then suggested that the General Court of Massachusetts repeal all laws derogatory to the monarchy, administer oaths of allegiance and justice in the name of the sovereign, allow freedom of worship for Anglicans, and eliminate church membership as a condition for the franchise.

The Bay colonists, particularly the commonwealth faction, were appalled by the king's suggestions. Many blamed Norton and Bradstreet for having given Charles the impression that Massachusetts was eager to please him. The stock of the moderates fell rapidly. Firmly in control, Endecott and his supporters studiously ignored the king's requests and got away with it for the time being. But divisions still existed in the colony and would become worse. Obstructionism would increasingly lead to visitations by royal appointees, and eventually one of those agents would succeed in playing upon the colony's divisions to speed the downfall of the charter.

CONNECTICUT'S QUEST FOR A CHARTER

While Massachusetts delayed acceptance of the Restoration and never seemed to submit with any sincerity, some of the other colonies had been more ready to make peace with King Charles. Rhode Island was the first in New England to accept the finality of the Restoration. In

October of 1660, Charles II was proclaimed in that colony, and Dr. John Clarke was chosen by the magistrates to travel to England in search of confirmation of the patent that Parliament had issued to Roger Williams. Connecticut was somewhat more reluctant to concede the collapse of Puritan hopes, but followed Rhode Island's example in March of 1661. Plymouth recognized the new regime three months later.

Only New Haven pursued a course of resistance similar to the Bay's. Without anything resembling a charter, the colony's position was extremely precarious. But the settlers openly demonstrated their unwillingness to accept the Stuarts' rule. Disregarding their earlier history of conflict with the Dutch, New Havenites first responded to the Restoration by opening negotiations with Peter Stuyvesant for permission to settle in what is now New Jersey. At the same time John Davenport welcomed Edward Whalley and William Goffe into his home and organized a network of colonists for shielding the two regicides. In June of 1661, Director General Stuyvesant and the Council of New Netherland granted the New Havenites permission to examine the site of their proposed settlement and agreed to grant any migrants free trade, free land, and free exercise of religion, though they would be subject to Dutch civil law. While awaiting word of ratification by the Dutch home government, the New Havenites also made half-hearted plans to seek a charter from Charles II and became the last New England colony to proclaim the king, doing so on 22 August 1661.

By the time New Haven belatedly recognized the royal authority events were already in progress that would lead to the dissolution of that strictest of the Bible Commonwealths. When Connecticut proclaimed the new monarch in March the legislature had chosen John Winthrop, Jr., to go to England in search of a charter. Winthrop had been his father's right hand in the preparation for and launching of the Great Migration and had come to Massachusetts himself in 1631 at the age of twenty-five. In the succeeding decades he had been instrumental in the founding of the towns of Ipswich, Saybrook, and New London. He was one of the assistants in Massachusetts from 1632 to 1650, an assistant in Connecticut from 1651 to 1657, and governor of the colony thereafter. An industrial pioneer, he established salt- and ironworks in New England and was noted for his scientific interests. Well traveled, moderate, a natural diplomat, he was well suited to represent his colony on a mission intended to gain for Connecticut a charter that would not only guarantee the colonists their rights but would also expand the colony's bounds to include New

Haven, Rhode Island, and parts of New Netherland. Arriving in London, he used his many connections there to gain access to the new powers of the realm.

The Connecticut governor needed all the help he could muster because of the questionable legitimacy of his colony's claims. The Warwick Patent, upon which the colonists based their right to govern, had never been seen and probably did not exist. Winthrop's task was either to gain royal confirmation of the Warwick Patent or to secure a new charter, and it soon became obvious to him that the latter was his only real hope. Even there he had to confront opposition—from John Clarke, who naturally wished to save Rhode Island from Connecticut's clutches; from a Captain John Scott, who appeared late on the scene, purportedly representing New Haven; and from enemies of the Puritans, such as Samuel Maverick, who advocated consolidation of the New England colonies and appointment of a governor-general.

The Connecticut charter was drawn up and dated 23 April 1661 and sealed on 10 May. It ratified the boundaries petitioned for by Winthrop and made no substantial change in the government of the colony. Discovering that a large tract of Rhode Island territory had been given to Connecticut, John Clarke appealed to the king for a further review of the document. Winthrop was forced to delay his departure from England and fight off this new challenge. He met with Clarke in Clarendon's presence but neither agent was willing to yield anything. Finally Winthrop succeeded in gaining Clarendon's permission to send the charter to Hartford, which Clarke opposed since it made it much more difficult to effect any changes in the document.

The Connecticut authorities, on receipt of the charter, almost immediately attempted to impose their rule on New Haven and the disputed Rhode Island territory. Residents of the New Haven colony were admitted to freemanship, and the Connecticut magistrates appointed officials in several towns within the jurisdiction of New Haven. Having been surprised to learn the contents of the Connecticut charter, Governor William Leete, John Davenport, and other leaders of the colony on Long Island Sound sent agents to England to protest while they maintained a posture of noncompliance with Connecticut's demands.

In April of 1663 Winthrop finally reached agreement with Clarke on the Narragansett territory. The settlement, proposed by a panel of five arbitrators, established the boundary between the two colonies at the Pawtucket River (the present line between the two states). This preserved Rhode Island's territory as secured by Roger Williams in the 1644 patent, but the Narragansett property owners (Connecticut citizens including Winthrop) were guaranteed title to their land and offered the option of being governed by Connecticut if they chose. Agreement having been reached, Winthrop used his influence to speed the approval of the Rhode Island charter, which was finally issued to Clarke on 8 July 1663. Substituting a governor to be elected semi-annually by a general assembly for the old position of president, the new charter preserved the essentials of government as provided for in the old patent.

When Winthrop returned to Connecticut he found that his troubles were far from over. Connecticut's other magistrates refused to accept the land settlement with Clarke and insisted on full control of the Narragansett territory. Rhode Island officials on receipt of their charter refused to accept Connecticut's pretensions and tried to assert their authority over the Narragansett proprietors. The result was a series of violent clashes along the Pawtucket River, which continued until royal action imposed a settlement a few years later.

At the same time New Haven and New Netherland were mounting a challenge to Connecticut's territorial ambitions. In September of 1663, New Haven appealed for support at the quarterly meeting of the New England Confederation in Boston. Massachusetts and Plymouth both supported her against the ambitions of Connecticut, but Winthrop and his fellow magistrates refused to accept the confederation's judgment. In October the Connecticut General Court called for the categorical submission of the New Haven towns. With Leete and Davenport leading the resistance, the New Haven General Court authorized the raising of £300 to finance a mission to England in search of a charter. All of the towns that had been in the colony's jurisdiction were assessed. When an attempt was made to collect funds in Guilford (which had accepted Connecticut's rule) armed militia from Connecticut rode south to protect the Guilford residents and almost became involved in a battle with the New Haven forces.

While this struggle between Connecticut and New Haven was developing, Winthrop and his fellow magistrates were engaged in a similar dispute with Peter Stuyvesant, who protested Connecticut's assertion of control over Westchester and Long Island. Despite Dutch willingness to negotiate, Connecticut remained firm. When the magistrates dispatched a hundred militia across the sound, Stuyvesant reluctantly acknowledged the English claim to most of Long Island.

By the end of 1663, Connecticut had succeeded in significantly expanding her jurisdiction, and it appeared as if final capitulation of the resisters must soon be forthcoming. In the process, however, the colony had fragmented the onetime unity of the New England Confederation. More serious, Connecticut's territorial conflicts had convinced Clarendon and other high officials that a royal commission would have to be sent to the region if tranquillity were to be restored to New England.

THE ROYAL COMMISSION OF 1664

Clarendon had apparently begun to consider the dispatch of royal commissioners during the months in which he was witness to the quarrel between Winthrop and Clarke over the Connecticut–Rhode Island boundary. Later reports of Connecticut's conflict with Rhode Island and New Haven seemed further evidence of the need for an on-site boundary settlement. Complaints of the Bay colony's failure to observe English laws formed another basis for the final decision, as did the desire of London merchants for the conquest of New Netherland.

In the spring of 1664, Charles II dispatched a force of four frigates and four hundred soldiers to America under the command of Colonel Richard Nicolls. Nicolls was instructed to capture New Netherland—though England was at peace with the Dutch—and to govern the new territory as deputy for the king's brother, the duke of York, to whom it was granted as a proprietary colony. Nicolls was also to head a four-member commission of inquiry, which was to settle Connecticut's boundaries, hear all other regional complaints, and exert pressure on Massachusetts to alter her system of government. The other commissioners were Sir Robert Carr, Colonel George Cartwright, and Samuel Maverick—the last-named member guaranteeing some anti-Puritan bias on the commission.

The charter of 1664 granted to the duke of York posed a serious new threat to Connecticut's pretensions. James Stuart was given, in addition to what had been recognized as Dutch New Netherland, a large portion of Maine, Martha's Vineyard, Nantucket Island, Long Island, and all of the mainland west of the Connecticut River. While Winthrop's cooperation with the commissioners won for Connecticut a favorable compromise, which moved the New York boundary westward to the Mamaroneck River, Connecticut was forced to cede her claim to Long Island, and the contradiction between the two charters was to be a source of future disputes.

When the dispatch of the royal commission became known in New

Haven, that colony's officials became concerned as to the effect that such a tribunal might have on their colony. They recognized that their hope of a separate charter was unrealistic, and, fearing the possible appointment of a royal governor or some other loss of liberties, the General Court voted in August of 1664 to yield at least temporarily to Connecticut's jurisdiction if the larger colony would defend New Haven against the actions of the commission. Connecticut held out for unconditional submission, and in September the commissioners of the New England Confederation recommended to New Haven that the colony yield. In December the remaining towns of the colony did submit, and New Haven abandoned all pretence of independence.

The residents of New Haven accepted the decision with differing degrees of grace. William Leete entered into the political life of Connecticut and eventually succeeded John Winthrop, Jr., as that colony's governor. But many New Havenites had always suspected the more lenient religious system of Connecticut and feared the effects of absorption. The Reverend Abraham Pierson led some of those diehards to settle in New Jersey (a separate colony carved out of New York and granted to friends by the duke of York). There, in Milford—later Newark—they attempted to establish the type of Bible Commonwealth they had lost. John Davenport was another who found Connecticut's rule unpalatable, and in 1668 he left the town he had founded for a pulpit in Boston.

While Connecticut thus acquired New Haven, the colony was less fortunate in its claim to the Narragansett region. In March of 1665 the royal commissioners decreed that the disputed territory belonged to neither Connecticut nor Rhode Island. Labeling it the "King's Province," they decreed it to be royal territory, though Rhode Island was requested to administer it until further notice.

When the Bay magistrates first heard of the dispatch of Nicolls at the head of an armed force, they feared that the troops were to be used against their colony. The charter was hidden, the forts in Boston harbor strengthened, and the militia summoned. When it became evident that the English troops were intended for use against the Dutch some of the tension eased. Ever since the king's earlier letter the broadening of the franchise had been occasionally debated in Massachusetts. With the arrival of the royal commission the General Court took a small conciliatory step by altering the requirements for freemanship. In place of the old requirement of church membership, the new law stipulated that anyone who was not a church member could be admitted to freemanship by a majority vote of the General Court, if he could produce a certificate from the minister in the town of his residence testifying that he was not vicious in his behavior and a statement from his town selectmen that he was a freeholder ratable at no less than ten shillings.

Beyond this enlargement of the franchise (and it would still be difficult for the nonorthodox to acquire freemanship) the General Court would not go. In fact, as it became known that the commission was instructed to secure changes in the charter and the election of Nicolls as governor, the strength of the commonwealth faction grew. The General Court refused to adopt an oath of allegiance to the king, refused to extend religious liberty to non-Puritans, and refused to allow appeals over the head of the General Court to the crown. When the commissioners attempted to sit as an appellate court, they were prevented from doing so, and the court petitioned the king for a recall of the commission. All of this was provoking to the commissioners themselves and to the king. Secretary of State William Morice wrote to the colonists that the king was unhappy. He suggested that since Governor Endecott "is not a person well affected to his Majesty's person or his Government, his Majesty will take it very well if [at] the next election any other person of good reputation be chosen in that place."

The loyalty of the colonists to Endecott was not to be tested, the governor having passed away. The royal reprimand did generate concern, however, and seemed to win support for the moderates. Nevertheless, when the commissioners departed in the fall of 1665 they had won no new concessions. Nicolls and his colleagues had succeeded in suspending the Bay's jurisdiction over Maine and in precipitating the slight broadening of the franchise. Beyond that they had been successfully resisted in everything they attempted. They recommended revocation of the Massachusetts charter as the only way of bringing the colony under the authority of the home government.

Fortunately for the Bay colonists this threat to their charter was to be blunted (as the threat in the 1630s had been) by the outbreak of war. The conquest of New Netherland had led to the Second Anglo-Dutch War (1665–1667). Preoccupied with the European struggle, the English government ignored the report of its royal commissioners. Furthermore, the years of war marked the period of Clarendon's political decline. In 1667 the one man in the government with the interest and ability to have coerced the Bay was cast out of power. Massachusetts in the same year sent Charles II twenty-four masts for the royal navy and quietly resumed the government of Maine.

THE IDEOLOGICAL EFFECT
OF THE RESTORATION

The original settlers of New England believed that they were a remnant set apart from the majority of their fellow Englishmen, chosen to preserve the true faith and thus serve as a beacon for worldwide reformation. The colonists of Massachusetts, New Haven, Connecticut, and Plymouth were brought together by their commitment to this ideal, and the progress of reform in England in the 1640s and 1650s had given them confidence in their mission.

The Restoration, demonstrating the frailty of the Puritan hold on England, planted doubts in the minds of New Englanders. The hold that Winthrop's vision of a "city on a hill" had had on the colonial imagination was shattered. The very men who had articulated that goal—the clergy and the magistrates—became somewhat suspect in their reading of history and of God's will. Just as 1660 marked the appearance of conflicting political views of how the colonies should deal with England, so too did it signal dispute over what God wanted of the colonies in the future.

Some colonists began to abandon all pretence of a religious mission and to regard New England as primarily a new world for secular advancement. Such men were likely to be royalists politically—seeking to develop closer political and economic ties with England as a means of advancing their own interests. Most New Englanders became more suspicious than ever of England and of the outside world. Preserving the purity of their own society became their prime concern. While they were no longer sure of when the millennium would come, they remained convinced that it would come and that the faith had to be preserved in the Bible Commonwealths in anticipation of that day. Some took this view to a more extreme point than others. John Davenport would devote the remaining years of his life to a defense of the New England Way in exactly the form expressed in the Cambridge Platform, while others, such as Increase Mather, would come to recognize the need for some adaptation and growth and some exchange with the outside world. But all of the members of the second and succeeding generations who sought to preserve their religious inheritance displayed a greater attachment to their homeland than did the founders. Whereas John Cotton saw the New Jerusalem coming in England, his descendant Jonathan Edwards had no doubt but that the millennium would dawn in New England. When the colonists struggled against English policy in the late seventeenth century and eighteenth century they did it not, as had their fathers, for England's sake, but for the sake of New England—"dear New England!" as Michael Wigglesworth expressed it, "dearest land to me!"

Their confidence shaken by the return of Charles II, New Englanders would divide over how to meet their problems. They would strike out more harshly against dissenters and then be forced to accept the presence in their midst of Baptists, Quakers, and Anglicans. They would fight each other over the question of extending baptism and from that divisive debate would spring other controversies over church membership, ordination, and open communion. They would see their afflictions as divine punishment for their shortcomings and carry self-indictment to a literary art in their jeremiads. Just as the unity of the New England polity had begun to crumble in the 1660s, so too would the ideological symmetry of the New England mind.

12 | CHALLENGES TO THE FAITH: PLURALISM AND DECLENSION

Stripped of confidence by the collapse of the English Puritan state, New Englanders became more divided in their attitudes toward religious dissent and, principally in Massachusetts, more repressive in their treatment of sectaries. What justification there is for regarding the seventeenth-century colonists as cruel bigots is drawn from events in the Bay between 1658 and 1692. Judged by European standards, earlier dissenters such as Roger Williams and Anne Hutchinson had been let off lightly—they were not executed, subjected to imprisonment, or even whipped. Quakers and Baptists who challenged the Bay colony's orthodoxy in the 1660s and after were not always so fortunate.

Yet if some Puritan leaders were harsh toward nonbelievers, they were no more tolerant of what they saw as their own failings (though less extreme in punishing them). The period that saw the execution of Quakers and imprisonment of Baptists were years in which the clergy fought each other over the question of baptism, and in which they developed the literary form of the jeremiad, verbally castigating themselves and their flocks for having wandered from the path of righteousness. The Puritans' intolerance was in part at least a symptom of their own insecurity.

"SHE HANGS THERE LIKE A FLAG"

First to feel the new harshness of the Puritan magistrates were the Quakers. But the punishment and execution of Friends was not simply a case of Puritans seeking to rid their society of threatening religious

138

influences. Banishment would have sufficed to keep error out of the colony had the Quakers accepted the exile imposed on them by the Massachusetts courts. As Governor Endecott explained it, the Friends were not executed for their religious beliefs per se, but for "their superadded presumptuous and incorrigible contempt of authority. They would not be restrained but by Death." At least one modern historian has agreed with the Salem magistrate. Daniel Boorstin has argued that "the Puritans had not sought out the Quakers in order to punish them; the Quakers had come in quest of punishment." While many missionary Friends showed little sign of the thirst for martyrdom detected by Boorstin, among the Quakers who came to Massachusetts were some of the most disorderly and unrestrained "heretics" to ever challenge the colony's orthodoxy. Friends disrupted Puritan worship services by interrupting sermons, by strolling naked down the aisles, and by other means calculated to focus attention on themselves and—presumably—their ideas. Fines were no deterrent, and when banished these Quakers returned. In effect they *did* mock the laws and authority of the Bay and provoked the magistrates to excess even before the confidence of those gentlemen was shaken by the Restoration.

In June of 1658, Christopher Holder and John Copeland, two Friends who had previously been whipped and banished from the Bay, returned to Massachusetts and were arrested in Dedham. A public disputation was held in Boston in an effort to convert the two prisoners while also offering a public refutation of Quaker beliefs. When Holder and Copeland remained unmoved by this demonstration, the magistrates ordered them each to have an ear cut off (not unusual punishment by the standards of the day) and to be once again sent from the colony. They were threatened with death if they returned, and in October the General Court legitimatized that threat by legislation establishing the death penalty for any who returned from banishment.

In September of 1659 William Robinson, Marmaduke Stephenson, and Mary Dyer were arrested, tried as Quakers, and banished. Mary Dyer—who had earlier been sent from the Bay as one of Anne Hutchinson's followers—returned home to Rhode Island, while Robinson and Stephenson traveled north to New Hampshire. But soon all three were reunited and back in Boston, bearing witness to the truth as they saw it. In October of 1659 they were tried by the General Court with Governor Endecott presiding, were convicted and sentenced to death. Mary Dyer, on the scaffold with hands bound and face covered, was reprieved, while her fellow missionaries were hung. But within a year she was again arrested in Boston and, refusing to pledge never to return if released, she was executed. "She hangs there like a flag," reported one contemporary, and certainly her execution was a beacon that brought still more Quakers to test their mettle against the Puritan magistrates. At the same time the hanging of a woman in Boston, no matter what the justification, shocked many members of the community and sparked a movement to replace the death penalty with a less odious form of punishment for Quakers.

Additional impetus for altering the law was provided by the Restoration. The Massachusetts moderates recognized that Charles II was unlikely to approve the execution of Quakers for failure to adhere to a religious system that the king himself found objectionable. Opponents of the death penalty in the General Court were able to gain an abatement of executions while the laws were reviewed. In May of 1661 the court replaced the death penalty with the "Cart and Whip Act," under the terms of which Friends could be strapped to the back of a cart and whipped from town to town out of the colony. Modified in 1662, that law remained the basic statute under which Quakers were dealt with for the next decade.

While the General Court was enacting this change, English Quakers had been persisting in efforts to sway King Charles to prohibit any persecution of Friends in the Bay—adding their voices to the other enemies of Massachusetts at the royal court. While not sympathetic to the sect's beliefs, Charles did order a stop to the execution of Quakers in Massachusetts and allowed Samuel Shattuck—an exiled Bay Quaker from Salem—to personally carry the royal order to Governor Endecott. By the time he reached the colony the law had been changed. The home government's only other intervention to protect the Friends— an order by the royal commission of 1664 that Quakers not be discriminated against in secular affairs—was ignored by the Puritan magistrates.

Despite the execution of a total of six of their number, the Quakers did manage some growth in the colony during the 1660s, thus confirming many of the orthodox in the belief that the Quakers were a real danger to the holy remnant. Nantucket Island in particular developed a reputation as a center of Quaker strength, but following its inclusion in the patent given the duke of York there was little that the Bay could do about it. In 1674 a Quaker meeting was established in Boston. The General Court responded in 1675 by passing a law prohibiting such assemblies in the colony. In 1677 the constables were ordered to search for and disperse all Quaker meetings. And throughout the 1660s and 1670s there were instances of punishment under the Cart and Whip Act.

Nevertheless there was growing evidence that the moderate political faction was willing to consider toleration. Certainly clergymen such as

Increase Mather and magistrates such as John Leverett, perhaps influenced toward liberality by their continuing contact with English dissenters, were aware of the value of uniting all non-Anglicans. In his 1677 election sermon to the General Court, Mather followed his exhortation that the government encourage orthodoxy with a statement that

> it is far from my design in speaking this to stir up the Magistrates to that which the Scripture calls *Persecution*: it were better to err by *too much indulgence* towards those that have *the root of the matter in them*, than by *too much Severity*. Nay, as to those that are indeed Heretical, I can for my own part say with Luther, *ad judicium sanguinis tardus sum*, I have no affection to *sanguinary* punishments in such Cases.

Some of this change in attitude was attributable to the changing image of the Quakers themselves. As time went on, the American Friends appeared less as enthusiasts and more as sober and pious Christians. This "finer sort of new Quakers," as Cotton Mather referred to them, were more restrained in their behavior, more orthodox in their theology, and more biblical in their religious orientation. Naturally they would receive a different reception than had Mary Dyer and her contemporaries.

Outside of Massachusetts the Quakers generally fared better. In Plymouth, overt government interference with the Friends was minimal after Isaac Robinson—the son of the Pilgrim pastor John Robinson—was sent to win back Quaker converts in Sandwich and was himself won to the new sect. New Haven passed rigid legislation against the Friends but was visited by few in the years before she lost her independence. In Connecticut, eight Quakers were expelled between 1656 and 1660, but the personal tolerance of John Winthrop, Jr., minimized the severity with which they were treated. After 1660 the Connecticut magistrates were far too concerned with appearing circumspect to indulge in a bloody persecution.

Along with Massachusetts, the New England colony in whose history the Quakers achieved considerable importance was Rhode Island. The antinomian exiles in the Aquidneck Island region had provided the most fertile ground in all the colonies for the organization of an American Quaker movement. Having reached many of George Fox's conclusions independently, former followers of Anne Hutchinson, such as her sister Catherine Scott, William Coddington, and Joshua Coggeshall, along with their families joined the Society and brought to it their social prestige and political influence. From their initial appearance in the colony the Quakers held high positions in Rhode Island government, and in 1674 Nicholas Eaton became the first of the colony's many Quaker governors.

Not all Rhode Islanders welcomed the spread of the Quaker influence, however, and foremost of those who placed themselves in opposition was the venerable Roger Williams. Denying the right of any government to impose religious beliefs by force, Williams nevertheless did not believe that all faiths were equally appropriate means of approaching God. A committed biblicist, he found the Quaker reliance on the inner light both foolish and dangerous. Further adding to his choler—as Perry Miller has intimated in his biography of Williams— was the nature of the Quaker converts. Friends such as William Coddington and his followers were among the very Rhode Islanders who had done the most to obstruct Williams's efforts in the 1640s to mold the various towns of the area into a single colony.

Thus, when George Fox visited Rhode Island in 1672, Williams challenged the Quaker leader to a debate. His letter, however, miscarried and did not reach Fox before the Englishman's departure. Williams was left to contend with three of Fox's disciples. Having rowed from Providence to Newport to state his views, he engaged the three Quakers in debate for three days in that town and a fourth day back in Providence. The "father" of Rhode Island was heckled persistently by an audience of Quakers and Baptists as he tried to engage in dialogue a trio who rejected the very authority of the Scriptures upon which he based his arguments. Williams won no converts. The debate was a sign of Quaker strength and also of the diminishing stature of Roger Williams in the colony he had served so well. The final irony was that the greatest acclaim for his published account of the debate came from Massachusetts.

THE BAPTIST CHALLENGE RENEWED

In May of 1665, Thomas Goold and eight others were rebaptised by immersion and organized in Charlestown a Church of Christ on antipedobaptist principles. Goold, a member of the Charlestown congregation, had become convinced of the error of infant baptism almost a decade earlier. In the intervening years he had listened to the arguments of the clergy and of his neighbors without being moved. He believed that the legitimacy of administering the sacrament to infants was something that good Christians could disagree over, and he wanted to maintain his membership and responsibilities in the Charlestown congregation. After he was censured by that church and warned by the magistrates, the local and colony officials ignored him until 1663, when friends of his from England persuaded him to hold private prayer meetings in his home. When Goold went still further and organized a new church, he forced the magistrates to take notice of his stand.

The colony's Court of Assistants gave Goold a hearing in September of 1665 and ordered the Charlestown Baptist and his brethren to cease their schismatic practices. When they refused to do so the General Court called Goold and four other members of the church in October. The five were convicted and disenfranchised and the court warned them that they faced imprisonment if they persisted in their errors. They refused to recant and their legal problems continued.

In the meantime the congregation had moved to a location on Noddles Island in Boston harbor, where they had acquired land. Sympathy for the Baptists had been growing in some quarters, which made it more difficult for the magistrates to deal with them. Some of the more conservative clergy and laymen who were at the time fighting a proposed extension of baptism (the Half-Way Covenant) were sympathetic to the Baptist insistence on a congregational community comprised exclusively of adult saints. Certainly the deputies in the mid-1660s rejected the assistants' suggestion that Goold and his brethren be banished.

In an attempt to win the Baptists back to orthodoxy or at least display their errors, the governor and council ordered a public disputation and appointed six orthodox clergymen to engage Goold and his followers in debate. The ministers were John Allen of Dedham, Thomas Cobbett of Lynn, Samuel Danforth of Roxbury, John Higginson of Salem, Jonathan Mitchell of Cambridge, and Thomas Shepard, Jr., of Charlestown. The debate was held in April 1668 before Governor Richard Bellingham and the assistants. All of the participants were agreed upon the basic Calvinist theology that formed the core of the New England Way. Beyond that the Baptists could not even agree among themselves. Goold and some of his followers denied that they sought separation from the Congregational churches, while others sought toleration as a separate but equal denomination, and a few rejected the validity of the Puritan churches and maintained that they alone possessed the truth. All were returned to prison, the clergy reported to the court against any toleration of the sect, and on 7 May 1668 the General Court banished Thomas Goold, William Turner, and John Farnum.

When the three took no steps to depart, they were jailed again pending their forcible ejection. But to the surprise of the magistrates sixty-six orthodox citizens of the Bay petitioned the General Court that the imprisoned Baptists be freed and tolerated. Then, in 1669, the magistrates received a letter signed by thirteen prominent English Congregationalists urging that the Baptists be tolerated, in part at least so as not to provide justification for further action against Congregational dissenters in England. In the same year Robert Mascall, an English Puritan divine and cousin of John Leverett of Massachusetts, wrote to inform the Bay leaders that English Congregational churches were practicing the sort of communion with Calvinistic Baptists that Goold had desired.

With sentiment in favor of the Baptists growing on both sides of the Atlantic it was no surprise that when Goold and his colleagues, on being released from jail to pursue personal business, fled to Noddle's Island they were allowed to remain there undisturbed in their semi-exile. When Governor Bellingham died and was replaced by the moderate John Leverett in 1673, the Baptists moved into Boston. When they built their own church in 1679 there was some minimal attempt to impede them, but in 1681 the General Court accepted their petition seeking permission to worship in the building. From 1682 on, there were no formal indictments brought against the Baptists in Massachusetts.

One Baptist congregation had won toleration. Baptist groups in other parts of the colony still found existence difficult if not impossible. It was not until the 1730s that a second Baptist church was successfully founded in the Bay, while outside the colony the sect mustered strength only in Rhode Island.

THE HALF-WAY COVENANT

While the magistrates of the Bay were attempting to suppress the spread of Baptist views in the 1660s, the clergy of the Puritan commonwealths were engaging in their own dispute over the nature of baptism. The decision of the Cambridge Assembly in 1648 to limit baptism to the children of the elect had not solved the problems that had led Richard Mather to propose extending baptismal privileges. Most clergy were against going to the type of parish system which prevailed at Newbury, with children of all professing Christians eligible for the sacrament. But in the 1650s a number of churches began to adopt the so-called Half-Way Covenant,* whereby the children of any baptized individual could themselves be baptized regardless of whether either parent had or had not been admitted to full communion in the congregation. Richard Mather's Dorchester congregation accepted the change in 1655 but retracted that acceptance in the following year on the advice of neighboring churches. Thomas Cobbett's Ipswich congregation adopted the Half-Way Covenant in 1656 and stuck with that decision. When Connecticut officials requested enlightenment on the subject from Massachusetts, the Bay's General Court in 1656 called a ministerial assembly to air the issue once again.

The assembly was held in 1657 with thirteen Massachusetts divines in attendance and four from Connecticut. New Haven, reflecting Davenport's conservatism, refused to participate. The assembly recommended that all baptized children, upon reaching maturity and swearing to the church covenant, should be able to present their offspring for baptism regardless of whether or not the parents had had a conversion that qualified them for full membership. In the following years a growing number of clergymen came to support this proposal, but the power of implementing it rested with each individual congregation. In most, lay opposition to the change was more than sufficient to block it.

The existence of two "endorsed" standards for church membership was certainly a weakness in the united front of New England Puritanism. To remedy this the Massachusetts General Court issued a call in December of 1661 for a synod "for settling the peace . . . in these churches of Christ." Over eighty lay and clerical representatives of New England churches were in attendance when the synod convened in 1662, the most glaring absence being that of John Davenport, who was preoccupied combating Connecticut's attempt to annex New Haven. Leading the revisionists, who were in firm control of the synod, were Richard Mather, Thomas Cobbett, John Norton, and John Wilson of Boston, John Eliot of Roxbury, and Jonathan Mitchell of Cambridge. The opposition to the Half-Way Covenant was led by two of Richard Mather's sons, Eleazer and Increase, with Increase in close communication with Davenport. The younger Mathers were overwhelmed. The synod approved the proposed change and forwarded that finding to the Massachusetts General Court, which

* The term "Half-Way Covenant," indicating that the baptized person would have some rights of full membership (the right to have his or her children baptized) and not others (the right to partake in the Lord's Supper), was an invention of the eighteenth century but has been applied retroactively by historians.

officially recommended the Half-Way Covenant to the churches of New England. But with each church autonomous, the "conclusion" of the synod marked merely the beginning of the struggle.

The course of the ensuing debate was most convoluted in the newly enlarged colony of Connecticut, where there were in effect three significant ecclesiastical factions. One, which historian Robert Pope has termed "presbyterialists," sought a parish type of church membership that would have gone beyond the Half-Way Covenant. Congregationalists were divided into supporters and opponents of the innovation, with a disproportionate number of the latter coming from what had been New Haven.

The most liberal faction, the presbyterialists, was the most threatening to the conservatives and yet showed the greatest potential for growth. The charitable approach to church membership that Thomas Hooker had advocated had undoubtedly left its mark on the colony, and once broadening of membership was proposed by some clergy it became easier to discuss still further changes. The General Assembly of the colony, upon receipt of a royal request that church membership be liberalized, reflected its accommodationist approach by suggesting to the churches in 1664 that all inhabitants who combined a belief in proper dogma with a life of good conduct be eligible for the "half-way" kind of membership—whether or not either of their parents had been baptized. This official support of the presbyterialist position gave further impetus to that movement.

Faced with this prospect of radical change in the standing order, the more tractable of those who had opposed all change capitulated to the Half-Way Covenant as a reform preferable to the greater danger posed by the presbyterialists. With the clergy still divided into at least two major groups, the General Assembly in 1669 announced that till "better light" was available to guide them the magistrates would tolerate any polity practiced by congregations adhering to the fundamentals of orthodox theology. This policy of toleration soon came to cover a variety of practices. At the conservative extreme were congregations such as that in Farmington, which refused to accept the Half-Way Covenant or any other modification of membership. Many churches did adopt the half-way reform as suggested by the synod of 1662. The First Church of Hartford was one of a number that adopted presbyterialist standards for church membership but limited the rights of nonregenerate members. At the other pole from Farmington were churches such as those in Wethersfield and Stonington, which not only went beyond the Half-Way Covenant in admitting all godly men to membership but which also allowed all such members to participate in the Lord's Supper. Thus, while virtually all of the churches adopted some form of extended baptism, pluralistic polity had become a fact of life in Connecticut by the end of the 1660s.

In Massachusetts, where there was no sizable support for a presbyterial polity, acceptance of extended baptism came very slowly and reluctantly. Previous historians of this period, often preoccupied with political concerns, were prone to view extension of church membership from the viewpoint of its effect on broadening the franchise and jumped to the conclusion that the laity must have welcomed an innovation with such liberally democratic possibilities. In point of fact, as demonstrated by Robert Pope, the core of opposition to the Half-Way Covenant in Massachusetts came from the laity. Why? There were probably a combination of motives at work. On the one hand the laity of the churches had been taught for years that the traditional standards were those desired by God. Having worked for decades to establish the validity of the New England Way, the clerical advocates of change were in the position of pointing out shortcomings in the work that they or their predecessors had performed earlier. If the clergy had been in error before, they might be again, and opponents of change were quick to make this point. More important, Edmund Morgan and Robert Pope have both found evidence of a heightened scrupulosity in the colony. Individuals whose personal histories would have prompted them to present themselves for membership in the climate of the 1630s were now less assured of the validity of their religious experience. This, rather than an actual decline in piety, might have been the cause of the decline in church membership. Lay men and women whose exclusion from the churches was a reflection of their own standards rather than those of the congregation were not likely to be in favor of liberalization. And if those who would benefit from the change were not eager, who would be? Support for this hypothesis can be drawn from the fact that in churches that did adopt the Half-Way Covenant there was a marked reluctance to utilize it.

Throughout the 1660s and into succeeding decades the battle raged in the various congregations of the Bay. In some cases congregational acceptance came purely from a desire to gratify a popular pastor and was rescinded on his death. In other cases the inability of pew and pulpit to agree led to schism and the establishment of competing churches. Both sides attempted to gain the support of the magistrates and other public officials, but the colony's secular leaders were no more capable of agreeing on the issue than their clerical counterparts. For a time the traditionalists were given an assist by the accession of John Davenport to the pastorate of the First Church of Boston. One of the principal architects of the New England Way, speaking from the most prestigious pulpit in the region, Davenport was expected to exert an important influence on the debate. But his very arrival in the First Church sparked a debate that further illuminated the fragmentation of Puritan unity.

John Davenport had become increasingly disenchanted in New Haven following that community's incorporation into Connecticut, and thus was eager to accept the invitation tendered by the Boston congregation. His own New Haven church had been reluctant to let him go, and when he arrived in Boston he found a significant minority of his new church opposed to his leadership because of his opposition to the Half-Way Covenant. Upon his installation the minority faction sought permission to secede and found their own church on half-way principles. Davenport refused to grant them the dismissal required and insisted that they accept the standards of First Church. The dissidents called an extralegal council of ministers from eastern Massachusetts to get support for their secession. This clerical council granted the dissidents its blessing, and a bare majority of the colony's magistrates was found to approve the formation of the Third Church of Boston.

Davenport was incensed by these developments. What had begun as a dispute over baptism had seen a ministerial council and a group of Massachusetts magistrates interfering in what he regarded as an internal dispute in the First Church of Boston. The council of ministers, Davenport concluded, had blatantly violated the principle of congregational autonomy. Davenport was still smarting over that affront when he accepted an invitation to deliver the 1669 election sermon to the General Court. He used the occasion to urge the members of the court and the laity to resist infringements upon the purity of the New England Way. At the height of his campaign, on 13 March 1670, Davenport died. His followers were able to mount a last major effort. Sympathetic deputies in the General Court gained majority support for a report severely criticizing the ministerial council for its approval of the secession.

Their authority challenged, the reformist clergy responded by actively campaigning for candidates of like mind in the elections of 1671. The lay opponents of the Half-Way Covenant, deprived of Davenport's leadership and further weakened by the death of Eleazer Mather in 1669 and the defection of Increase Mather in 1671, were incapable of maintaining their political strength. The new house of deputies retracted the previous year's critical report. With that vote the organized colony-wide opposition to the Half-Way Covenant ceased, and the traditionalists retreated to a rearguard defensive action in their own churches.

Despite this turn of events there had been no significant extension of baptism by 1671, and in the ensuing five years the opponents of change were successfully able to block adoption of the Half-Way Covenant in all major congregations. But in 1676 there began a decade and a half of crises in the Bay, beginning with King Philip's War and ending with the witchcraft hysteria. By the end of the century probably four out of every five churches had accepted the reform, while some congregations had gone even further in opening access to baptism and also to the Lord's Supper. Searching for reasons for God's alienation from them as reflected in their afflictions, many were persuaded by the clergy that among their other sins they had failed to properly discipline the children of the covenant. By bringing more citizens into the covenantal relationship it was argued that more effective discipline could be maintained in the society. Furthermore, the loss of the Bay's charter convinced some of the political desirability of bringing more citizens into a close relationship with the churches.

Widespread adoption of the Half-Way Covenant did not necessarily result in widespread utilization. In at least some congregations it was not truly effective in broadening the church base. What the debate did achieve was to further weaken the homogeneity of the New England Way by opening the floodgates to all forms of membership extension and by setting the clergy in fierce debate among themselves with a resulting loss of prestige for the ministerial class.

"DECLENSION" AND THE REFORMING SYNOD

For the Puritan leaders who continued to believe that their society was a partner in a national covenant with God, the series of reverses that began with the Restoration were signs of God's displeasure with New England's sins. The Restoration itself, the debate over baptism, the visitation of the royal commission, the spread of Quaker and Baptist influence, growing secularism as manifested in the adoption of some of the London fashions in clothes and conduct, the outbreak of King Philip's War, the great fire of 1676—these and other misfortunes and changes were seen as punishment for the shortcomings of the covenanted people. Bewailing their sins, calling upon the people to repent and return to the way of their fathers, the clergy increasingly played the role of Jeremiah.

Historians have often indulged in discussion of whether or not the clergy were accurate in describing the latter part of the seventeenth century as a time of declension. Certainly from the point of view of the twentieth century one is struck not by a sense of decay but of social, economic, and even religious growth and vitality. But given the historiography of the Puritan, it was a time of declension. New Englanders were a people in a covenant relationship with God that required a high level of purity and a strict maintenance of the standards of the New England Way. Deviance from that goal was a sign of decay, the extent of the decline measurable by the extent of the deviance. With English controls prohibiting strong political action and Congregational inhibitions precluding coordinated ecclesiastical activity, the clergy were thrown back to the jeremiads, bewailing in those sermons the society's fall from grace and exhorting the people to repentance.

Not all the Puritans despaired, however. Governor John Leverett on one occasion in 1675 rebuked Increase Mather for having proclaimed in a sermon the depravity of Massachusetts. Leverett, who had served under Cromwell in England and who had been the Bay's agent at Whitehall in the early days of the Restoration, was more positive in his estimation of what New England had achieved. And for others, also, the form of the jeremiad began to mask a growing appreciation of New England's strengths. By emphasizing the heights from which their society had fallen, many displayed considerable pride in where the society still was. Thus, they softened the sense of disappointment in their declension and recognized positive values in their contemporary pursuits.

The feeling of loss was great enough in the late 1670s, however, to prompt Increase Mather and several of his clerical colleagues to ask the Massachusetts General Court to call a synod that would address itself to two questions: "What are the evills that have provoked the Lord to bring his judgements on New England?" and "What is to be done so that those evills may be reformed?" This Reforming Synod of 1679 met for its first session in September. A committee that included Urian Oakes, Increase Mather, Solomon Stoddard, and James Allen prepared a report of the session's findings which was subsequently endorsed by the General Court. This statement of "The Necessity of Reformation" cited various shortcomings of the population that lay behind God's "Controversy with his New England people," including neglect of religion in churches and families, intemperance, worldliness, and lack of public spirit. It called upon all to make further efforts to reverse these trends, recommending renewals of church covenants, firmer congregational discipline, increased support of education, and similar remedies that would strengthen the bases of Puritan culture. In the years that immediately followed, many churches were stirred to renewed efforts, many young people were brought into the churches, and clergymen remarked on an improvement in the religious tone of the region.

The revival of piety was one of the assembly's accomplishments, however shortlived. Another was the preparation of a confession of faith for the New England churches. The same committee that prepared "The Necessity of Reformation" was entrusted with this task. Under the direction of Urian Oakes and Increase Mather, both of whom had been in England during the Protectorate, the synod adopted with slight modification the Confession of Faith of the English Congregational Savoy Conference of 1658. In June 1680 the General Court approved this action and ordered the confession printed.

Despite these actions of the Reforming Synod, the religious spirit and uniformity of the founders was not to be recaptured. The Puritan churches were increasingly forced to compete and justify themselves in a world that was increasingly pluralistic and secular. That task, which clerical leaders had begun to assume in the 1660s and 1670s, would be made still more difficult by the political upheavals of the following decades.

13 | AN OPPRESSED PEOPLE: NEW ENGLAND'S ENCOUNTERS WITH KING PHILIP, GOVERNOR ANDROS, AND THE WITCHES

While struggling with the religious crises of the post-Restoration period, the New Englanders also experienced three major conflicts, which tested their endurance, altered their government, and at the same time reinforced the anxieties of those who believed the society to be in decline. From the forests of New England came the first real Indian uprising in the region's history. In England the renewal of consolidation efforts led to the revocation of the colonies' charters. And in the troubled times of the early 1690s the citizens of Essex county Massachusetts became convinced that there were witches in their midst. By the end of the century the direct Puritan control of New England society, curtailed by the Restoration, was at last toppled, and in succeeding generations the preservation of Puritan ideals became a task of the various social institutions of the "peaceable kingdoms"—the small towns that dotted the New England landscape.

KING PHILIP'S WAR

From the time when Plymouth's first governor, John Carver, signed a treaty of peace with Massasoit, the chief of the Wampanoag tribe, the history of New England's Indian relations was one of remarkable, though not unblemished, amity. The Puritan settlers were not interested in exterminating the Indians. A number of colonists labored hard to bring to the Indians what they viewed as the twin blessings of Puritan faith and English civilization. Colonial officials passed legislation protecting Indian rights and supporting the missionary activities of clergymen such as John Eliot and Thomas Mayhew. What conflict there was between 1620 and 1675—most notably the Pequot War—was not racial in nature and was marked by the active participation of some Indian tribes on the side of the colonists. That expansion of the settlements caused erosion of Indian culture and leadership was neither planned by the Puritans nor unwelcome to many Indians. By the 1670s some four thousand natives were living in the area of English settlement, many of them in "praying towns" which John Eliot had been authorized to found.

Some Indian leaders found their own power and influence threatened by Puritan expansion. In the interaction between the two cultures, Indian values and traditions were being slowly eroded. The once independent native tribes of New England were gradually reduced to dependence on the English economy. Many Indians sought assimilation into colonial society, adopting the white man's dwellings, clothing, and religion. All of this had to appear threatening to many tribal chieftains and religious leaders. They were further alienated by the undoubted offences inflicted on the tribes by some colonists, not all of whom were apprehended and tried by the New England authorities. If some Indians suspected and feared the white man, some New Englanders looked down upon the Indians and had little concern for the natives' rights. Regardless of the forbearance of most white and red leaders, malcontents on both sides could find incidents to sustain their racist hostilities. As the century progressed and the English population grew and expanded, such incidents multiplied.

Among the discontented chieftains was Metacomet—King Philip to the colonists—the son of Massasoit and the chief of the Wampanoags. Generally conceded to have been weak, deceitful, vain, and ambitious, Metacomet had been suspected in 1667 of conspiring with the French and Dutch against the English. In 1671 observers at the Indian village of Mount Hope noticed warlike preparations among Metacomet's braves. The Plymouth authorities summoned the chief to appear before them at Taunton. They demanded that his people surrender their guns, which he was forced to agree to.

Though signs of Indian discontent persisted, there was no further scare until 1675, when the Indian Sassamon warned Plymouth's Governor Josiah Winslow of a new conspiracy being engineered by Metacomet. Raised under strong Christian influence, Sassamon had wavered between the two cultures, retaining contacts in both. Shortly after informing Winslow of Metacomet's plans he was murdered. An Indian eyewitness identified three of Metacomet's braves as the guilty parties. They were tried, convicted, and executed.

The Wampanoags were incensed by the executions and on 20 June 1675 the Indians fell on the English settlement of Swansea. King Philip's War had begun. The immediate objectives of the colonial authorities were to prevent other tribes from joining Metacomet and to keep the Wampanoags bottled up on the Mount Hope peninsula. Emissaries, including Roger Williams, went to neighboring tribes to urge their neutrality. Rhode Island stationed boats to block the tribe's escape by water, while Connecticut sent troops to guard the land route. A combination of inexperience and intercolonial jealousies allowed Metacomet to escape from the Mount Hope peninsula. Shortly thereafter he was again surrounded and again he eluded his pursuers. His early successes were encouraging to other tribes, such as the Narragansetts, some of which began to enter the struggle against the English.

By midsummer Brookfield, Northfield, Deerfield, and other Massachusetts towns had gone up in flames. Governor Winslow led a winter campaign against the Narragansetts, engaging and defeating them in the Great Swamp Fight, but sustaining 20 percent casualties in his own forces. While heartening to the colonists, the victory did not significantly relieve the pressure on the frontier. By the spring of 1676 the area of English settlement had been contracted to within seventeen miles of Boston. Every inhabitant of Massachusetts between the ages of sixteen and sixty was made liable to a military draft. Other colonies came to the support of New England with food supplies to sustain the numerous refugees pouring into the seacoast towns from the frontier. Meanwhile, starvation proved the Indians' greatest enemy. The "praying Indians" who had been held suspect by most colonists during the early stages of the struggle were gradually utilized against Metacomet to good effect. The tide began to turn in the summer of 1676 and Metacomet's death in August at the hands of one of the Christian Indians broke the back of the rebellion. Though the fighting continued on the northern and eastern frontiers till 1678, the southern New England tribes had capitulated by the end of 1676.

The effects of the war were sobering. At least thirteen frontier towns were totally destroyed and six additional ones partially burned. Five hundred of the Bay's five thousand males of draft age had been killed or captured, as had many women and children. The economic loss was equally staggering. The war underscored the increasing colonial jealousies that prevented cooperation between the former sister commonwealths.

THE DOMINION OF NEW ENGLAND

The attack on the charter of Massachusetts, first launched in the late 1630s and renewed in the mid-1660s, was mounted by the colony's enemies once again in the 1670s. Sir Ferdinando Gorges pushed his claim to Maine, which had been seized by Massachusetts. Robert Mason simultaneously revived his family's title to New Hampshire. English merchants complained of violation of the Navigation Act by New Englanders. Other critics raised the charge that the colony continued to discriminate against Anglicans and other non-Puritans while considering itself an independent commonwealth. They reminded the government that the royal commission of 1664–1665 had recommended revocation of the charter.

Following the Third Anglo-Dutch War (1672–1674) King Charles had aligned himself firmly with the Earl of Danby and the Anglican, divine-right conservatives in Parliament. Once again the king embarked upon a policy of centralization and control, highlighted in colonial affairs by the appointment of a new Privy Council committee, the Lords of Trade and Plantation. This new group had broader authority and a more efficient organization than its predecessors. Seeking to improve on earlier attempts to regulate the colonies, the Lords of Trade found the main obstacle to be the rights allowed the colonists by their various corporate and proprietary charters.

The mounting chorus of complaints against Massachusetts led the Lords of Trade to investigate the relations of the Bay to the home government. Concluding that "this is the Conjuncture to do something Effectual for the better Regulation of that Government, or else all hopes of it may be hereafter lost," the Lords recommended that the king command the Bay government to send agents to answer charges against their colony. Edward Randolph, an aspiring civil servant with connections to the Mason family, was instructed to carry the royal demand to New England.

In Edward Randolph the Massachusetts colonists met an antagonist who perceived his own future as closely dependent on the overthrow of the Bay government and who dedicated himself totally to that end. Arriving in Boston in June 1676 he remained for over three months, observing local conditions and contacting leaders of the royalist and moderate factions. His report to the Lords of Trade was prejudicial to Massachusetts and stated that there would be substantial local support for royal intervention. He thereupon began collecting further information to be used against the Bay. Meanwhile Peter Bulkeley and William Stoughton arrived in London to represent the colony in hearings before the Lords Chief Justices. Despite their efforts, the court's decision in 1677 rejected the claims of Massachusetts to New Hampshire and Maine.

Randolph next presented the Lords of Trade with evidence that the Navigation Act had not been enforced in the Bay, that the magistrates denied appeals from their courts and refused to administer a proper oath of allegiance, that the religious requirement was still in effect for enfranchisement, and that the colony illegally operated a mint. He demanded investigation of these charges and of the validity of the colony's charter. Bulkeley and Stoughton attempted to undermine Randolph's credibility, but most of these charges had been made too often by too many individuals for that strategy to be effective. By the spring of 1678 the Lords of Trade had come to the conclusion that the Bay government was irredeemable. Having explored the possibility of issuing a supplementary charter to amend the original grant to the Massachusetts Bay Company, the Lords of Trade requested opinions from the attorney general and the solicitor general on the validity of the charter. Both advised that there was sufficient grounds to institute quo warranto proceedings for its repeal. At the same time the Lords of Trade sought to institute immediate regulation of the Bay's commerce by recommending the appointment of Edward Randolph as collector of customs in Boston.

While this attack on their government was being mounted in England, the colonists themselves did nothing to aid their cause, and actually hindered it. While Randolph was complaining of the Bay's refusal to administer an oath of allegiance to the king, the General Court strengthened the enforcement of its oath of fidelity to the colony. The court also, in October 1677, declared that the Navigation Act was in force "by the authority of this Court." This implicit rejection of Parliament's authority to legislate for the colonies was based upon the lack of colonial representation in Parliament so that "the lawes of England are bounded within the four seas, and do not reach America." Such expressions were true reflections of the commonwealth philosophy, but in the circumstances they only hastened the pursuit of quo warranto proceedings by the Lords of Trade.

The English government was shaken by Titus Oates's revelations of a "popish plot" in 1678, and preoccupation with that affair delayed implementation of the decisions reached by the Lords of Trade. But Randolph finally received his appointment and arrived in New England in October of 1679. His first task was to inaugurate royal government in New Hampshire. Following the decision against Massachusetts in the dispute over New Hampshire and Maine the Bay leaders had stolen a march on the crown and purchased from Gorges his rights to Maine. Robert Mason, however, in return for recognition of his rights in the land, cooperated with the Lords of Trade in having New Hampshire revert to the crown. In January of 1680 Randolph formally brought that colony into existence as the second royal colony in America (Virginia had been the first).

Following completion of his work in the north, Randolph took up his customs post in Boston and began to seize vessels suspected of violations of the Navigation Act. In addition to his official functions, Randolph also labored at bringing into being a domestic faction that would support English attempts to further restrict the liberties of the Bay and the power of the magistrates. In attempting this the English agent found a considerable number of New Englanders who were amenable to his approaches.

In the two decades following the Restoration, the disunity of New England society had grown steadily more pronounced. While the conservative commonwealth faction still had the best claim to be the popular party, it had become less and less representative of upper-class sentiments. In this period of rapid growth in the colonial population and economy, men such as Joseph Dudley and Fitz and Wait Winthrop —all sons of governors—were less satisfied with the life style of provincial New England, less sure of colonial values, and increasingly attracted to the standards of Stuart London. Merchants increasingly were dependent on their commerce with the outside world and believed in seeking an accommodation with that world across the Atlantic which the commonwealthmen regarded with suspicion. Others felt themselves denied the power due them by their wealth or breeding, as a result of the stranglehold the conservatives held on the political process. Alienated by cultural, economic, or personal factors, such individuals were among those whom Randolph was able to interest.

Faced with Randolph's accumulation of evidence against them and the growing forces of discontent in the colony, the magistrates agreed to the English government's demand in 1681 that agents again be sent to Whitehall to represent the colony. But even this step was taken only after bitter debate, and the court denied the agents authorization to discuss any modifications in the charter. With Massachusetts thus unwilling to compromise, the Lords of Trade initiated quo warranto proceedings against the colony. Randolph cooperated fully in Boston, but even with his help the writ was not returned to England within the time period necessary for action in the common law courts. Thwarted at the quo warranto proceedings, the Lords of Trade turned to the more complex task of securing a writ of scire facias from the Court of Chancery. On 23 October 1684 the decree of dissolution was handed down by the justices, and the Massachusetts Bay Company ceased to exist.

The impact of the charter loss was not immediately felt in Massachusetts because the Lords of Trade and the Privy Council had failed to devise an alternative form of government. It was not until the following year that a provisional government was agreed upon. Part of the explanation for the delay was the death of Charles II in February of 1685 and the confusion caused by Monmouth's Rebellion and its suppression by the new king, James II. Charles had been in favor of making Massachusetts a royal colony and appointing Colonel Percy Kirke as governor. After the king's death a new policy began to develop among the Lords of Trade. Kirke was abandoned as the choice for governor, and plans were made for the annexation of other territories to the Bay. While that strategy was being advanced, Joseph Dudley was appointed president of a provisional council to govern the colony.

Dudley assumed office in May of 1686. Edward Randolph served as the council's secretary, while the membership consisted of prominent colonists who had been sympathetic to Randolph's earlier efforts against the charter government. Included in the new government's jurisdiction at this time were Massachusetts, New Hampshire, Maine, and the "King's Province." Within two weeks Dudley and his colleagues had succeeded in reorganizing the system of local government, the courts, and the militia. Many officials of the charter government were reappointed. In general, Dudley's council, comprised of native New Englanders, knew how far they could go without alienating a significant portion of the population. Some Bostonians, such as Samuel Sewall, were distressed at the reappearance after so many years of St. George's cross in the colony's flags, and the introduction of Anglican worship and marriage services, but most accepted the counsel of such leaders as Increase Mather, who advised Sewall and others to tolerate such innovations.

In December of 1686, Joseph Dudley was superseded by Sir Edmund

Andros, the newly appointed governor of what was thereafter to be known as the Dominion of New England. Plymouth, which had existed at the monarch's tolerance, was added to the jurisdiction. Rhode Island's charter had been the object of court proceedings; though not yet concluded, Andros was instructed to include Rhode Island in the Dominion. In the spring of 1687 Connecticut was ordered included. A majority of that colony's General Assembly were opposed to yielding, so, in October, Andros journeyed to Hartford to seize control of the government—though the charter was hidden from him. In the spring of 1688, New York and New Jersey were added to the Dominion, which then stretched from Maine to the Delaware River. All of this territory was to be ruled by a royal appointed governor with an appointed council. All representative legislatures were eliminated.

The Dominion was an experiment in imperial consolidation. The Lords of Trade hoped that it would bring the American colonists more firmly under the king's authority, would foster economic growth, and would facilitate defensive measures against the growing threat of the French and the Indians. But success depended on Sir Edmund Andros, whose task it was to overcome the natural resistance of peoples stripped of the self-government to which they had become accustomed. Andros did not have the temperament for winning the support of the people, nor did he start with a clean slate. Autocratic by virtue of his military background as well as by nature, as governor of New York during King Philip's War he had tried to take advantage of Connecticut's difficulties to seize territory conferred on that colony by the Winthrop-Nicolls agreement of 1664. He had been stopped only by a show of force by the Connecticut militia. To the ranks of those who had never forgiven him for that action he soon added new enemies through the adoption of arbitrary policies.

Andros was unperceptive of the atmosphere surrounding him and moved decisively into areas where action was bound to stir resentment. The judicial system was made conformable to that of England; the press was subjected to censorship; the Church of England was given a preeminence in the colony. Whereas Dudley had been content to allow Anglican services to be conducted in the Boston Town Hall, the Anglican Andros was not. He demanded that the Congregationalists in the community either turn over one of their meetinghouses to the Church of England or contribute to building one. When this failed he forced his way into Samuel Willard's Third Church of Boston (the "Old South") on Easter Sunday of 1687. From that date on the

Church of England had priority, and Willard's congregation had to wait for the conclusion of Anglican services before being allowed to use their meetinghouse for Sabbath worship.

Further resentment was stimulated by the governor's tax and land policies. Under the old charter, provincial taxes had been levied by the General Court of Massachusetts and equivalent bodies in the other colonies. Under the Dominion, representative government had ceased to exist and the taxing power rested in the hands of the governor and council. Dudley had held off from taking any action, but the Dominion needed revenue. Andros, without seeking the requisite approval of the council, in 1687 imposed poll and land taxes upon residents of the Dominion. Opposition to the levy was strong, particularly as the tax was directed against the land.

The strongest resistance came from Essex county and specifically from Chebago parish in Ipswich, where the Reverend John Wise provided leadership. Wise, the first son of an indentured servant to have graduated from Harvard, was a physically active, popular leader, with a strong instinct for defending the rights of the people. The tax had been approved neither by a representative assembly nor by the council, nor had the rates been set by the town meetings. All of these points were used effectively by Wise and others in stirring their neighbors to noncompliance.

Andros acted swiftly against the dissidents. Wise and the others were arrested, imprisoned, and arbitrarily tried and fined. As the protest had centered in the town meetings, Andros restricted town meetings to one assembly per year for the sole purpose of selecting community officials. Furthermore, the towns were prohibited from collecting funds for the support of the churches.

Among the new governor's instructions was the stipulation that all new grants of land were to be subject to a quitrent and that all existing land titles (which in New England included no requirement of quitrent) be reviewed for confirmation. Reconfirmed grants could also be made subject to quitrents, and the revenue generated from these sources was intended to finance many Dominion activities. Thus Andros by 1688 had begun to cast doubt on the validity of all property grants made under the old charters. The prospect of a new financial burden of quitrents was overshadowed by the possibility that Andros might see fit to deny some citizens confirmation of their titles.

While Andros did achieve valuable results in strengthening the region's defenses, his administration became increasingly unpopular. In an attempt to counter the governor's reports of local resistance and also to gain relief from Andros's oppression, Increase Mather made plans to travel to England. Randolph brought a series of legal actions against the Boston clergyman in an attempt to block his departure, but Mather managed to evade the authorities. Fleeing to Charlestown, then to Plymouth, he finally embarked for England.

The England in which Increase Mather disembarked was itself on the verge of throwing off a tyrant. When James II had succeeded his brother Charles to the throne, he had had the advantage of a friendly Parliament and a tested, efficient ministry. Though his Roman Catholicism—a product of his stay in France during the interregnum—was held against him by some, earlier attempts to exclude him from the succession had won him sympathy. When the duke of Monmouth, the illegitimate son of Charles II, led an invasion to seize the throne he was easily suppressed. But James—like his father Charles I—did not know when assertions of divine-right monarchical authority became counterproductive. And his desire to extend political rights to Catholics alienated an ever-growing segment of the English aristocracy and governing middle class. Still, whatever his arrogance and despite his promotion of Catholics, James might have been tolerated if his queen had remained childless. But the birth of a son to the royal couple in June of 1688 presented the nation with the prospect of a continuing catholic succession. Leaders of the Protestant interest sent an invitation to William of Orange, ruler of the Netherlands and husband of James's daughter Mary, urging him to assert his claim to the throne of England. In November 1688, William's army landed in England. James's troops went over to the invader, and James fled to the continent. The Glorious Revolution was swift and bloodless.

In New England, Indian attacks in the summer and fall of 1688 had forced Andros to leave his capital and undertake a defense of the frontiers. The militia resented being pressed into service, and popular opinion was outraged by the Catholic faith of some of the appointed officers. While Andros was absent, rumors began to circulate in Boston of William's proposed descent on England. In early April of 1689 it was known that the invasion had occurred, but the outcome still remained in doubt. By then Andros had returned to a city which was itself on the brink of revolt. Shortly after sunrise on the eighteenth of April small groups of armed men gathered in the streets of Boston. Andros signaled from the Town Hall for a barge to transport him to the *Rose*, a royal naval vessel. But the barge was seized by the townsmen. Andros fled to the garrison house on Fort Hill. Randolph and other councilors were seized and jailed.

While the governor was isolated and besieged, the council chambers in the Town Hall filled with leaders of the revolt. Among them was

Simon Bradstreet, the last elected governor of the Bay under the old charter. Bradstreet, who had come to Massachusetts with his wife Anne in 1630, was a personal link with the ideals of the Great Migration. Also present was Wait Winthrop. Like others who had chafed under the oligarchic control of the old commonwealth faction, welcomed its overthrow, and been rewarded with places on the Dominion council, Winthrop had found Andros no more willing to share power than the old governors had been. Andros had eventually alienated all but those who were most dependent on him personally, and Winthrop's presence in the Town Hall was proof of that. With him and Bradstreet were the Reverend Cotton Mather (Increase's son), the prominent landowner Elisha Cooke, and about twenty others.

A Council of Safety was formed, with Bradstreet as president. The council issued a proclamation which accused Andros of having precipitated the violence by his arbitrary rule and called upon the government to surrender. News of the rising in Boston had quickly spread to the surrounding communities, and their militia responded in much the same way as they would in April of 1775 upon the outbreak of another rebellion. Surrounded by a growing army, cut off from the harbor and the garrison on Castle William, Andros surrendered to the Council of Safety late in the afternoon and the revolt came to a successful end, having been as bloodless as the toppling of James II.

When official word reached New England of King James's abdication and the proclamation of King William and Queen Mary as cosovereigns, it lessened the chance that the leaders of the Boston revolt would be treated as traitors. But the colonists still had to decide how to order their government. Very few New Englanders hoped that the new monarchs would maintain the Dominion. Each colony attempted to resuscitate its former government and sent to Increase Mather materials that would enable him to place the overthrow of Andros in the most favorable light.

In Massachusetts, the Council of Safety issued orders for the election of town delegates to a convention; it in turn recalled Governor Bradstreet and the other officials elected in 1686. They agreed to rule under the colony's old laws, pending further word from England. In Plymouth, which had no valid charter to fall back on, authority could not be wielded effectively. Some of the citizens hoped that eventual incorporation into a larger jurisdiction would be their fate. Deprived of popular support, the activities of Plymouth's government in the years that followed were minimal. Connecticut and Rhode Island were free from such concerns. The legality of their inclusion in the Dominion had always been questionable, and in 1690 the crown's legal advisers handed down opinions that neither colony's charter had been legally vacated.

From his first audience with the new king in January 1689 Increase Mather was faced with a variety of problems. One was the new monarch's indifference to colonial affairs. Mather also had to combat the efforts of Edmund Andros and Edward Randolph, both of whom were returned to England in 1689 and who devoted their efforts to vindicating their conduct and blocking restoration of the old Bay charter. Finally, Mather was to be plagued by the presence in Massachusetts of a strong minority led by Elisha Cooke, which limited Mather's flexibility by insisting that anything short of restoration of the old charter would be intolerable.

An initial aid to Mather's efforts came when the Bay government, reversing a previous indifference to the "French menace" in Canada, sent an expeditionary force under William Phipps to attack the French settlement at Port Royal. Phipps had had little military experience but was well embarked on a meteoric rise in colonial affairs. Born of poor parents in Maine in 1650, he had been apprenticed to a ship carpenter as a youth, acquiring considerable knowledge of the sea and the shipping industry. Moving to Boston, he married a wealthy widow. His wife's inheritance enabled him to pursue a quest for sunken treasure in the Caribbean. Displaying considerable ingenuity, Phipps recovered the rich cargo of a sunken Spanish galleon. Suddenly prosperous, he went to London in 1687 and was knighted (King James being pleased with the royal share of the salvage). Returning to Boston, Phipps had joined the opposition to Andros. Appointed to command the force against Port Royal, his organizational ability and continuing good luck enabled him to force the French garrison to capitulate in May 1689. Buoyed by this success, Massachusetts participated with representatives of other northern colonies in an intercolonial conference in New York City in May 1690. The conference approved a two-pronged attack on French Canada. Fitz Winthrop was to command an army of New York and Connecticut militia and Indian allies in an overland attack on Montreal, while Phipps was to direct an amphibious assault on Quebec.

In England the effort to secure a charter had encountered further delay. Mather secured a letter from William in August 1689, in which the king approved the steps the colonists had taken against the Dominion, and succeeded in getting a provision for the restoration of the old Bay charter included in the Corporation Bill. But when William prorogued Parliament before that bill's required third reading, the last real hope for the charter restoration died. Early in 1690

Elisha Cooke and Thomas Oates were sent to assist Mather, but by their resistance to compromise they hindered more than helped the mission. Throughout 1690 nothing was accomplished as William was occupied with an Irish rebellion and other affairs, and the agents awaited word of what they hoped would be a conquest of Canada.

Unfortunately for the cause of the charter, the attacks on New France failed. Winthrop found that the Indian allies were less eager to fight than had been expected (partly because of the return to power of the feared French governor Frontenac), and the logistical support for the operation was totally inadequate. The leaders of the army fell to quarreling, and the invasion bogged down at the southern end of Lake Champlain. Phipps was no more fortunate. Sailing from Boston with some twenty-two hundred troops, including the combative John Wise serving as chaplain, he landed his army opposite Quebec and demanded that citadel's surrender. Frontenac rejected the demand. A week's siege included two skirmishes that failed because of poor leadership and discipline. The expedition's supplies were soon depleted. Phipps gave up the attempt and sailed away—unaware that the prospect of starvation would soon have forced Frontenac to capitulate.

Early in 1691 the Massachusetts agents in England were thwarted again when William departed for Holland. In his absence, however, Mather was able to win Queen Mary's promise to intercede with her husband. By the fall of the year a compromise charter had been worked out. Under it Plymouth was included in Massachusetts but New Hampshire became a separate royal colony. The king retained the power to appoint the Massachusetts governor. The lieutenant governor and secretary of the colony were to be chosen by the governor. The General Court was revived. The charter mandated annual meetings of the legislature, though the governor had the right to adjourn, prorogue, or dissolve its sessions. The lower house was to consist of four deputies from Boston and two from each other town, to be elected by adult males who were forty-shilling freeholders or who possessed property valued at forty pounds. The Court of Assistants was replaced by a comparable Governor's Council of twenty-eight members chosen by the deputies (as under the old charter) but over whose selection the governor had a veto. The governor also had a veto over all legislation. All acts were also to be sent to England for approval. Judges, sheriffs, and local magistrates were to be appointed by the governor and council.

Judged by the standard of the old Bay Company charter, the new Massachusetts government was taken from the people and placed in the hands of the king, to be exercised by his appointed governor.

Elisha Cooke and others insisted on viewing the matter in that light. But judged against the Dominion, Increase Mather had achieved considerable success. Land titles were confirmed. Town meetings were again allowed to flourish. The General Court once again guaranteed to the people participation in legislation and taxation. And, as a concession to Mather, the Boston clergyman was allowed to name the first royal governor, with only one stipulation, that it be a military man. He chose the most promising member of his own congregation, William Phipps, who had joined him in England after the failure of the Quebec assault.

WITCHES IN SALEM AND PHIPPS IN BOSTON

On Saturday evening, 14 May 1692, Increase Mather and William Phipps returned to Boston with the new charter. Their welcome was muted by the observance of the Sabbath eve, but also by popular disappointment at the terms of the new charter. Having experienced a taste of the old charter freedoms since the fall of the Dominion, many were loath to relinquish them. Beyond that, the first council had been appointed by the king, with Mather's advice, and its composition was a further irritant to the Cooke faction. A half dozen of the new councillors were members of Mather's congregation—to the virtual exclusion of the emerging "old charter party," including Elisha Cooke. Equally harmful to the new government was the support extended to it by the surviving Anglican faction. Confronted with this complex political situation, Governor Phipps was informed upon disembarking that there were witches in Salem Village.

Salem witchcraft has attracted a disproportionate amount of interest from American historians. Over the years the executions for witchcraft have been blamed on the clergy in general, the Salem pastor, the Mathers, the girls who claimed to be afflicted, and the slave Tibuta. The facts are relatively straightforward, the interpretation of them far from simple.

The Reverend Samuel Parris was minister of the parish in Salem Village, the small rural village in the western jurisdiction of the town of Salem, which is now Danvers. Early in 1692 it was discovered that the clergyman's daughter and niece, and several of their friends, all very sick, had been experimenting with the occult. With medical science unable to cure their illness, some in the community jumped to the conclusion that the girls were afflicted by witchcraft. Pressed to identify their afflicters, the girls named the Parris's slave Tibuta and two older women of dubious reputation. The three accused were interrogated by magistrates John Hathorne and Jonathan Corwin. One of the women, Sarah Good, challenged the magistrates and acted in an offensive manner, while Tibuta confessed to practicing witchcraft. The afflicted girls fell into fits as the "witches" were being interrogated, and the confusing terror of the scene coupled with Tibuta's confession was enough to convince the magistrates that the devil was loose in Essex county.

Fear and accusations soon spread, and shortly after his arrival Governor Phipps appointed a special Court of Oyer and Terminer in which the accused could be tried. Deputy Governor William Stoughton (serving as chief justice), Wait Winthrop, and Samuel Sewall were among its prominent members. After a slow start, in which it appeared that the judges would follow the clergy's advice to proceed with care, the judges too seemed to become caught up in the hysteria that surrounded the obviously suffering accusers and the proliferation of new confessions to having practiced witchcraft. Soon the executions began and the accusations continued to multiply. Respectable citizens such as John Proctor and Rebecca Nurse went to the gallows. Giles Corey refused to plead and was crushed to death under a gradually increased load of stones. (The torture was acceptable by standards of the day; by refusing to plead despite it, Corey avoided the forfeiture of his goods that would have occurred if he had been convicted and thus saved his family their inheritance.) By the end of the summer the situation was clearly out of hand and accusations were less credibly being hurled at prominent citizens far from Salem. Captain John Alden (son of John and Priscilla) was jailed, but he escaped and fled to New York. Dudley Bradstreet, son of the former governor, was charged and fled. Samuel Willard of the Third Church of Boston was named, as was Governor Phipps's wife.

Part of the reason for the proceedings' getting out of hand lay in Stoughton's acceptance of spectral evidence, and particularly his insistence that the devil could not assume the spectral shape of an innocent person. Both Increase Mather and Cotton Mather had objected to that position but the court followed the lead of Stoughton (who had once been a clergyman himself). Reports by hysterical victims that they were tormented by the spectre of any person was sufficient justification for the indictment, and often the conviction, of the accused. The clergy of the colony for the most part objected to this, but they hesitated to apply pressure to Phipps, perhaps because they feared to jeopardize their influence on the governor—which they saw as much more important under the new charter. When they did belatedly act and Phipps called a halt to the proceedings in September of 1692, the court had tried and convicted twenty-seven residents of the Bay, most of them from Salem. Nineteen had been hung. Close to a hundred additional men and women were awaiting trial, while still more had been accused and not yet charged. Fifty had confessed to witchcraft and were thus saved from execution (as the judges saw it, a confessed, repentant witch could be saved—an unrepentant witch was deserving of death).

During the last few decades it has at last become possible to interject common sense into the witchcraft hysteria. It is now recognized, for instance, that witchcraft was a commonly accepted phenomenon throughout Europe and America both before and after 1692 and that the executions in Salem do not compare in numbers to those in England and France. Because people believed that witchcraft was efficacious, many practiced it and, in a limited sense, it worked. Chadwick Hansen contends,

It worked then as it works now in witchcraft societies like those of the West Indies, through psychogenic rather than occult means, commonly producing hysterical symptoms as a result of the victim's fear, and sometimes, when fear was succeeded by a profound sense of hopelessness, even producing death.

"The behavior of the afflicted persons," he writes, "was not fraudulent but pathological. They were hysterics, and in the clinical rather than the popular sense of that term." Working from facts such as these Hansen has enabled us to see the afflicted girls not as liars but as persons genuinely afflicted by fears that resulted in hysteria. The clergy did not instigate the panic, they tried to bring it under control. Some of the accused who confessed *had* been guilty of attempting to invoke supernatural powers to achieve their ends.

Hansen left unsolved the question of why the troubled victims projected the specific individuals named as the source of their afflictions. Granted that some of the accused were "guilty" of practicing witchcraft, most were not. Historians Stephen Nissenbaum and Paul Boyer have focused on the history of social conflict in Salem before 1692 as a means of better understanding the nature of the crisis. From the 1660s the agrarian interests of most of the villagers had led them to seek an autonomous existence from the ever more commercially oriented seaport town of Salem. But the villagers were themselves divided. Many of those in the eastern half of the community—particularly innkeepers along the Salem-Ipswich Road, such as John Proctor—saw their fortunes dependent on the town and set themselves against the movement for autonomy. The internal quarrels that resulted were allowed to fester because the governmental institutions that might have composed these differences were not allowed to exist. The two factions—the prospering eastern families and the declining western farmers (who suffered from the combination of increasing population and stable acreage)—engaged in a continuing struggle for control of the village and its only separate institution, the church. This factionalism was intense enough to have had a role in triggering the witchcraft hysteria and in determining its course. Boyer and Nissenbaum find that in Salem itself the afflicted were drawn from the ranks of the oppressed western farmers, and their accusations were leveled against those who were geographically and socially identified with keeping the village in the town.

In the aftermath of the executions some, such as Samuel Sewall, came to recognize that a miscarriage of justice had occurred. Some contemporaries attempted to use the episode to blacken the reputation of the Mathers and thus weaken the political faction with which they were identified. Many viewed the whole episode as a further sign of God's displeasure with his people. And the governor's manifest inability to control the situation was the first real evidence of Phipps's unsuitability for his position.

William Phipps repeatedly offended the citizens of Massachusetts by his clumsy handling of the government and by his personal misconduct. A good deal of the Maine roughneck remained in the Massachusetts governor. He lost his temper and cudgeled a man in the streets of Boston. He assaulted the captain of an English ship. He used street profanity in his official papers and insulted the General Court. In England, Joseph Dudley conspired against Phipps, and few colonists were willing to defend him. In 1694 Phipps was recalled to London to answer complaints against him. He died there in the following year. William Stoughton governed in his absence and continued to govern until the new appointee, Richard Coote, the earl of Bellomont, arrived in 1699. Upon Bellomont's death in 1701, Joseph Dudley was appointed governor of Massachusetts. With Bellomont and Dudley, all hope that the old Puritan leadership could guide the head of state was gone forever.

PART THREE

PURITAN CIVILIZATION IN THE AMERICAN WILDERNESS

14 | THE BASES OF PURITAN SOCIETY: TOWN, FAMILY, SCHOOL

The period of Cromwell's Protectorate had formed a type of high watermark for the New England Puritan experiment. Buoyed in their interpretation of their role by the recent course of events, the settlers were confident of their rectitude and of the stability of their institutions. The collapse of the English Puritan regime in 1660 insinuated doubts into the New England mind and made the colonists more suspicious of change. The religious and political history of the region took off in new directions, which colonial leaders viewed as evidence of decline. But while they might have seen their experiment in creating a Christian commonwealth as a failure, they had in fact succeeded in creating enduring institutions of social and cultural life.

In comparison with the other regions of British America, the Puritan colonies had from the outset a discernible character that lasted well over a century. An Englishman looking at early New York, Virginia, or any of the other mainland colonies would have been hard pressed to predict their pattern of growth. Even Pennsylvania, which was founded with a sense of purpose not dissimilar to that of the Puritans, changed greatly in its first seventy-five years. But New England, though changes took place and though its own leaders were often skeptical of their people's constancy, succeeded better than most human societies in holding on to its original values, traditions, and institutions.

That the Puritans succeeded in preserving their traditions almost intact for a century or more was no accident. Far more self-consciously than their neighbors in the Middle Colonies and the South, the Puritans organized themselves so that succeeding generations would know and revere the standards of the founders. The towns, the churches, the families, and the schools of the Bible Commonwealths all had specific responsibilities in the transmission of social and religious values. Those institutions reveal not only how the Puritans lived but how their descendants learned to imitate them.

THE TOWN—A "CHRISTIAN, UTOPIAN, CLOSED, CORPORATE COMMUNITY"

The New England town has a commanding place in the folklore of America, celebrated by countless politicians and historians as one of the cradles of democracy. But only in recent years has the application of demographic and other social science techniques revealed to us the true nature of life in the towns and villages that spread across the New England landscape. Out of these studies has emerged a picture of communities that were much more traditional, English, primitive, and conservative than had previously been recognized.

The England from which the Puritans came was predominantly a land of rural villages and hamlets. Most Elizabethan communities were small—some seventy families, each averaging between four and five members. Most of the villagers lived in close proximity in a central community surrounded by fields and woods. If the land was still tilled as in the Middle Ages, the villagers cultivated it in common, with each family assured the harvest of a designated portion. In communities where the fields had been enclosed and the land divided into family farms, the work was still often performed in common. Some of the villagers practiced various crafts in addition to working the fields. The principal figure in most such communities was the local lord or squire. Living apart from the village in his manor, he dominated the economic and religious as well as the social life of the region. John Winthrop, for example, had held such a position in Groton.

In the period just before the Great Migration, the local institutions of Stuart England had been subjected to growing pressure by Charles I's attempts to impose governmental centralization. The monarch's efforts to reduce the powers of local corporations, congregations, and train bands only served to strengthen the countryman's attachment to his threatened way of life. Bringing that background of conflict to America, the early colonists labored to create local institutions capable of withstanding any undue outside influence.

Townships were granted to groups of colonists by the General

Court. Usually, but not always, the core group came from the same region of England or, in the case of later townships, from older New England towns. The land they were assigned averaged about 36 square miles—being much larger than a comparably populated community in England. In one of the first modern studies of a New England town, Sumner Chilton Powell concluded that the first settlers of Sudbury, Massachusetts, held firm to the English open-field system of agriculture. Since Powell's study, Philip Greven has detected the same process at work in early Andover, Kenneth Lockridge in Dedham, John Waters in Hingham, and Edward Perzel in Ipswich. The early Puritan farmer did not build a farm in the wilderness but, rather, followed tradition and built his home in a nuclear village while farming assigned lots in the surrounding countryside.

Because of the generous size of the township, the first settlers divided but a portion of the land and left the remainder for future division. Each head of a household was granted a home lot in the village. The inhabitants communally determined the size of each individual's lot on the basis of his socioeconomic status. A house-holder's share in the division of home lots in turn established his proportion in future divisions of the various fields, meadows, and woodlands. At this point some modification of the English pattern becomes apparent. Whereas the typical English farmer was a tenant, New England villagers almost invariably held their land in fee simple.

After receiving their land grant, apportioning home lots and farm land, setting aside land for a common, a graveyard, and a meeting-house, the New Englanders still had not completed their work. For whereas their Old World counterparts were populated by a relatively mobile group of families brought together by circumstances, the villages of Massachusetts and her sister colonies were closer to being what Kenneth Lockridge has labeled "Christian Utopian Closed Corporate Communities":

Christian because they saw Christian love as the force which would most completely unite their community. Utopian because theirs was a highly conscious attempt to build the most perfect possible community, as per-fectly united, perfectly at peace, and perfectly ordered as man could arrange. Closed because its membership was selected while outsiders were treated with suspicion or rejected altogether. And Corporate because the commune demanded the loyalty of its members, offering in exchange privileges which could be obtained only through membership, not the least of which were peace and order.

The Puritans gathered together in communities motivated by religion. That tie, institutionalized in political covenants, the churches, and the schools, kept the first generations of settlers in Massachusetts, New Haven, and Connecticut in their towns. While settlers in other parts of America, including parts of Plymouth, were drawn to the frontier and were highly mobile, such was not the case where abundant land coincided with the utopian drive of Puritanism. In towns like Dedham, Massachusetts, few men left or joined the community after its founding, save by death and natural increase. The degree of mobility was not only less than that in the other colonies, but also less than in England.

Reflecting the Christian utopianism of the New Englanders, and forming the political basis for their towns, were written covenants. When the settlers of Dedham founded their community in 1636 they stated their aims in a covenant which asserted that "We whose names are hereunto subscribed do, in the fear and reverence of our Almighty God, mutually and severally promise amongst ourselves and each other to profess and practice one truth according to that most perfect rule, the foundation whereof is everlasting love." To insure the homogeneity of the community the covenant stipulated that "we shall by all means labor to keep off from us all such as are contrary minded, and receive only such unto us as may be probably one heart with us." But, recognizing as good Puritans that even the best of men might fail to agree, the settlers pledged

That if at any time differences shall rise between parties of our said town, that such party or parties shall presently refer all such differences unto some one, two, or three others of our said society to be fully accorded and determined without any further delay, if it possibly may be.

This provision for arbitration of disputes was followed by the signatories' agreement that each would bear his proportionate share of the labor and cost of government and a stipulation that all newcomers to the town be required to subscribe to the covenant.

The concerns manifest in the Dedham Covenant and the many like it were for peace and order. The administration of the towns was similarly motivated. The purpose behind allowing broad participation in the town meetings was not to facilitate the expression of divergent viewpoints, but to provide the broadest possible base for political consensus. Having participated in the decision-making process, the citizens felt obliged to accept the results. But despite the broad franchise, affairs in the early decades of settlement were managed primarily by selectmen, who were generally elected from the families who had taken the lead in the town's founding. Later, as the founding generation passed away, the number of candidates for leadership increased, and issues became more troublesome, the selectmen were granted less independence of action and the town meeting took more authority to itself. But even then, leaders of the community attempted to prepare proposals in a way that would receive the greatest popular support.

Also contributing to consensus was the church. The meetinghouse— used for town meetings and divine services—usually was located in a geographically prominent position, symbolic of the place held by religion in the community. The pastor and teacher played key roles in shaping and articulating the ideology, hopes, and values upon which the citizens acted. Furthermore the congregation's ministers educated the populace in Christian doctrine and ethics, provided an intellectual window to the outside world, and served as forces of conciliation in community disputes.

The peacefulness of the New England towns was not permanent. Some communities were torn by internal disputes at a relatively early date—the Hingham unrest in the 1640s is a case in point. More often, the growth of population within a geographically restricted area gradually eroded the order of the community. By the end of the seventeenth century the open-field agricultural system had given way to individual farms in communities such as Dedham and Andover. The further divisions of land, after the initial settlement, had presented many householders with the difficult task of cultivating a number of fields increasingly distant from each other and from their homes. Gradually, but with increasing momentum land deals with neighbors led to a consolidation of individual holdings. That development in turn led to desertion of the central village in favor of residence on outlying farms. This dispersion of population weakened the homo-geneity of the community and inhibited communal supervision of the inhabitants. Alternate centers of population developed, creating conflicts over such issues as the routing of roads and the location of new meetinghouses. In the larger townships, some of these satellite centers eventually gained recognition as separate parishes and then as autonomous townships.

Dispersal was not the only response to a swelling population. By the second generation in some towns, and certainly by the maturing of the third generation, the community's land had long since been divided. Partible inheritance had to give way to primogeniture, as the individual farms became too small to divide profitably. Younger sons were faced with the choice of seeking a career other than farming or moving to a town with land yet to divide. Maturation thus came to be equated with economic independence, in contrast with the seventeenth century when many sons were accustomed to living on their father's land until his death. As time went on the mobility of the New England population increased.

Neither dispersal nor mobility, however, caused the colonists to reject the ideal of the New England town. Forced to seek their fortunes elsewhere, the sons and daughters of New England migrated with friends and neighbors to form communities modeled on those they had left behind and often bearing the same name. Thus the overpopulation of the towns, while producing greater class differentiation and other undesirable results, also encouraged the spread of New England culture.

THE FAMILY: A LITTLE COMMONWEALTH

"A Household," wrote the English Puritan Robert Cleaver, "is as it were a little commonwealth, by the good government whereof, God's glorie may be advanced, the commonwealth which standeth of severall families, benefited, and all that live in that familie may receive much comfort and commoditie." Cleaver's statement, typical of Puritan thought in the New World as well as the Old, highlights three of the functions of the family for New Englanders: as an agency for the worship of God, as a supporter of civil order, and as a source of mutual comfort for its members. In these respects the Puritans were engaged in modifying and even reversing traditional English views on the nature of marriage and the family.

Marriage, the basis of family life, was a subject that attracted the attention of numerous Puritan authors. Whereas the Catholic church had celebrated matrimony as a sacrament that created an indissoluble union between man and wife, the Protestant Reformation had led to a denial of the sacramental basis of marriage, opening the possibility of dissolving the union for sufficient cause. In some respects the Anglican church had carried forth the spirit of the Reformation, allowing divorce in cases of desertion or adultery. It would be hard to imagine Henry VIII's church doing less. But in other respects the Church of England remained committed to the Catholic position, adhering to the view that marriage was a sacrament ordained by God for the purpose of procreation. Here the Puritans strongly disagreed. As James Johnson has shown in a study of English Puritan marriage doctrine:

Essentially the concept of marriage that develops in Puritanism at the beginning of the seventeenth century has these characteristics: (1) marriage is an ordinance of God but no sacrament; (2) it is the normal state of man, with dispensation to remain single a special gift of grace to particular persons; (3) it is a social estate, the microcosm of all human society, and at the same time a trial ground for salvation; (4) the lord of the family is the husband/father/master, but because of the existence of mutual duties the wife's position often approaches equality with her husband in certain respects; (5) depending on context, the purpose of marriage is now procreation, now companionship, with a significant emphasis on the latter emerging on the basis of God's wish to remedy Adam's loneliness in Eden.

Placing companionship as the primary purpose of marriage was the most radical shift from the Catholic-Anglican position and could easily lead (as in the thought of John Milton) to justification of divorce on grounds of incompatibility, though it did not in early New England.

In the colonies, the Puritans were able to act upon these beliefs. Marriage was made a civil contract, performed before agents of the state. Family life was strongly encouraged, the early colonists going so far as to assign single men and women to live with families as part of those households. The family was regarded as a religious society with the obligations of group Scripture reading, prayer, and catechizing. The family was also the school of first instance, primarily responsible for the socialization of its members and for their education in the rudimentary skills of reading and writing.

Within the family the husband was without question the master. He was prince and teacher, pastor and judge in his household. The law gave him significant authority to govern and discipline those in his care, both the members of his natural family and any apprentices living with him. He was the legal representative of his family. In addition to conducting religious exercises, which included family discussion of Sabbath and lecture-day sermons, daily prayer, and Scripture reading (in which the father was to his household as a clergyman to his congregation), the husband was required by law to support his family adequately. And he was enjoined to love his wife, to comfort and support her, so that marriage would provide companionship for both partners.

Love was the cement of the Puritan family and sex was viewed as one of the means of expressing that love. The stereotype of the Puritan as having been prudish and condemnatory about sex has no basis in fact. While the colonists insisted that intercourse be limited to married couples and were harsh in penalizing promiscuity and sexual deviancy, such attitudes reflected their family-centered concept that sexual relations must be an expression of love. As their diaries, letters, and other writings make evident, the Puritans were a good deal more comfortable discussing sexual matters than are many of their descendants.

There is no doubt that New England Puritans believed women to be naturally subordinate to men. But the Puritan emphasis on companionship as a purpose of marriage was both a reflection of an improving status for women and a cause of further equalization. Combined with the socioeconomic environment of the New World, it led to a noticeable improvement in women's status. The reasons for this liberalization (in comparison to England) are readily identified. Despite the largely familial nature of the Great Migration, the sex ratio in Massachusetts and the other Bible Commonwealths was markedly different from England's. Whereas there was a surplus of females in the mother country, with a resultant undervaluing and exploitation of women in general, in New England the situation was reversed. In the 1630s there were probably three men for every two women. Another influence was the great need for labor in the colonies, which led to greater economic opportunities for women than were available in England. Puritanism was also important. "Souls have no sexes," wrote Robert Bolton, and the possibility that a woman could be admitted to church membership while her husband was not helped to undermine some of the distinctions between the sexes. In fact a majority of the "visible saints" in seventeenth-century New England were women. Evidence of the improved status of women was manifested in a number of other ways: Women were much more likely to marry above their class in the colonies; there was an increasing tendency to treat women as individuals before the law; educational opportunities, though limited, were greater than in England; and women held greater responsibilities in marriage.

Whereas prevailing English attitudes on marriage stressed the authoritarian role of the husband, New England thought reflected the Puritan emphasis on relationships based on love. As historian Roger Thompson has pointed out, "Rather than the common English idea that marriage made men brutes, American Puritans told their congregations that men who maltreated or tyrannized over their wives were brutes." While the theory of male supremacy was retained by the colonists—and was reflected in such areas as their views on the political and intellectual capacity of women—it was only imperfectly adhered to within the family. The demand that a potential spouse be "lovable" (one did not marry for love, but should choose a mate for whom one could develop love) gave a woman a larger role in selecting her spouse. Subordinate to her husband, she nevertheless often helped make family decisions. In her role as parent she stood equal to her husband in authority and responsibility. That Puritan marriage was not simply an institution for the subjection of women is obvious in the correspondence of John and Margaret Winthrop and the poetry of Anne Bradstreet.

Relations between parents and children were also characterized by a blend of authoritarianism and love. The Puritans believed in the innate depravity of man from birth and, after a relatively comfortable first year of life—warmed by swaddling and the heat from the kitchen fire, rocked to sleep and regularly breast fed—the child was subjected to an increasingly firm discipline. As John Robinson had once explained,

there is in all children, though not alike, a stubborness, and stoutness of mind arising from natural pride, which must, in the first place, be broken and beaten down; so that the foundation of their education being laid in humility and tractableness, other virtues may, in their time, be built thereon.

But if physical punishment was frequently the lot of the child, the Puritan parent, like the preacher, sought not only to instill responsible behavior by terror, but also to encourage it by means of good example. Parents reasoned with their children, prayed with them, taught them their early lessons in reading and writing, and held up to them the example of a godly life.

In addition to being the basic unit of economic production and a source of emotional strength for its members, the Puritan household was an important instrument of acculturation. The closeness of human association in the colonial family made that role inevitable. New England homes of the seventeenth century were generally small and almost always crowded. In most cases they contained not more than three rooms. One or two bedrooms would sleep parents, children, and servants, as well as visitors. The kitchen served as an all-purpose room, with a large fireplace around which the family performed its numerous indoor activities: cooking, baking, brewing, eating, spinning, knitting, sewing, making candles, praying, reading, and conversing. The home offered the family some privacy from neighbors but little for its individual members.

If the home environment seemed close and confining, outdoor activity scarcely offered a more extended range of social contact. Male members of farm households spent their days working together in the fields or making and repairing their farm implements. Women—in addition to their domestic duties—were generally assigned the management of the family's home lot, including the barnyard, garden, and orchard. Children were pressed into labor as soon as they were able. In the towns the businesses of most artisans and merchants similarly commanded the labor of all members of the family.

If the values and responsibilities of the colonial New England family were appreciably different from those of its English counterpart, so too were the demographic patterns. While the typicality of some town studies has been questioned, thus delaying any firm conclusions, it is nevertheless evident that many long-held assumptions about early American family history are no longer tenable. For years students of the family wrote of early marriages, high infant mortality, and early adult death as characteristic of life in the seventeenth and eighteenth centuries. Greven in his study of Andover, Demos in his research on Plymouth, and Lockridge in his examination of Dedham have demonstrated that the early settlers did not marry at a much younger age than their Old World counterparts. Demos has demonstrated that in colonial Plymouth the age at marriage for men averaged from twenty-five to twenty-seven, while most women married between twenty and twenty-two. These studies have also demonstrated that families usually had from seven to ten children, born at fairly regular two-year intervals (which suggests abstinence or artificial means of birth control). Infant mortality was about one in ten, which is less than half of what is today considered normal in the nonindustrial world. More startling is the longevity of those who survived childhood. The improved standards of nutrition and relative absence of disease helped prolong life to about seventy for men and almost that age for women. Twenty percent of the first and second generation males in Andover survived into their eighties.

EDUCATION IN THE BIBLE COMMONWEALTHS

The New England family, beyond providing social indoctrination, was the first in a series of educational institutions that culminated in the colleges of Harvard and Yale. In England the Puritans had been noted for their respect for learning, demanding it of the clergy, encouraging it among the laity, and spreading it by the endowment of schools and lectureships. Knowledge, they believed, was important for reasons of religion—God revealed himself in nature, history, and the Scriptures, and it was man's responsibility to study and learn the lessons thus provided him. Education was also important if men were to know and obey the law and protect their rights against potential tyrants. The New World heightened the need. Surrounded by wilderness, subjected to the lure of an alien (Indian) life style, burdened with responsibility to be a "city on a hill," the colonists strove to preserve and pass on their values.

In 1642 the Massachusetts General Court required the selectmen of every town "to take account from time to time of all parents and masters, and of their children, especially of their ability to read and understand the principles of religion and the capital laws of this country." Connecticut passed similar legislation in 1650, New Haven in 1655, Plymouth in 1671. Reading and writing were taught in the home, usually by a parent, occasionally by an elder brother or sister. Family reading sessions around the hearth in the evening offered the children of some households excellent opportunities to improve their skills. Some women of the colonies provided a welcome service to families in which the adults were illiterate by teaching reading and writing to their children for a small fee. Such domestic classrooms became known as "dame schools."

Concerned that families were not satisfactorily fulfilling their duties, and determined to provide further education for boys who had learned the rudiments, the Massachusetts General Court in 1647 passed another law:

It being one chief project of that old deluder, Satan, to keep men from the knowledge of the Scriptures, as in former times by keeping them in an unknown tongue, so in these latter times by persuading them from the use of tongues, that so at least the true sense and meaning of the original might be clouded by false glosses of saint-seeming deceivers [it is ordered] that every township in this jurisdiction, after the Lord hath increased them to the number of fifty householders, shall then forthwith appoint one within their town to teach all such children as shall resort to him to read and write [and requires also] that where any town shall increase to the number of one hundred families or householders, they shall set up a grammar school, the master thereof being able to instruct youth so far as they may be fitted for the university.

In the first decade after the enactment of the "old deluder Satan" law, apparently only one-third of the fifty-household towns maintained a "petty school," the inhabitants perhaps believing that they were making adequate provision for the teaching of reading and writing in their own homes. Though the extent of compliance later declined, all eight of the hundred-family towns of the 1650s established grammar schools. As with the earlier educational legislation, the other Bible Commonwealths shortly followed the leadership of the Bay.

There had been grammar schools, of course, before the 1647 law required them. The town of Boston engaged Philemon Pormont as schoolmaster in 1635, and several other communities started their own schools soon after: Ipswich and Charlestown in 1636; Cambridge in 1638; Dorchester, Newbury, and Salem in 1639; New Haven and Hartford in 1642. These and the schools that followed them were generally taught by college graduates who were awaiting calls to pastoral posts; career schoolmasters such as Ezekiel Cheever were a rare exception. The typical schoolhouse was sparse and small, perhaps 20 feet long, slightly less in width, with a 6-foot ceiling. Windows were few. Desks were attached to the walls and light and heat were both provided by a large fireplace—excessive for those near it and insufficient for those far away.

New England boys first entered these schoolhouses at the age of seven or eight. (Later in the seventeenth century some towns began to admit girls.) Because the purpose of the grammar school was to prepare pupils for college, its curriculum emphasized Latin and included at least an introduction to Greek, and, in some schools, to Hebrew as well. Instruction was year-round and stressed the rote memorization of certain texts. The daily routine in one such school— the Hopkins Grammar School in New Haven—is described by historian Lawrence Cremin:

The master and scholars are enjoined to attend every morning from six to eleven and every afternoon from one to five in summer and from one to four in winter. The master is instructed to begin each day with a short prayer and then to seat his pupils in the schoolroom "according to their degrees of learning." He is also asked to examine them every Monday on the preceding day's sermon and to catechize them every Saturday from one to three in the afternoon.

Seven or eight years of such drill prepared the more promising pupils for attendance at Harvard. Founded in 1636, the college had gotten off to an uncertain start, from which it had been saved by the presidency of Henry Dunster (1640–1654). Dunster insisted upon a four-year program of studies and himself taught all the courses until qualified graduates emerged to assist him. While Puritanism permeated the course of studies and the colonists looked to the college to perpetuate an educated ministry, Harvard was not a seminary, and more than half of the students in its first fifty graduating classes did not enter the ministry.

The college curriculum was modeled upon that of Oxford and Cambridge, especially Emmanuel College at Cambridge, where twenty-nine of the first generation colonial leaders, including Henry Dunster, had studied. The curriculum paralleled that of Oxford and Cambridge in its attachment to Logic, Rhetoric, Ethics, Metaphysics, Greek, Latin, and the Natural Sciences. To those traditional subjects the Harvard overseers added unusually thorough courses in Hebrew and Aramaic, to enhance scholarly investigation of the Scriptures. Students learned these disciplines from lectures and from textbooks and compendia of learning such as those written by Johann Alsted and Petrus Ramus. Oral declamation forced students to organize and articulate their thoughts logically and persuasively, while disputations stimulated analysis and intellectual agility.

The students who entered upon this course of studies in the seventeenth century were given college rank and status according to the "Supposed Dignity of the Families" upon their first admission. Violation of college rules could be punished by degradation in the class. During their years at the college, students were not allowed to reside in private homes. College authorities insisted on campus residence because it facilitated closer moral supervision and because it fostered a sense of community.

Harvard's lapse from strict orthodoxy worried the Mathers and their supporters at the close of the seventeenth century, but throughout that century and the next Harvard, and, later Yale, managed admirably to "advance learning and perpetuate it to posterity." From those schools came the leaders of New England society, civil as well as ecclesiastical. From the remarkable school system, which bore witness to the Puritan concern for learning, came the men and the cultural environment that enabled New England to eclipse the other regions of colonial America in literary and scientific achievement. But more important to the Puritans, the schools meshed with the efforts of towns, churches, and families to capture and fill the minds of generations of New England youth with an attachment to the values and hopes of the founders. Accordingly, while the surface life of the colonies changed, much of the Puritan tradition persevered to help shape a new nation.

15 | ART AND SCIENCE IN COLONIAL NEW ENGLAND

The intellectual heritage that led the Puritans to establish an educational system also encouraged New England scholars in the task of investigating man and nature and communicating their findings in writing as well as in oral sermons. While Puritan colonists thus pursued tasks to which many of their English brethren likewise set themselves, the New World environment did modify the intellectual life of the colonists. Separation from the stimulus and criticism of Stuart England would deny American authors the chance to perfect their thoughts and modes of expression. On the other hand, the sense of mission of the Bible Commonwealths perhaps served to stimulate many to articulate their goals and beliefs to an extent they would not have felt in England. More significantly, in the areas of architectural development, scientific investigations, and technological innovations the physical environment of North America presented new problems to be solved and placed a premium upon creativity. Out of the blend of Puritan ideology and New World environment there emerged an intellectual life which, if sometimes provincial, was nonetheless deeply rooted and broadly based.

LITERARY EFFORTS

In discussing the English Puritans, Owen Watkins has commented that

they valued literature not for its own sake, but just in so far as it promoted right attitudes and right conduct. Their creative energy was mostly taken up with interpreting the concepts and values they considered crucial to human destiny, and so their chief publications were sermons, treatises, and handbooks—doctrinal, devotional, practical, and controversial. But

184

they also believed, with many ancient authorities, that "examples are more powerful than precepts," and thus the esteem given to expository works was shared by history and biography.

While this might be a somewhat narrow description of a tradition that included John Milton, John Bunyan, and Andrew Marvell, it focuses upon what was most important to the Puritan artist—his message. And even in the more carefully crafted works of a John Milton, the didactic purpose stands out clearly. In this respect, the New England colonists were no different from their English brethren. The authors of the Bible Commonwealths devoted their efforts primarily to the production of sermons, religious tracts, diaries, biographies, and histories.

The most important literary form for the American Puritans was the sermon. The colonial clergy had learned from English predecessors such as Richard Sibbes and William Perkins to cultivate pulpit oratory as a fine art. Whereas sermon artistry meant stylistic ornamentation and logical subtlety to Anglicans such as John Donne and Lancelot Andrewes, the criteria by which Puritans judged their efforts were exegetical and practical. The minister's words were the central element in religious services, the purpose of which was to convey the word of God and his grace. For this to be accomplished the message had to be logically organized and clearly presented.

Each sermon—whether prepared for delivery on the Sabbath, a lecture day, or a special occasion (such as a fast day or election day)— opened with a biblical text. Then, according to the standard form, the preacher would "open" the text, collect the doctrine, give reasons to prove it, and finally show how it should be applied. In the first part the clergyman would begin by placing the text in its scriptural context. Then he would open the text by the explanation of various key words. (Thomas Hooker, preaching on one occasion from Proverbs 8:32, explained that "hearken" connoted hearing, understanding, retaining, and subjecting the will to God.) Having clarified the text, the minister stated the doctrine, frequently simply rephrasing the text. Following the doctrine came the second principal part of the sermon, the "proof." Here, frequently enumerating the various points, the minister would reinforce the validity of the textual doctrine by bringing to bear his broad knowledge of the Scriptures, drawing upon the Old and New Testaments to cite similar passages supportive of the doctrine. Having stated and proved the authenticity of his doctrine, in the last part of the sermon the preacher would turn to its "uses." Here, also enumerating his points, he stressed the utility of the doctrine and how it should be applied by his listeners to their everyday lives. Frequently rather general, these applications could be sharply relevant, as when John Davenport addressed his New Haven congregation shortly after the Restoration on the need to shelter true Christians fleeing from persecution in Europe.

The care that went into the preparation of the sermons was considerable. A New England pastor would frequently pray and meditate on his text, consult his library of scriptural commentaries and theological and secular works for proofs and illustrations of his points, and carefully write out the sermon. An hour or more in length, its organization had to be logical and clear to facilitate the note taking of the congregation; its phrasing had to be plain and simple, using homely metaphors from the everyday lives of the audience so as to ease comprehension. The sermon had then to be memorized for delivery, rather than read, so that the preacher's contact with his listeners would be more direct.

The better sermons of a Cotton, a Davenport, or an Edwards reveal the logical organization and direct, plain style that was the Puritan ideal. Many were printed as delivered. Others were combined, with slight revisions, to form the contents of published treatises. Samuel Willard's *Compleat Body of Divinity* was a published edition of 250 lectures in which that pastor had sequentially analyzed the key points of Puritan theology.

Next to the sermon, the most explicitly didactic works of the colonists were diaries and biographies. The former were confessional self-examinations in a written form. In the first instance they were intended for the author's own assistance. By charting his spiritual progress he was able to have a record both of his human frailty and of God's mercifulness to him, thus preventing him from falling into the sins of pride and despair. Published, or circulated privately in manuscript, these personal records could lead unbelievers to desire grace, stir slothful Christians to piety, and give hope and sustenance to men or women experiencing trials similar to those weathered by the author.

The diaries also formed the basis for details in the biographies of eminent clergy and civil leaders. The purpose of these efforts—the most notable being the sketches included in Cotton Mather's *Magnalia Christi Americana*—was to edify readers by demonstrating the journeys of individual souls toward God and their success in carrying out the Lord's purposes. Like medieval hagiography, such biographies were largely stylized. In them the author invariably stressed the events leading to the saint's conversion, that climactic episode itself, and the virtues he displayed thereafter. Comparisons were often drawn between the subject of the biography and figures from the Old Testament. Yet for all the stylization involved, the authors generally held sincere affection for their subjects (often men personally known to them) and this emotion shines through to leave a real impression of the force that a John Cotton or an Increase Mather exerted on his contemporaries.

If the spiritual biography traced the progress toward grace of a notable individual, the historical writings of the colonists were similar attempts to trace the covenantal progress of the Bible Commonwealths. Edward Johnson, John Winthrop, and William Bradford in the first generation, and Cotton Mather and William Hubbard later in the colonial period, all wrote out of a concern to make sense of the history of the colonies. Believing that God's plan was revealed in the unfolding of daily events, these historians were careful in their recording and, at their best, remarkably objective in their narrative. Objectivity was essential so that even if the meaning of events was indiscernible at the time of their occurrence, those events might nevertheless be preserved for the examination of later generations.

The first published history of New England was Edward Johnson's *Wonder-Working Providence of Sion's Saviour in New England*, published in London in 1654. The author was a ship's carpenter with little formal education who had been among the early settlers of Massachusetts and been elected militia captain of Woburn. Written when the Puritan cause was at its zenith in Old and New England, his work is a vigorous if ungrammatical paean to the work of "Christ [who] creates a New England to muster up the first of his forces in." Johnson's concern was with the way in which New Englanders made their progress from being the "Forlorne of Christs Armies . . . overpowered with multitudes [and] forced to retreat to a place of greater safety," through their tribulations of the 1630s, to their sharing in Christ's triumphant overthrow of the Antichrist. It is the theme of the pilgrim's progress applied to a people. Johnson was a participant in that journey, and in the 1650s he was capable of looking back in exultation. While his fervor and militant rhetoric might jar the twentieth-century reader and his accuracy falls below the standards of Bradford and Winthrop, he compensates with other strengths. His eye for detail is excellent, his narrative often enriched by it; and his depiction of the antinomian controversy, though not literally true in all detail, captures vividly the fears of the orthodox and the fervency of the Hutchinsonians.

William Bradford's narrative *Of Plymouth Plantation* was not published until 1856 but had frequently been drawn upon by historians that included William Hubbard and Thomas Prince. While his theme also was the struggle between God and Satan, that thread is much less obtrusive than in Johnson's work. The manuscript was composed in two parts: the first, relating the Pilgrims' journeys from Scrooby to the New World, was written in 1630; the second, carrying the story to 1646, was prompted by the Puritan triumphs in England. Bradford's purpose was to narrate the story of the Pilgrims' piety in the face of adversity, hoping that future generations might be stirred to emulation, but he lets the story of their struggles convey that lesson rather than overtly lecturing the reader. In the judgment of historian Kenneth Murdock,

He had an untutored knack for a good story, a knack for the orderly knotting up of every thread he started to trace, and, as a special gift, rare among Puritan writers, a vein of humor. . . . Bradford's phrasing is not that of the imaginative artist, wide-ranging in metaphor and simile, nor that of the scholar, ransacking books for illustrations and parallels, but that of the man whose ears were full of the plain speech of English farmers and who was bred to relish simple rhythms and words with the sense of familiar life.

It is this lack of flamboyance, coupled with a scrupulously accurate and humble presentation of facts, that makes the Plymouth governor the most readable of colonial authors.

Close to Bradford in simplicity and unadorned grace of expression was his fellow governor John Winthrop. Written in the form of a journal, Winthrop's account has been published as *The History of New England from 1630 to 1649*. Filled with factual information concerning the political events of moment and such remarkable acts of providence as the destruction of a copy of the Anglican Prayer Book by a garret mouse which left the Bible untouched, the *History* is one of the most valuable sources for reconstructing the early years of Massachusetts and the nature of the New England mind. While the personal warmth evident in Winthrop's letters is lacking in the journal, his style reminds us of Bradford's in its sparseness and plainness, qualities lacking in the works of most of the period's authors.

Cotton Mather, writing later in the colonial period, stood firmly in this historical tradition, though his style was unique and his wordiness unmatched. The publication of the *Magnalia Christi Americana* represented the culmination of an effort begun in 1693. Divided into seven "books," the massive tome begins with a study of the founding of the colonies; proceeds with separate parts offering biographical sketches of New England's eminent governors and divines; then presents "books" on Harvard and on the New England Way; continues with a part treating shipwrecks, apparitions, and other remarkable acts of providence; and concludes with a review of the wars of the Lord against Roger Williams, Anne Hutchinson, the Indians, and other threats to God's chosen people. The whole often appears to be a disjointed and uneven compilation rather than a coherent history. Mather's erudition intrudes upon the reader's consciousness and detracts from the author's purpose. His filiopietism leads to distortions. Nevertheless, this sustained jeremiadlike lamentation for New England's past glories contains passages of taut and moving prose, is occasionally subtle in its analysis of the New England Way, and carries an overpowering sense of conviction. As Samuel Eliot Morison once commented: "Almost anything you can say about the *Magnalia* will be true, in part; for it has a bit of everything, in matter, style, and method."

Reading the biographies and histories authored by the Puritans, one frequently encounters brief passages of poetry. As a literary form the poem was familiar to the Puritans—particularly those who received a heavily classical university education—and they were not adverse to using it for a purpose. But the poetry of such authors as Edward Johnson and Cotton Mather had little to recommend it to later generations, and was probably found seriously wanting by their own contemporaries. But despite the colonists' preference for prose composition, New England produced at least three poets who wrote extensively in that medium and whose works merit inclusion in anthologies of American literature.

The Puritan poet who came closest to sharing the concerns of the sermon writers and historians was Michael Wigglesworth. Wigglesworth had been born in England and migrated to Connecticut with his parents in 1638. He attended Harvard, received his bachelor's and master's degrees, and in 1656 was called to minister to the Malden congregation just outside Boston. His diary, written while a tutor at Harvard, displays elements of introspection and morbidity that went beyond what was normal for a devout Puritan. In his own day he was best known as the author of three poetical works: *Meat Out of the Eater, God's Controversy with New England*, and *The Day of Doom*. The last, published in 1662, became one of the most popular volumes read in the colonies, its sales unequaled by any American literary work until Benjamin Franklin's *Way to Wealth. The Day of Doom*, based upon a dream that Wigglesworth had in 1653 while a student at Harvard, was an epic of 224 eight-line stanzas. It opens with a depic-

tion of the "security of the World before Christ's coming to judgment."
In the fifth stanza,

> . . . at midnight broke forth a light,
>   which turned the night to day,
> And speedily a hideous cry
>   did all the world dismay.
> Sinners awake, their hearts do ache,
>   trembling their loins supriseth;
> Amazed with fear, by what they hear,
>   each one of them ariseth.

From that turning point the poet goes on to depict in great detail
"the Great and Last Judgment": God's sudden appearance, his summons
of the living and the dead, his redemption of "sound believers," and
his punishment of the damned (the various categories of sinners are
carefully inventoried). Though his language is generally tight and
apt, the poem's swift ballad meter and internal rhymes strike modern
sensibilities as unsuitable. Yet in its day it was widely hailed and
memorized by many as an act of devotion.

Less explicitly didactic than Wigglesworth, but a far more capable
poet, was Anne Bradstreet. As Robert Richardson has persuasively
argued, "she wrote from what might be called the Puritan sensibility, . . . and her best poetry gains rather than loses by being considered as the product of that sensibility." The daughter of Thomas
Dudley, Anne had been raised on the estate of the earl of Lincoln,
where her father was steward. At the age of sixteen she married Simon
Bradstreet. Together with her father, they migrated to Massachusetts
in 1630. Her spirit initially rebelled against the harshness of the
wilderness, but she was able to master those feelings and dedicate
herself to meeting the needs of her husband and the eight children
they raised. She also managed to write poetry, though made to feel
"I am obnoxious to each carping tongue/Who says my hand a needle
better fits." With the support of her family she was able to overcome
these prejudices against expressions of female intellect.

Her first volume of poems, *The Tenth Muse Lately Sprung Up in
America* . . . , was published in London in 1650. Her second volume,
containing revisions of her early work as well as new poems, was
published in 1678, six years after her death. The early poems, containing comments on historical events, philosophical love, and similar
interests, were filled with ineffective literary devices. They also reflected her inability to reconcile love of this world and the need to
rely on the next. In her later work, however, particularly "Contemplations," she achieved a simpler, more lyrical expression as well as a

resolution of the tensions within her. "Contemplations" is a poem of thirty-three seven-line stanzas, containing a series of sustained and ordered reflections on nature and the supernatural. Ultimately, the temporal world is found wanting:

> O Time the fatal wrack of mortal things
> That draws oblivious curtains over kings,
> Their sumptuous monuments, men know them not,
> Their names without a Record are forgot,
> Their parts, their ports, their pomp's all
> > laid in th' dust
> Nor wit nor gold, nor buildings scape time's rust;
> But he whose name is carved in the white stone
> Shall last and shine when all of these are gone.

The poem, as Richardson interprets it,

comes to rest in a gentle and evocative poetic reference to the selective and unknowable ways of the Puritan God. The poem is a demonstration, in the form of a recorded experience, that nature itself generates belief. In seventeenth-century New England this could only mean that the world itself leads the mind of man to acknowledge God. . . . It accepts both worlds, perceives their connection, and acquiesces in that connection.

Edward Taylor, like Wigglesworth and Bradstreet, was born in England. He grew up in the period of the Puritan revolution and Cromwell's Protectorate. He attended Cambridge University, taught school for a period, migrated to Massachusetts in his twenties, and completed his education at Harvard. He graduated in 1661 and accepted a call to be pastor in Westfield. There he served for fifty-eight years, until his death in 1729. His considerable number of poems were written as spiritual exercises and were not discovered and published until the 1930s. Intensely theological, the poems are sensuous, meditative, logical, and mystical. The vividness of the metaphors and the earthiness of some of the language are unlike any other colonial literary productions. In the "Prologue" to his "Preparatory Meditations" he writes:

> I am this crumb of dust which is designed
> > To make my pen unto Thy praise alone,
> And my dull fancy I would gladly grind
> > Unto an edge of Zion's precious stone.
> > And writes in liquid gold upon Thy name
> > My letters till Thy glory forth doth flame.

The poems that followed were attempts by Taylor to bring himself to the proper frame of mind and state of grace for the celebration of the

Lord's Supper. They lead the reader to a deeper understanding of the variety of Puritan postures in the presence of God, and are all the more remarkable as works of art for not having been designed as such.

THE VISUAL ARTS AND MUSIC

The visual arts in colonial society were rarely produced purely for the purpose of conveying aesthetic pleasure. Almost without exception the surviving artistic treasures of the colonists are in architecture, furniture, silverware, and other objects whose primary purpose was functional. The reasons for this have little to do with ideology. Except for the painting and statuary of saints, the Puritans had no objection to the arts. But the struggle of winning a livelihood from the wilderness left little energy or financial patronage for nonpractical activities. Particularly in the seventeenth century, the artistic genius of the settlers was limited to the decorative design and ornamentation of functional objects.

Architecture has been the most enduring artistic legacy of the seventeenth century. Having been forced to spend their first winter in caves or in holes dug out of the ground and covered over, the first settlers in places like Plymouth and Salem initially constructed homes of sawn timber with thatched roofs. But these dwellings, despite their sizable fireplaces, were inadequate protection against the New England weather. The demands of the climate soon led to structural modifications: the clapboard exterior and the lime-plaster interior. Later, the thatched roof was replaced with shingles.

The basic New England home of the 1640s became known as the "saltbox." Built around a huge central chimney with a number of fireplace openings, these structures in many cases began as small, two-room dwellings. Second stories, when built, often protruded over the ground floor; the overhang, originally a European urban space-saving device, was at first copied literally in New England and was retained in later designs for decorative effect. As a family grew, the saltbox could evolve through the construction of lean-to and other additions. Ceilings were generally low, to retain the heat. That was also one reason for the small windows in these homes; the high cost of importing glass was another. Many colonists merely used wooden shutters to cover their window openings, others chose to employ oiled paper.

Despite their functionalism, these seventeenth-century homes often possessed a simple grace that makes them architecturally pleasing to this day. As time went on and the settlers came to know prosperity, refinements of design revealed greater concern for aesthetics. Corner pendants, decorative iron door latches and hinges, and other such additions made their appearance. Gables began to be used, to enhance appearance as well as to provide additional room. In the eighteenth century the utilization of the gambrel roof, pedimented Doric-columned doorways, and painted facades revealed conscious attempts to imitate the style of Georgian England.

As with domestic architecture, the design of New England's meetinghouses likewise reflected functional concerns first. A large room with a pulpit at the center of one wall and a large table for the Lord's Supper were all that were strictly necessary for a Puritan house of worship, and in the early years of settlement that is all that was available in some communities. As time went on designs became more complex. Since the Puritans rejected the doctrinal beliefs that determined the design of medieval churches, they came to America without any preconceived models of meetinghouse design. Consequently, their creations reveal considerable variety. As architectural historian Marian Card Donnelly explains,

According to the size and prosperity of a town, its meeting house might . . . have one or more galleries, built-pews, a belfry, and some architectural ornament. Sizes and shapes of the buildings varied, as did the types of roof, which included gabled, cross-gabled, and hip roofs, with or without dormers, platforms, and turrets.

Designed for town meetings as well as for worship, many were similar in design to English town halls and market halls. Their interiors were marked as Protestant by the absence of statuary, stained glass, and other ornamentation; and Puritan rather than Anglican by the arrangement of seats to face the pulpit rather than the communion table. The meetinghouse, like domestic structures, was generally constructed of the plentiful wood of the region.

The cabinetmakers, goldsmiths, and other artisans of the seventeenth and eighteenth centuries were frequently highly skilled in the decorative beautification of their products. While the chairs, tables, and chests of Puritan New England primarily show artistic characteristics common to England and Holland, some regional creativity did develop, the so-called "Hadley chests," for instance, being distinctive products of the cabinetmakers of that Massachusetts town. John Hull, one of the wealthiest merchants of Boston and the colony's mintmaster, was also the first in a tradition of skilled Boston goldsmiths that would include Jeremy Dummer, John Covey, John Dixwell, and Paul Revere.

Often neglected in surveys of art, but unjustly so, are the works of domestic artistry such as the needlepoint, patchwork bed coverlets, and embroidered hangings created by the colonial housewives. Showing tasteful design and skillful execution, these items reflect the desire to beautify their surroundings that was shared by most of the Puritans.

Painting was one art form that made little headway in the colonies, it being decidedly a luxury beyond the means of the colonists to patronize. It should be pointed out that this was not an effect of Puritanism, there being ample examples of English art patronized by the Puritans. In New England there is little evidence of native artists before the 1670s; these tended to be either amateurs who combined painting with other skills or journeymen limners of little talent. An example of the former was John Foster, the proprietor of the first printshop in Boston, who evidently executed portraits of Richard Mather, John Davenport, and others, and who made a woodblock engraving of Mather. Limited to portraiture, early New England painting seldom displayed anything exceeding workmanlike competence.

Just as the Puritans rejected physical ornamentation in their meetinghouses because it might distract the worshipper's attention from God, so too they prohibited music from their services. But Englishmen of the Elizabethan and Stuart ages were extremely musical—even more so than their twentieth-century descendants—and it would have been unusual if those tastes had not been brought to the colonies. The citizens of the Bible Commonwealths took pleasure in singing madrigals as well as psalms and delighted in the music of lutes, violins, trumpets, flutes, virginals, and other instruments. Even in the churches the singing of psalms without musical accompaniment was part of services. Developing tastes were reflected in the late seventeenth-century movement to replace the "lining-out" form of communal singing with "singing by note."

In art and architecture, as in their literature, the Puritans were primarily practical. Their environment and their ideas led them to emphasize the simple and functional. Graceful ornamentation, when it did not detract from those criteria, was encouraged to the extent that economics allowed. They similarly saw value in musical entertainment, provided of course that it did not distract from the business of life. Their bent for practicality, which determined much of the region's artistic development, was also to influence the growth of science.

SCIENCE

English university graduates of the sixteenth and seventeenth centuries, Puritan as well as Anglican, saw no incompatability between science and religion. They were confident that the study of the creation could only add to man's knowledge of the creator. Whatever the ultimate effect of the Enlightenment upon Christianity, the men who sought to extend the frontiers of seventeenth-century science did so in the belief that they were advancing God's cause. That same spirit and incentive was present among the New England colonists.

Harvard's adoption of the English university curriculum meant that New England youth were exposed to subjects that today would be distinguished as arithmetic, geometry, physics, astronomy, and botany. Puritans proved more receptive to the developing scientific revolution than did many other groups. As early as 1659, New England almanacs propagated the new astronomy based on Galileo's findings, rather than the Ptolemaic view of the universe. The curriculum at Harvard reflected that commitment as well. Likewise, the works of Descartes and Newton found favor in the Massachusetts college. In fact, Newton's mathematical formulation of the law of gravitation was made possible in part by Bostonian Thomas Brattle's observations of the elliptical orbit of the comet of 1680.

The academic pursuit of science was encouraged by Thomas Hollis's endowment of a professorial chair in mathematics and natural philosophy at Harvard in 1727. The first Hollis Professor, Isaac Greenwood, introduced new courses in mathematics to the curriculum, published an arithmetic text, and wrote a manuscript for algebra studies. Greenwood was succeeded by John Winthrop IV, who held the Hollis chair until his death in 1779. During his long career he published six pamphlet volumes, contributed eleven papers to the English Royal Society, and was recognized for his learning by the award of an honorary degree from Edinburgh University. He encouraged his English friends to donate scientific equipment to Harvard, including a telescope that had belonged to Edmund Halley. He was perhaps the first American to teach Newton's calculus and was responsible for the introduction of "pure science" to Harvard. Thomas Clap, a contemporary of Winthrop, introduced Newtonian science to Yale during his tenure as rector there.

While individuals such as Greenwood and Winthrop could be classified as professional scientists, most colonial scientific activity was performed by amateurs. The first and one of the most notable of those figures was John Winthrop, Jr. That extraordinary statesman was also a highly motivated scientific investigator. A friend of many of the founders of the Royal Society, he was among the first members of that institution. A student of alchemy, astronomy, botany, medicine, and chemistry, he sought to apply his knowledge to improving the lives of his neighbors. He was particularly looked to for aid as a physician, at a time when the practice of medicine was primitive.

Other colonists followed Winthrop's lead in combining scientific observation with their primary careers. The Reverend Gershom Bulkeley of Glastonbury, Connecticut, practiced medicine and conducted chemical experiments. Merchant Thomas Brattle filled much of his time with astronomical observations. His brother William likewise had an interest in science and was admitted to the Royal Society on the basis of his reports. The lawyer Paul Dudley prepared papers for the Royal Society on the habits of whales, New England earthquakes, the preparation of maple sugar, and a variety of other topics. But next to Winthrop, the region's most impressive amateur scientist was Cotton Mather.

Cotton Mather was elected a fellow of the Royal Society in 1713 on the basis of his observations of natural phenomena. His treatise *The Christian Philosopher*, published in 1720, was a mixture of Christian piety and scientific discussion which argued that science was an incentive to religion. *The Angel of Bethesda* was a lengthy manuscript compilation of extant medical knowledge, which he completed in 1724 but which was unpublished at his death. He studied and wrote shorter pieces on subjects ranging from rainbows to rattlesnakes. But his most famous act of faith in science was his commitment to inoculation as a protection against smallpox, the dreaded disease of the colonial period.

Mather had heard from an African slave of the use of inoculation in Africa and had later read an article on similar Turkish practices in the *Transactions of the Royal Society*. He won Dr. Zabdiel Boylston to the belief, and when a smallpox epidemic struck New England in 1721 the two urged the use of inoculation, Boylston experimenting with the method on members of his own family. While many clergymen supported the practice, most physicians were strongly opposed. Hysterical citizens, convinced that inoculation would spread the disease, directed bitter verbal attacks against the two crusaders. A primitive bomb was thrown through Mather's window. But while about 15 percent of the six thousand who contracted the disease by natural means died, mortality among those who had been inoculated was only 2 percent. Some resistance remained, but the Mather-Boylston experiment paved the way for the eventual control of smallpox in the Western world.

Medical experiments were, of course, eminently practical, as were many of the other efforts of these amateur scientists. John Winthrop, Jr., used his knowledge in the founding of salt- and ironworks in New England. Joseph Jenkes of Saugus, Massachusetts, patented a water wheel to harness one of the region's prime power sources. Rather than daunting them, this new country stimulated the colonists' interest with its marvels and sparked their ingenuity. While they were too far removed from the centers of scientific activity to develop true genius, as in literature the New England Puritans succeeded in making contributions to science that would stir the emulation of later generations.

16 | RACE RELATIONS

The Puritans were not alone in their American wilderness. Before they came the land had been farmed, the wildlife hunted, the streams fished by the Indians of the region. And, later in the 1640s, white New Englanders gradually followed the lead of their Dutch neighbors and of their fellow Englishmen to the South by importing black men and women from Africa. New England thus developed a racial heterogeneity that has remained typical of America to this day.

WHITE AND RED: COEXISTENCE AND CONVERSION

The seal of the Massachusetts Bay Company depicts an Indian standing on the American shoreline asking Europe to "Come over and help us." There is no reason to believe the seal had any basis in fact. The Puritan belief that the natives desired their help was a gratuitous assumption based on the conviction that any heathen instinctively longed for Reformed Christianity and English culture. Hence New Englanders believed they had a divinely ordained mission to spread Puritanism to all men—Indians as well as Englishmen. The charter of the Bay Company, moreover, charged the colony's officials to "wynn and incite the Natives . . . [to] the onlie true God and Saviour of Mankinde."

The objects of this solicitude lived mainly along the coast and waterways of New England. The Indian population probably numbered about twenty-five thousand in 1615 but a devastating plague—undoubtedly contracted from European fishermen—had reduced the number to perhaps fifteen thousand by 1620. All were of the Algonquian family, but they were divided into at least ten major tribes. In the north, inhabiting western Maine, were the Abenakis. Present-day Vermont and New Hampshire were peopled by the Pennacooks. The Massachusetts reigned in the eastern region of the colony of that ⁄

198

name, while central Massachusetts was the territory of the Nipmucs, with the Pocumtucks to their west. The arm of Cape Cod was occupied by the Nausets. The Wampanoags dominated what became the heart of the Plymouth colony. Present-day Rhode Island was the tribal territory of the Narragansetts. The Pequots, Wappingers, and a loose group designated the "River Tribes" each held portions of the land that was to be settled as the Connecticut and New Haven colonies.

All of these tribes were essentially regional, moving only with the seasons among a number of semipermanent campsites. The staple of their diet was corn, although they did hunt and fish extensively (the Abenaki, however, differed in being more dependent than the other tribes upon the hunt). Individual tribes were led by a chieftain called a sachem or sagamore. Lesser sachems ruled over the various divisions of a tribe. The powwows, or medicine men, were religious leaders whose political and healing functions often took precedence over spiritual duties.

Most New England commentators described the natives of the region as tall, full-bodied, and handsome. Their complexion was light enough that close observers of Indian life such as Roger Williams believed that they were born white and bronzed as they aged through exposure to the sun and the repeated application of stains for ceremonial purposes. The Puritans found the Indian to be courteous and hospitable to strangers. They also considered him lazy and prone to drunkenness.

The helpfulness of the Indians proved valuable to the English. Their skills, strength, and knowledge of the area were sufficient to have created serious problems for the English had they opposed the Puritan colonization, but they welcomed the newcomers and assisted them in adjusting to the New World. The record of assistance tendered to the Pilgrims by Samoset and Squanto was duplicated many times in the experience of other colonists. From the natives the Puritans learned how to plant corn and other New World vegetables, where to fish and hunt, and other lessons that contributed to the low mortality rate of the early New England settlements.

On their side, the Puritan leaders tried to treat the Indian with respect and fairness. That their concepts of fairness were shaped by their English Puritan heritage was to be expected. The New Englanders did not seize Indian lands. The tribes had claims to most of the land in New England, but much of the region was not held as the territory of any tribe, and the natives initially had no objection to the spread of white settlement into unclaimed land if the settlers were friendly. In fact, the possibility of gaining military assistance from the Europeans against hostile tribes encouraged chieftains like Massasoit to welcome the newcomers. In cases where the settlers coveted land claimed by the Indians, the laws of the colonies required acquisition by the colonial government, not by individuals. Unscrupulous frontiersmen were thus held in check. Deeds for particular plots had to be specific in their provisions, translated into the native language, and reviewed by designated colonial officials. Payments were cheap by European standards of land value but were in keeping with the needs—metal tools, cloth, utensils—of Algonquian society. There were violations of these procedures later in the century, when the swelling population made government control less effective and when attitudes toward the Indian had deteriorated appreciably. In such instances the Indians were cheated, although prosecution and conviction of the perpetrators often occurred.

In many cases, native tribes submitted by treaty to the protection of the Puritan colonies and thereby became subject to colonial laws. While legislation denying the Indian firearms and whiskey and exempting natives from military service were clearly discriminatory, the Indian generally received equal treatment under law in the New England colonies. There is, of course, no way of judging the subtler forms of prejudice among magistrates and jurors, or of measuring the handicaps imposed on Indians by the language barrier or foreign concepts of crime and justice. But the records do show that Indians often won property and other disputes in Puritan courts, and whites who cheated, raped, or murdered Indians were—during the earlier decades at least—prosecuted and punished with the same rigor as if their victims had been white. There are at least two instances before 1676 in which whites were executed for the murder of Indians.

Economically, the Indians welcomed the advent of the white man. The sale of land brought welcome aid to some tribes and caused no initial hardship. New tools and materials made a strong impact on native society. Knives, hatchets, needles, awls, hoes, textiles, and other such items of European manufacture led to marked improvements in the Indian standard of living—as did guns when they could be obtained. That this influx gradually created a dependency upon English sources contributed in the long run to the undermining of native society. But such was not the intent of the Puritan traders, nor did most of the Indians, when they recognized this consequence, reject the trade.

In their political, legal, and economic relations with the Algonquian tribes of the Northeast, the Puritans tried to deal with the Indian as an equal. Assuming that the Indians were born white and became darker only from ceremonial staining and the sun, the New England colonists were free of racist attitudes toward them. This was due partly to the widespread belief that the Indian tribes were descendants of the lost tribes of the Jews, whose conversion would signal the advent of the millennium. But if they did not view the Indian as racially inferior, they certainly judged him culturally inferior and gradually mounted an effort to "raise" him to the level of Englishmen by bringing him the blessings of civilization and Christianity.

In the first decades of Puritan settlement there was little effort to convert the natives, though individuals such as Roger Williams did develop close relationships with certain tribes. Part of the lack of missionary effort stemmed from the colonists' preoccupation with their own survival, but mainly it reflected the difficulties of the task. In the first place, Congregationalism made no provision for missionaries: the New England preacher was ordained to minister to the needs of a specific congregation: there was no general ordination for missionaries. Consequently, work among the Indians had to be an added activity for heavily burdened clergymen. Another difficulty was inherent in the nature of Puritan theology: Puritanism was one of the most subtle and intellectually demanding variants of the Christian faith. Englishmen found mastery of the Puritan theology exceedingly difficult; American Indians must have found it more so. Compounding this problem, but in itself a separate obstacle, was the need for missionaries to master the Algonquian language. And finally there was the inevitable resistance by the Indians themselves to an alien faith. Both Christianity and English culture threatened to undermine Indian beliefs and customs. Most of the natives, and especially the chiefs and religious leaders, resented the settlers' efforts at proselytizing. Given these problems, it would have taken a remarkable man to make major progress in the conversion of the Indian.

One such individual was John Eliot. Eliot was born in England in 1604 and educated at Jesus College, Cambridge; he taught school for a year in England, and migrated to America in 1631. After remaining a year in Boston, where he substituted as pastor for John Wilson during the latter's absence to bring his family to the colonies, Eliot was called to be teacher of the Roxbury congregation, where he shared ministerial duties with Thomas Welde. In the early 1640s Eliot began to learn the Algonquian language. His tutor was an English-speaking Indian who had been captured and pressed into servitude in the Pequot War. He began to practice his skill among the local tribes. He soon made a strong impression on the subsachem Waban—who sent his eldest son to be educated in the Dedham grammar school—and on 28 October 1646 Eliot conducted his first religious service in the Algonquian language in Waban's village. Thereafter he increased his visits to the Indians, gradually increasing his audiences and winning their respect for him and his faith. Word of his success spread through the colonies and to England. Aided by propaganda from colonial spokesmen and the efforts in England of Edward Winslow, a movement sprang up in Parliament for the support of missionary activity which culminated in 1649 with the creation of the Society for the Propagation of the Gospel in New England. The society (rechartered after the Restoration as the New England Company) was to raise funds in England to be dispensed by the commissioners of the New England Confederation. With this support Eliot and his missionary allies began to expand their work.

The Roxbury clergyman believed that conversion to Puritanism must be accompanied by adoption of English habits and life styles. This in turn required him to draw converts away from their tribes and set them up in Europeanized villages. Accordingly the General Court of Massachusetts in 1646 authorized the purchase of land for the settlement of Christian Indians, and in 1651 the first "praying town" was established in Natick. The converts planted crops, built a bridge across the Charles River, erected a meetinghouse, homes, and a palisaded fort. Their model, down to the method of assigning house lots and formulation of a covenant, was the Puritan New England town. Civil government, on Eliot's suggestion, was copied from the Old Testament, with one leader chosen for the "hundred" (the whole village), one for each of the subgroups of "fifty," and ten as rulers of "tens." In 1652, Eliot sought to organize a church of his converts, but their conversion narratives were not sufficiently convincing to the observers from neighboring congregations. The converts' intellectual assent to Puritan doctrine was unquestioned; it was the presence of saving grace that was in doubt. Eventually a church covenant was signed by members of the Natick congregation in 1660. By the eve of King Philip's War there were fourteen such praying towns in the Bay, accommodating about eleven hundred Indians who had adopted the life style and religion of the Puritans. Throughout New England there were perhaps twenty-five hundred Indians who had nominally adopted Puritanism—approximately 23 percent of the native population.

An important aid in spreading Christianity to the tribes was Eliot's translation of the Bible into the Algonquian language. Here again Puritanism set high standards: converts must be able to read the Word. Early in his missionary career Eliot had contemplated translating the

Scriptures. The task was monumental. Since the Algonquian language was without a written form he had first to develop a written vocabulary while still learning the language himself. Moreover, the native language and English were often discrepant in syntax and vocabulary. Nevertheless, Eliot mastered these difficulties sufficiently to publish an Algonquian catechism in 1654. Finally, in 1661 the press at Cambridge ran the first copies of the New Testament in the native tongue, followed by the Old Testament two years later.

While Eliot stands out among the Puritan apostles to the Indians, he was by no means alone. The Mayhew family on Martha's Vineyard were equally dedicated. From 1647 until his death at sea ten years later, Thomas Mayhew, Jr., carried on a vigorous and successful missionary effort. After his death his father, Thomas Mayhew, Sr., took up the task. The first Indian church on the island was established in 1659. By the eve of King Philip's War most of the Indians on Martha's Vineyard and the nearby islands of Nantucket and Chappaquiddick were nominally Christian, with close to a hundred communicants. Later, a third generation of Mayhews—Matthew and John—continued the work.

In addition to these, Richard Bourne, William Leveridge, and the younger John Cotton in Plymouth; James Fitch, Abraham Pierson, and Thomas James in Connecticut and New Haven jurisdictions; and others all aided in the task of conversion. Indians were Christianized, Anglicized, and sent to New England schools. An Indian College was established at Harvard, though a relatively small number of Indians attended and only one graduated, dying of consumption a year later.

Critics such as Neal Salisbury and Francis Jennings have argued that altruistic rhetoric merely disguised the political and economic roots of Puritan Indian policy and that the "effect of the missionaries' work was to help clear the few Indians who remained, thus opening up still more land and assuring the settlers' safety." But John Eliot, Thomas Mayhew, and the others cannot be understood simply as agents of Puritan imperialism. To be sure, Eliot viewed the natives as "living in a state of sin, and repentance was necessary to be saved." But he and every other Puritan clergyman would have said the same of himself and the members of his congregation. The Puritans thought *everyone* should share in what they considered the blessings of Christianity; at the same time they deplored forced conversions and religious symbols that had no substance. They hoped, initially at least, to make every Indian into a full-fledged New England Puritan. It is not surprising that they failed. They did, however, have some success, and as one student of early Indian-white relations has observed,

It is hard to chastise the Puritans for failing to do better a job that their contemporaries did not perform as well. . . . The suspicion and hostility of the pre-Pilgrim period was changed during the early decades of Puritan settlement into an atmosphere of amity and cooperation, and that atmosphere remained prevalent until 1675.

King Philip's War was a turning point. While the earlier Pequot War had been essentially a conflict between the Puritans and a large segment of the Indians against a single tribe, the clash with Metacomet was far more of a race war in the eyes of the colonists, and it certainly was a graver threat to the survival of the English settlements. Because a large portion of the Indians turned against the English, and because the outlying settlements suffered fearfully from the atrocities of war, the pervasive attitudes among the Puritans turned bitter. During the war the praying Indians had to be relocated to an island in Boston harbor and guarded against the populace. And despite the aid of Christian Indians in bringing the uprising to an end, the broad support that had brought much success to the missionary effort could not be recaptured after the war. By 1700 the Puritans had begun to regard the Indians as a race apart. An emerging racism, based on fear of the Indian and a suspicion that he would never accept Christianity or English ways, justified a more callous treatment of the native tribes. Atrocities attributed to the Indians allied to the French in the eighteenth century were used to justify similar atrocities against the Indians. The charitable impulse of the earlier decades was all but forgotten.

THE SELLING OF JOSEPH:
SLAVERY IN PURITAN SOCIETY

It was considered acceptable in the seventeenth century for European states to bind prisoners of war into slavery or some other form of servitude. When Oliver Cromwell defeated the Scots at the Battle of Dunbar and then again at Worcester, he sent some of his captives to New England as servants. Similarly, following the defeat of the Pequots in 1637 the colonists had shipped some of the defeated Indians to the West Indies to be sold as slaves. The master of the ship *Desire* exchanged them for a cargo of "some cotton, and tobacco, and negroes, etc." Thus John Winthrop recorded in his *Journal* what was probably the arrival of the first slaves in New England. The year was 1638. There is no direct evidence that these blacks were treated as slaves by the Puritan colonists, but since they were probably acquired as slaves in Barbados, it is fair to assume that they would not have been sold for a lesser term of service in Boston.

Within three years the presence of slaves was enough to warrant a clause on slavery in the Body of Liberties. But the growth of the black population was slow. By 1700 there were only about one thousand blacks in New England. Indeed, throughout the colonial period the chief connection of the Puritans with African slaves came through the seaport merchants' involvement in the lucrative slave trade.

No stigma attached to participation in the slave trade; indeed, some of the great Boston and Newport fortunes were based on it. Yet in the New England colonies themselves slavery was not popular. Slaves were granted greater equality before the law than elsewhere in British America, and there was widespread concern for improving the status of the black servant. In part, these characteristics of the institution in New England were based on economics; in part they were the result of Puritanism.

In contrast to the economic life of the Southern colonies, there was in New England no staple crop that required large-scale cultivation by gangs of laborers. The New England farm could generally be operated without calling upon outside labor; when help was necessary, the supply of indentured servants was sufficient to meet it. By the third generation the concern of the colonists was, if anything, that farm holdings were becoming too small to be profitably worked by the average size family. While some farms in Massachusetts and Connecticut did utilize small amounts of slave labor, they were clearly the exceptions. The only agricultural area in which there was noticeable utilization of slaves was the Narragansett territory of Rhode Island—the "King's Province." There, a considerable number of blacks were employed in the dairy farming, horse breeding, and cattle raising that were peculiar to that region.

Overall, the slave population rarely exceeded 3 percent of the New England labor force during the colonial period. Most of those slaves were employed in the seaports such as Boston and Newport. There, they were hired out by their owners (frequently the shipowners involved in the slave trade) to work alongside free blacks and whites in a variety of occupations, including building, fishing, and whaling, and in the ropewalks, shipyards, distilleries, and other centers of industry in the community. They were able to develop certain skills and to acquire such privileges as were customary whenever slaves were hired out for skilled or semiskilled work in an urban environment.

While in New England there were fewer economic and social incentives to debase the black population than in Virginia and elsewhere, the Puritans also demonstrated somewhat less of the English racial bias against blacks than other seventeenth-century colonists. The Massachusetts law of 1641 guaranteed to slaves "all the liberties and Christian usages which the law of God established in Israel doth morally require." This meant that black slaves had the same protection against maltreatment as did white servants. The slave, in contrast to Southern practice, was married by civil authorities, and his marriage was binding in the eyes of the law. When accused of crimes by his master or others, the slave had a right to trial by jury. No master was free to arbitrarily inflict punishment upon his slave.

Recognized as a legal entity with rights before the law, the slave was also recognized as a person with a soul. Though segregated in meetinghouses and burial grounds, free blacks and slaves were allowed a role in the spiritual life of New England. Besides being included in family and congregational religious services, blacks were admitted to membership in the churches on the same basis as their white masters and neighbors. In 1641 a black female servant became a member of a New England church. Others followed, though not in the same proportion as whites. In theory at least, no racial bar to salvation was erected or envisioned by the Puritans—whites, Indians, and blacks were all eligible for God's saving grace. As Cotton Mather expressed it: "God is no respecter of persons," and "Negroes may be the elect of God."

A number of prominent New England clergy encouraged the spiritual progress of the region's black population. John Eliot urged improved treatment for slaves and attention to their education so as to better fit them for religious instruction. Cotton Mather taught black slaves and organized a Society of Negroes, which met at his home for prayers, catechizing, and instruction. Nevertheless, neither Eliot nor Mather, nor most of those who shared their concern criticized the institution of slavery. It was recognized in the Scriptures and the clergy advised those who had that unfortunate calling to submit and strive to serve their masters better.

One colonist whose apprehension of slavery's evils went deeper was Samuel Sewall. The son-in-law of John Hull, Sewall was one of the colony's richest merchants. He served as a magistrate and had been one of the panel of judges who condemned the witches at Salem. In 1700 he was serving as a judge of the Superior Court of Massachusetts. He had, he confided in his *Diary*, been "long and much dissatisfied with the Trade of fetching Negroes from Guinea and had a strong Inclination to write something about it." A Boston citizens' committee had been agitating for the imposition of a forty shilling per head tax on the import of slaves. That attempt to inhibit the growth of slavery, combined with the circulation of a petition for the "freeing of a negro and his wife unjustly held in Bondage," may have influenced Sewall to publish in Boston in 1700 the first tract against slavery written in America, *The Selling of Joseph*. His central premise in the volume was that "These Ethiopians, as black as they are; seeing they are the Sons and Daughters of the first *Adam*; the Brethren and Sisters of the Last *Adam*, and the Offspring of GOD; They ought to be treated with a Respect agreeable." "Originally and Naturally," he argued, "there is no such thing as Slavery." "Joseph," he recalled to his biblically versed audience, "was rightfully, no more a Slave to his Brethren, than they were to him, and they had no more Authority to *Sell* him than they had to *Slay* him."

While opposed to slavery, Sewall was not flattering to slaves. He accused them of laziness, untrustworthiness, and restiveness, and argued that they were less profitable employees than indentured servants. And while he believed in improving the treatment of blacks, and demonstrated that commitment in his personal conduct, he did not believe in assimilation. Nevertheless, Sewall was in advance of his day. More citizens of the Bay sided with John Saffin, who defended slavery in *A Brief and Candid Answer to . . . The Selling of Joseph* (Boston, 1701). Slavery, albeit in a mild form, continued to exist in New England until after the American Revolution.

The Puritans believed that all men were born with the stain of Adam's sin. Naturally depraved, man was doomed to a life of sin. Even saving grace could not completely restore the perfection of the soul; sanctification was never perfect in this life. While they hoped to establish a "city on a hill" more perfect than man had yet known, they did not believe that even a chosen people would be free from error. In the area of race relations they are clearly culpable when judged from the perspective of the present day; they failed to achieve equality and understanding between diverse races and cultures. The John Eliots and Samuel Sewalls may have come closer than most of their contemporaries to establishing better ethnic relations, and yet in the end they too failed. That failure is also part of the Puritan legacy.

PART FOUR |

NEW DIRECTIONS

17 | NEW DIRECTIONS: PURITANISM IN THE NEGLECTED DECADES

The fifty years following the cessation of the Salem witch trials is the most neglected period in the history of colonial New England. Isolated between the drama of the seventeenth century and the oncoming of the American Revolution, the early eighteenth century has too often been viewed as merely the anticlimax of the former or the prelude to the latter. But for those who lived then it was neither. It was a time of painful growth and adjustment, marked by new directions in politics, economics, and religion, and by strong attempts to recapture the past. Those who experienced the turmoil of the period were, to a greater or lesser extent, captives of the Puritan century, but their heritage was one that demanded action. The cumulative roles played by many led to the birth of a new nation, and it is fascinating to note the emerging rhetoric that anticipated later Revolutionary arguments. However, few if any even dreamed of creating a new nation or a new kingdom of God on earth.

Politically, the decades between the Glorious Revolution and the Great Awakening were relatively tranquil in some parts of New England. Both Connecticut and Rhode Island held charters insuring colonists the right to self-government, and not until the 1740s did factional divisions mar the consensus between rulers and ruled along the southern coast of New England. But Massachusetts was faced with a new charter that almost inevitably set the people against the crown, the legislature against the governor. Denied the self-rule to which they had been accustomed, the Bay colonists were confronted with a royal governor endowed with great legal powers but denied by royal instructions the flexibility that would have given him political strength. The General Court was capable of serving as a worthy antagonist to the chief executive. Rather than uniting to serve the common weal,

211

the government of Massachusetts was divided by continuing strife between the people's spokesmen and the king's. But even that generalization is too sweeping, for, as in the years before the revocation of the old charter, the "popular leaders" of Massachusetts were themselves divided by personal jealousies and differences over tactics. Against the backdrop of this political struggle Massachusetts history continued to unfold as economic differentiation grew, the colonies were drawn into the imperial wars, the administration of the colony changed due to population growth, and fiscal crises emerged out of economic growth.

DECADES OF READJUSTMENT AND CHANGE IN MASSACHUSETTS: 1692–1742

During the 1690s and early 1700s the orthodox leaders of Massachusetts Puritanism were sorely pressed to defend and revitalize the faith of their fathers. The charter obtained by Increase Mather lessened the voters' control over their government and thus diminished the prospects of continued state support for the Bay's Puritan churches. While such governors as Phipps and Stoughton had some sympathy for the objectives of the godly, the term of each was short and troubled. Later English governors had no incentive to sustain Puritanism. Furthermore, the disagreement between Mather and Elisha Cooke continued after their return to the Bay. With Cooke at its head the "old charter party" in the General Court took a line that was opposed both to the royal governor in politics and to the Mathers in religion. Facing new threats to orthodoxy, the Mather party would itself be forced to resort to innovation in their attempts to restore true religion.

The most feared challenge to traditional Puritanism came from the Connecticut River valley, where Solomon Stoddard guided the Northampton church. Educated at Harvard and graduated there in 1662, he had become the college's first librarian. Poor health led him to spend the years 1667–1669 in the Barbados Islands. On his return to New England he was called to the Northampton congregation to replace the deceased Eleazar Mather. Whereas Mather had been one of the foremost opponents of the Half-Way Covenant, Stoddard supported that innovation and brought the congregation quickly to his viewpoint.

In the ensuing years the Northampton pastor became known as a compelling orator, a stern moralist, and a spokesman for frontier interests. He blamed the affliction of King Philip's War on the tolerance and worldliness of Boston. He urged firmer measures against the Baptists and other religious dissenters, and also against the Indians. He was sharply critical of the relaxed moral standards of the times, particularly the growing materialism and opulent life style of the colony's political and economic leaders. The Mathers would have agreed with him on much of this if Stoddard had not broken from the orthodox clergy in his sacramental theology and in his ecclesiology.

Stoddard took his first step away from orthodoxy in his 1687 tract *The Safety of Appearing at the Day of Judgement in the Righteousness of Christ*. Denying the possibility of detecting the elect, he repudiated the very concept of limited membership and limited communion. While continuing to maintain that salvation was a gift of God and limited to a select number, he urged all professing Christians who led scandal-free lives and were familiar with true doctrine to avail themselves of all the ordinances provided by Christ—baptism, the Scriptures, preaching, private prayer, and the Lord's Supper. While partaking of these was not a seal of salvation, each of them could serve as a converting ordinance. The logic of this position pointed far beyond the Half-Way Covenant toward a Presbyterian type of parish membership, with the sacraments open to all. In certain respects this policy of "open communion" was scarcely an innovation. The Windsor church had once practiced it but abandoned it in 1647, while the First Church of Hartford had open communion from the 1660s to the 1730s. What set Stoddard apart was not the opening of communion but his contention that it was not merely a seal of the covenant, that it could also serve as a means of conversion for those not yet justified—a contention that his own Northampton church rejected in 1690 at the same time that it authorized the practice of open communion.

Stoddard's views on the Lord's Supper attracted criticism from the Mathers and other eastern clergy. The orthodox viewed as equally serious the Northampton clergyman's polity proposals, which appeared in his 1700 treatise *The Doctrine of Instituted Churches*. Drawing inspiration from the Old Testament, Stoddard sought to have the instituted church organized on a national basis. It would be governed by a synod consisting of elders representing the constituent churches and responsible for maintaining sound doctrine and for the training and placing of ministers. Regional synods would act as administrative agents of the national body. Within the individual congregation, the minister and ruling elders would hold authority in matters of doctrine and discipline. Though ruling elders would receive their power from the congregation, the minister would receive his from God through the agency of the national synod. The prime functions of the minister were to preach and administer the sacraments to all professing Christians who sought them.

In many respects Stoddard's plan bore a close resemblance to Presbyterianism, and Increase Mather did view Stoddard as leading a western movement for Presbyterianism. But Stoddard himself rejected Presbyterianism, looking for Old Testament rather than New Testament precedents for his national church. And the Presbyterians of New England were equally emphatic in disavowing themselves from Stoddard and his insistence on conversion through sacramental ordinances. In his own Connecticut Valley, clergymen like Westfield's Edward Taylor were allies of the Mathers. When the Hampshire Association was formed in 1714 its emphasis was toward Presbyterian-style discipline. While Stoddard was a prime mover in its organization, he had by then shelved his plan for an instituted church and did not view the association as a vehicle for extending the use of "converting ordinances."

Rebuffed by his own congregation and by the colonial clergy, Stoddard by 1710 had begun to seek a new way of reaching the unconverted masses of New England. While he still viewed receiving the sacraments as vital preparation for conversion, he began to argue that saving grace was conveyed primarily through the preaching of the Word. The sermons of ministers who themselves possessed saving grace was to be the means of reviving the faith. Stoddard's sermons had brought revivals to Northampton in 1679, 1684, and 1696 and would again bring a harvest of souls in 1712 and 1718. He found himself supported by many of his colleagues in his new approach. While his influence was never such as to warrant the title "pope" bestowed on him by some historians, Stoddard came to assume an importance along the Connecticut River comparable to that of the Mathers on the eastern shore.

While Stoddard's influence was rising on the frontier, the conservative clergy were also forced to deal with the growth of a liberal spirit in Boston and Cambridge. While Increase Mather had been absent in England, control of Harvard had rested in the hands of tutors John Leverett and William Brattle, who shared a dislike of dogmatism and an attachment to a more liberal and catholic attitude toward the faith. Many students, including the young Benjamin Colman, found their views refreshing and persuasive. Upon the president's return, he restricted that spirit, adding to his unpopularity in some quarters. The liberals found ready allies in Elisha Cooke's party. While Cooke's motives were predominantly political—an antipathy toward the secular influence of Increase and Cotton—some of the key figures in his faction, such as the merchant Thomas Brattle, were also concerned with changing the college leadership for religous reasons.

The liberals were gratified when William Brattle was called in 1696 to be pastor of the Cambridge congregation. Two years later the Brattles and the Leveretts united with other Boston merchants to organize a new church in the city, and they chose Benjamin Colman to be their pastor. After graduating from Harvard in 1692, Colman had continued his studies in England, where he had made the acquaintance of numerous English nonconformists. The Boston liberals recognized the presence of local opposition to their plans and advised Colman to seek ordination in England. He accepted Presbyterian ordination and set sail for New England. The new church, the fourth Puritan house of worship in Boston, was erected on land donated by Thomas Brattle. In the fall of 1699 its members explained their views to the community in the "Brattle Street Manifesto."

The new congregation asserted its allegiance to the Westminster Confession of Faith. They declared their intention to have the pastor read the Scriptures without commentary and to utilize set forms of prayer. All children were to be baptized and public examination of candidates for membership was eliminated. Communion was to be open. All members were to share in the choice of pastor and the governance of the church. These rights of governance were explicitly granted to women as well as men. Though opposed to the new church, the Mathers were powerless to interfere with its formation.

In 1698 the liberal attack on Increase Mather's Harvard presidency had been renewed with an unsuccessful legislative attempt to require the college president to reside in Cambridge. In 1700 a new charter was approved for the college that included the residency requirement. For six months Mather attempted to live in Cambridge, but he then returned to his Boston congregation and resigned from the college. Capitalizing on the fact that the charter did not require the other officers to be resident, the Cooke faction arranged for the vice-president, Samuel Willard, to act as president while still being allowed to live in Boston and minister to the South Church. Under the leadership of Willard and John Leverett (who succeeded him in 1708), the liberal cause continued to advance at Harvard.

The Mathers had no greater right to claim exclusive possession of the Puritan tradition than did Samuel Willard, Benjamin Colman, or Solomon Stoddard. All were faced with a slackening of popular interest in religion and each sought new ways to make the faith important again in the lives of the people. Though the Mathers took more care than others to wrap themselves in the mantle of the founders, they were themselves willing to innovate to achieve their goals. And, peculiarly resembling Stoddard, they first sought institutional remedies to the decline of religion before they too were drawn to the path of persuasion.

Even before the loss of the old charter had deprived the churches of stable support, critics had identified congregational autonomy as one of the weaknesses of the New England Way, thwarting all attempts to impose uniformity on recalcitrant churches. Whereas the state had previously lent its weight to synodical platforms such as those of 1649 and 1662, after the loss of the charter the full burden of enforcing orthodoxy fell on the churches themselves. Some New Englanders, impressed by the developing union of English dissenters, began to look more favorably upon some of the controls provided by Presbyterianism. A comparable influence was exerted by the indige- nous tradition of clerical consociation dating back to the earliest days of the colonies. Late in 1690 an association of interested Boston area ministers was established in Cambridge. Every six weeks they would meet together to discuss common problems, attempt to resolve them, and lend each other mutual assistance.

Increase Mather had become strongly committed to the idea of clerical association through his contacts with leading English dissenters. He may also have remembered the Cromwellian supervision of the ministry by triers and ejectors, which had been approved both by Congregationalists and by moderate Presbyterians. While in England in 1691, Mather played an important role in bringing together Mathew Mead and John Howe for the drafting of the "Heads of Agreement," which was designed to serve as the basis for a union of English Con- gregationalists and Presbyterians. That union was short-lived, but in New England, Increase and Cotton Mather worked to make the "Heads of Agreement" the basis for uniting the fragmented elements of American Puritanism. It was their hope that ministerial associ- ations might establish some control over the individual churches in their respective regions.

Nurtured by the Mathers, the association movement gained strength, with ministers in other regions of Massachusetts organizing themselves along the lines of the Cambridge group. Many clergymen were con- cerned about what they saw as a decline of religion, and the association movement seemed a concrete plan for dealing with that problem. The movement was given further impetus in 1704, when twenty-seven ministers signed a circular letter calling for the various associations in the colony to be strengthened and recommending that they develop closer relationships with one another. In September of 1705 representatives of the five associations based at Cambridge, Weymouth, Salem, Sherborne, and Bristol met in Boston and drew up the "Proposals of 1705." This document called for the formation of associations in areas where they did not exist and the organization of the clergy of the associations into a standing council. The associations would provide for discussion of disputed issues and would also examine and recommend candidates for the ministry, supervise the member churches and advise them when necessary, and withdraw from fellowship with any offending congregation that persisted in error.

Despite its initial broad support, the proposals were not effectively implemented. New associations were formed, but standing councils were not adopted, nor were the associations able to exert any significant authority. Part of the explanation for this failure lay in the identification of the association movement with the Mathers. Many of the old charter party had never ceased to mistrust Increase and Cotton and instinctively reacted against whatever they proposed. Also important was the opposition of a group, led by John Wise, who wished to preserve congregational autonomy. Critical of the plan from the outset, Wise published *The Churches Quarrel Espoused* in 1710 and a *Vindication of the Government of the New England Churches* in 1717. Both were strong defenses of congregational autonomy, the *Vindication* pointing to the writings of the ancient church fathers, the "noble nature" of the Cambridge Platform, and—significantly—the "Light of Nature," as support for his contentions. Wise gained considerable support from clergy who viewed with skepticism the move to limit their power; bereft of the backing of the state, the proposals failed.

Thwarted in their attempt to restructure the churches of Massachusetts, the Mathers turned to other means of revitalizing religion. In the 1710s, Cotton Mather began to dispense with theological disputation and to work toward achieving an ecumenical pietistic consensus. Seeking a new "Christian Union," he saw its base as the common practice of piety. The effort owed much to the similar movement in late seventeenth-century England to establish societies for the reformation of morality, and something, as well, to the developing pietism of the continent. *Bonifacius. An Essay Upon the Good* (1710) was but one expression of his concern. In addition to the printing of manuals on the good life, Mather organized nondenominational benevolent societies that resembled the types of revival-generated activities typical of nineteenth-century American Protestantism. Ridiculed by some, misunderstood by others, Cotton Mather's call to the saints to unite in improving their society did lead to a healing of some of the divisions of Boston society. Mather himself began to find charitable things to say about the Quakers, and in 1718 he participated in the ordination of the Baptist minister Elisha Callendar.

Political events were also bringing Bostonians together. The appointment of Joseph Dudley as governor of Massachusetts in 1702 had been greeted with displeasure by both the old charter party and the Mathers' party, both groups remembering Dudley's efforts in getting the old charter revoked and his conduct as deputy governor of the Dominion. Almost immediately upon taking office, Dudley removed Elisha Cooke from his judgeship on the Superior Court and fired Elisha Cooke, Jr., as clerk of that court. When, in the following year, the elder Cooke was elected to the council, Dudley negatived his selection and that of his allies. In each of the next twelve years Cooke was named to the council by the lower House, and each year Dudley rejected him. Having set himself in opposition to the old charter party, Dudley attempted to build his own support from among merchants who were in competition with the Brattles, the Sewalls, and their allies, and he used his patronage to secure adherents to his cause. But he and his merchant allies opened themselves to charges of poor administration and abuse of power. By 1707 the Mathers had emerged as the strongest critics of the ethical shortcomings of the Dudley regime, uniting with their former opponents in Cooke's camp.

Adding to Dudley's difficulties was the multiplicity of problems with which his administration was faced and the lack of freedom imposed on him by his English authorities. The governor had to contend with an escalation of French and Indian attacks on the frontier, a continuing trade decline that had begun with the Glorious Revolution, a growing colonial debt, and runaway inflation brought about by the steady depreciation of the colony's bills of credit. But the English authorities didn't seem truly concerned about the colony; their instructions to Dudley denied him the latitude needed to deal with these problems, dictating instead that he insist on an enlargement of the governor's prerogatives. As a result, administration demands merely fed the opposition. By the close of Dudley's tenure in 1714 a fundamental political division had been created in Massachusetts. Using terms derived from the political rhetoric of the English Commonwealth tradition, the colonial leaders began to refer to themselves as the "country" party, and the governor and his supporters as the "court."

As historian Timothy Breen has described them, "the 'Court' faction consisted of men who for a variety of personal reasons had rejected the voluntaristic elements of Puritan political theory. This group tended to discourage, even to fear, mass participation in government affairs." Numerically small, the court faction was built around those who held patronage positions, merchants who profited from government contracts, Anglicans, and cultural Anglophiles. Their opponents, the country party, emphasized the need for popular participation in government and the need for holding all magistrates accountable.

In Massachusetts, Elisha Cooke, Jr.—Harvard graduate, physician, and prosperous landlord—emerged by 1710 as the leader of the country party. The old division with the Mathers was forgotten, and on the political front the younger Cooke was able to unite Boston. Once again the city selected men from the Mathers' faction to represent the community in the General Court. Using their power to thwart Dudley in the Bay and utilizing London friends such as Henry Ashurst to convey the governor's failures to the ministry in England, the country faction played a key role in Dudley's recall in 1714.

The administrations of Dudley's immediate successors—Governor Samuel Shute (1716–1722), Lieutenant Governor William Dummer (1722–1727), and Governor William Burnet (1727–1729)—were even less successful. All three followed instructions in trying to force the General Court to establish a permanent fixed salary for the governor, but the country faction easily blocked their attempts. Cooke attacked the king's claim to pine trees growing on private property (reserved by the English law for the use of the royal navy) as an infringement on the rights of the private property owner. And he agitated for an increase in the issue of bills of credit to ease the effects of the colonial currency shortage. Moving on these fronts, he was able to keep his faction united politically, in spite of disputes over Cotton Mather's advocacy of inoculation during the 1721 smallpox epidemic and the uproar created by the attacks on the clergy by James and Benjamin Franklin in their *New England Courant*. None of the governors was able to master the political opposition and each was in turn replaced.

Governor Jonathan Belcher (1730–1741) was able to make some limited headway in the early years of his administration. With the help of one of his appointees, William Shirley, he was able to encourage the challenge to Cooke's leadership mounted by younger Boston merchants such as Thomas Hutchinson and Andrew Oliver. But, as the decade wore on, it became obvious that Shirley and not Belcher had the support of the court faction, while at the same time the problems of the colony placed the governor in a steadily deteriorating position.

William Shirley, appointed governor in 1741, was the most successful of the royally appointed governors of Massachusetts. Part of his success was due to the leadership losses of the country faction—the death of Cooke in 1737 and the impoverishment of many of Boston's leaders following the enforced closure of a land bank they had organized. He was also aided by the further escalation of the war with the French. The increase of military activities brought a sharp rise in the governor's power, due to the resultant increase in patronage positions and his influence in the awarding of military contracts. At the same time Shirley took advantage of the growth of a viable county system of administration in Massachusetts to extend his influence through appointment of justices of the peace. Politically astute, the new governor also recognized the need to make concessions to local interests and was thus able to blunt the edge of an opposition that was itself somewhat muted by wartime patriotism. Nevertheless, the potential of the country party remained, for the colonists had learned to subordinate religious and other differences to the need for political unity.

CONNECTICUT POLITICS AND RELIGION: 1689–1734

The situation of Rhode Island and Connecticut differed radically from that of the Bay in that both of the charter colonies were free from the onus of a royal governor and thus, except for being required to abide by the Navigation Acts, virtually autonomous. With more freedom to act, the officials of both colonies were less likely to draw comparisons between themselves and the founding generation and were less weighted down by their history. Both, in the early eighteenth century, were relatively free of the factionalism that characterized their northern neighbor, and when political divisions did develop in the 1740s they did so as a result of conflicting ambitions among the colonial leadership rather than differences over the nature of political life.

While Connecticut was free from royal control, the colonists' recollection of the ease with which they had been absorbed into the Dominion of New England kept them from forgetting that they were part of the empire. Consequently, the attitude taken toward the mother country by the colony's early eighteenth-century leaders was one of caution and moderation. Even while they took steps to legislate a stronger system of church government they balanced that with an adoption of the English Toleration Act and other gestures of apparent liberalization designed for English consumption.

One step taken by the Connecticut magistrates in support of true religion was their chartering of a new Puritan college. The idea for such an institution had earlier been urged by John Davenport, but had been allowed to die. At the turn of the century the Reverend James Pierpont, Davenport's clerical successor at New Haven and husband of Davenport's granddaughter, revived the notion of a Connecticut college and met with encouragement from fellow clergymen. Though this new movement was firmly based in Connecticut, their loss of leadership at Harvard led the Mathers to give encouragement and support. In the summer of 1701, Pierpont and his colleagues began actively to solicit a charter, which the General Assembly soon granted. The charter placed absolute control of the college in the hands of a Board of Trustees, which was to number between seven and eleven, all of whom were to be Connecticut clergymen over the age of forty. On 11 November 1701 the trustees officially established their collegiate school. While their broad purpose was to educate young men in the arts and sciences so as to serve state as well as church, the board specifically announced its desire to "promote the power and Purity of Religion and Best Edification and peace of these New England Churches." To insure against the latitudinarianism of Harvard they specifically stipulated the use of William Ames's *Medulla Theologicae* and the Westminster Confession in the curriculum.

During its early history the college was a barely functioning concern. Its permanent location was undecided—at various times instruction was carried on in Saybrook, Killingsworth, Milford, East Guilford, Wethersfield, and New Haven, with Saybrook being the principal site. For much of the time there was no rector (president), and effectual control of the college was maintained by young and inexperienced tutors. Jeremiah Dummer succeeded in soliciting donations from Englishmen for the college library, but the books remained packed away, awaiting a decision on the school's site. Finally, however, the problems were ironed out. Between 1717 and 1719, New Haven was selected as the home of the school, it was named Yale College after one of its benefactors (Elihu Yale), the library was united with the students, and a rector, the Reverend Timothy Cutler, was installed.

While Yale had been undergoing its protracted birth, the trustees of the college had midwifed another plan to protect orthodoxy. At their 1703 meeting they proposed that the clergy of the colony petition the General Assembly to endorse officially the Confession of Faith of the Westminster Assembly as incorporated in the statement of the Massachusetts Reforming Synod. At that time the proposal failed to gain the support of the colony government, but in May of 1708 the assembly agreed to a request by Governor Gurdon Saltonstall—

himself a former clergyman and close associate of the Yale Trustees —that a synod be called to meet during the college commencement at Saybrook. Eight of the twelve ministers chosen to sit in the synod were trustees of the college, and they dominated the assembly's deliberations.

The synod recommended a statement that included three sections. The first adopted the 1658 Savoy Confession of the English Congregationalists. The third endorsed the 1691 "Heads of Agreement." The second section contained the real meat of the proposal. Divided into fifteen articles and primarily reflecting the thought of James Pierpont, it called for the establishment of ecclesiastical consociations in each county. These consociations would have the task of overseeing local congregations and would include lay representatives as well as clergy. Ministerial associations would also be established in each county and be given the responsibility of approving ministerial candidates. A general ministerial assembly would meet annually. Congregations not participating in this system would be declared not in communion with the established churches.

This Saybrook Platform was accepted by the Connecticut General Assembly with the provision that it not be binding on any church that did not wish to accept it. Within a year the counties of Hartford, New London, Fairfield, and New Haven had all formed the appropriate groups. A compromise between Congregational and Presbyterian principles, the document was an imperfect disciplinary tool. But the large number of churches accepting it offered hope that orthodoxy could— at least in those churches—be maintained, especially since being declared in noncommunion would deprive dissenting congregations of the tax and other privileges of establishment. Thus, not only did Connecticut Puritans adopt a platform where the Mathers had failed but in Connecticut control of the state by the godly gave some strength to the new structure. As a result, Connecticut would gradually evolve toward a closer affinity with the Presbyterianism of the Middle Colonies than with the Congregationalism of the Bay.

18 | ENLIGHTENMENT AND EVANGELICALISM

Even while the Mathers and their Connecticut counterparts were seeking ways of rekindling the faith of their fathers, Puritanism in New England was being undermined by new currents of thought being imported from Europe. The Enlightenment, often dated from the publication of Isaac Newton's *Principia Mathematica* in 1686 and Jock Locke's *Essay Concerning Human Understanding* and *Two Treatises on Government* three years later, represented in its essence a challenge to the traditional reliance upon authority in religious and secular life, and carried an assertion of man's ability to discover the secrets of the universe and exert some control over his destiny. Pushed to its logical extreme, the Enlightenment would later become a philosophical movement totally antithetical to the Calvinist world view that lay at the core of New England Puritanism. But in the early eighteenth century, in England and in the colonies, many were attracted to the philosophers' claim to have discovered natural laws, their optimistic view of man, and their skepticism toward all orthodoxies. Though John Wise's *Vindication of the Churches* rested heavily upon a natural law philosophy, in the Anglo-American world the Enlightenment left its mark more particularly upon Anglicans. In the eyes of New Englanders, the most noticeable sign of the new ideas was the rapid growth of the Church of England, particularly in Connecticut.

ANGLICAN GROWTH IN PURITAN COLONIES

The expansion of Anglicanism had causes that went considerably beyond Enlightenment philosophy. The formation in England in 1701 of the Society for the Propagation of the Gospel in Foreign Parts (SPG) was a direct response to the need for an expanded church

223

effort in Virginia, but the society's activities soon spread to the north. In 1702, George Keith, a former Presbyterian turned Quaker then Anglican, arrived in Boston as an SPG missionary. Over the next decades he was followed by others, much to the chagrin of the Congregationalists and Presbyterians, who complained that these purported missionaries were devoting their energies to the populated Puritan regions rather than to the unchurched frontier. But despite the concern of the established clergy, Anglicanism in the first two decades of the century made few real advances. Its strength remained limited to royal officials and their circle of supporters. In Connecticut as late as 1722 there was not a single full-time Anglican minister in the colony. But in that year the Church of England was to register its most spectacular achievement of the colonial period.

The books collected by Jeremiah Dummer for Yale had provided the Connecticut college with an excellent—and modern—library. Many of the donations were by Anglicans and included Church of England theological treatises. The Arminian, latitudinarian theology contained therein was far more compatible than Calvinism to the progressive thought of the Enlightenment. Timothy Cutler, the rector of Yale, had been gradually moving toward the Church of England even before he accepted the leadership of the college—perhaps having been influenced in that direction in the days when his father had been one of Andros's firmest supporters. Cutler and the Yale graduate and tutor Samuel Johnson became the center of a group of seven ministers who met regularly to read and discuss Anglican works. Rumors about the prevalence of Arminian teachings at Yale began to spread. The possibility of a confrontation over the issue attracted large crowds to the 1722 commencement. When during the exercises Rector Cutler concluded his prayer with the phrase "and let all the people say, amen," his use of that phrase from the Book of Common Prayer signaled his apostasy. On the day after the commencement the trustees listened to Cutler, Johnson, John Hart, Samuel Whittelsey, Jared Eliot, Daniel Brown, and James Wetmore declare that they were "persuaded of the invalidity of the Presbyterian [and Congregational] ordination, in opposition to the Episcopal." Governor Saltonstall called a meeting of the trustees and other clergy to attempt to confute the dissidents. But the clergy of New England had become more accustomed to citing church platforms than to thoughtful theologizing, and they were a poor match for Johnson and the others, who had painstakingly studied the issues. Though public pressure won Hart, Whittelsey, and Eliot back to orthodoxy, the other four made plans to go to England to be ordained.

Timothy Cutler returned to the colonies to accept a parish in Boston. Samuel Johnson returned to Connecticut, where he became the driving force behind New England Anglicanism. As vicar of the Anglican parish in Stamford, he guided the growth of his denomination so that within twenty years there were seven priests and over two thousand Anglican communicants in Connecticut. All the priests had graduated from Yale, following Johnson's own path. In fact Johnson encouraged Bishop George Berkeley—an important Enlightenment philosopher and later bishop in the Church of England—to donate books and scholarship funds to Yale.

During this period of growth Johnson worked diligently to insure the toleration of the Church of England. Though Connecticut had adopted the English Toleration Act of 1708, Anglicans were classified as dissenters in the colony. They therefore had to register with town clerks, and their taxes were applied to the support of the established Puritan churches. From 1725 to 1727 Johnson waged a campaign against these provisions, complaining repeatedly to the English authorities and threatening the colonial magistrates with charter revocation. As a result of his efforts, Governor Joseph Talcott and the assembly moved to forestall English action by legislation allowing any person who regularly attended Anglican worship to have his taxes directed to the Church of England clergyman. Though from Johnson's viewpoint the law was imperfectly administered, it was a major achievement and paved the way for similar concessions for Baptists and Quakers.

While most members of New England's Anglican establishment had been drawn from the upper classes, Johnson and his SPG associates in the 1720s had their greatest success among the lower classes of the region, men and women for whom the increasingly middle-class Puritan churches had little appeal. But success brought its own problems, and the Anglicans found that their distance from England's bishops posed numerous difficulties. Johnson worked diligently for the appointment of an American bishop; his efforts aroused the suspicion and ire of his non-Anglican neighbors but met with little response in England. That failing, he began to borrow from the Puritan tradition from which he had departed. Beginning in 1734 he organized meetings of the regional Anglican clergy in a fashion reminiscent of the Mathers' associations. He encouraged the use of lay preachers as a means of utilizing potential candidates for the ministry until they could go to England for orders. And he accepted the strengthening of parish vestries as a way of filling the power vacuum created by the absence of bishops.

JONATHAN EDWARDS AND THE GREAT AWAKENINGS

While the Church of England was making notable strides in expanding its New England base, "Arminianism" had been spreading as well. While it is perhaps true that Arminianism as properly understood did not exist in New England outside of the Anglican church, it must be recognized that the use of the term by English and American Puritans had seldom been precise. What had happened in many corners of New England under the direct and indirect influence of the Enlightenment was a growing emphasis on man and his morality. Religion was becoming more rational, and preachers increasingly described the conduct expected of men in a way that could be interpreted as meaning that man could influence his own fate. Even Cotton Mather's injunctions to "do good," though intended as statements of what was required of the elect, could be read as prescriptions for earthly and eternal happiness. A result of the New Englander's growing worldliness as much as being an effect of the new rationalism, the appeal to the mind had replaced the appeal to the heart in many of the region's pulpits. The suggestion that man could save himself or that acting as if one were saved might hasten conversion, whether preached by Samuel Johnson or a member of the New Haven ministerial association, was anathema to many clergymen. One such was Jonathan Edwards.

Edwards had one of the more interesting ancestries in colonial New England. His maternal grandfather was Solomon Stoddard. His forebears included Winthrops and Mathers and, on his mother's side, Thomas Hooker and John Davenport. His own grandson would be Aaron Burr. The son of the Reverend Timothy Edwards and his wife, Esther, Edwards was born and educated in the small rivertown of East Windsor, Connecticut. As a youth he showed strong interest in the natural world and in the practice of piety. Just before reaching the age of thirteen he was sent to Yale College. Following his graduation he remained for a further two years of study, during the second of which he underwent a conversion experience. From 1722 to 1724 he served as pastor to a parish that had split from the First Presbyterian Church in New York City, leaving when the division was healed. After two years as a tutor at Yale, he was called as an assistant to his grandfather, Solomon Stoddard, in Northampton. When Stoddard died in 1729, Edwards succeeded him as pastor.

Invited to deliver a public lecture in Boston in 1731, Edwards took the occasion to launch into a strong defense of traditional Calvinism, particularly the doctrine of man's total dependence upon God. While such a message would hardly have been startling a hundred years earlier, it was a measure of the century's changes that it did strike some in his audience as new. Elaborating on the same theme in a series of sermons at Northampton, Edwards in 1734 began to reap a harvest of conversions which soon spread to other towns along the Connecticut River. The energies of the new converts were directed to extra prayer meetings, charitable works, and other pietistic activities. But if the doctrine of man's dependence on God could breed exhilaration and release for those who believed themselves saved, it could breed despair in others. Some of the momentum of the revival was lost when Edwards's uncle Joseph Hawley committed suicide in the spring of 1735.

The Northampton revival was little different from those that Stoddard and other clergymen had seen in their congregations, little different from the awakening that had followed John Cotton's arrival in Boston in the 1630s, but there was a sense of expectancy in New England that fed upon the publication of Edwards's *A Faithful Narrative of the Surprising Work of God* (originally written as a letter to Benjamin Colman). Many saw in Edwards's description of the revival the beginning of a great design of the Lord, perhaps the beginning of the millennium. The reception of George Whitefield in New England in 1740 seemed further evidence of a providential design. An English Anglican priest and an associate of John and Charles Wesley in what would become the Methodist movement, Whitefield had begun preaching to large audiences in Savannah, Georgia, and gradually made his way north, attracting crowds of up to twenty thousand. One of the most powerful orators of his age, Whitefield's religious appeal was to the heart. Unsophisticated theologically, his preaching nevertheless drew emotional responses and conversions whenever he appeared. His presence served as a catalyst, igniting revivals in numerous New England churches. He was welcomed by Edwards in Northampton, and by the faculties of Harvard and Yale. Inevitably he attracted imitators.

First to follow Whitefield into New England was the Reverend Gilbert Tennent, who toured the region from December 1740 to March 1741. A graduate of his father's Log College and an ordained minister of the Philadelphia Presbytery, Tennent met with remarkable success. The appeal to the heart was once again sweeping New England. But Tennent went further than Whitefield in his message. Arguing that "the case of such is much to be pitied, who have no other but Pharisee-Shepherds, or unconverted Teachers," he elaborated on the dangers of an unconverted ministry, declared that such "natural men" had no place in the pulpit, and questioned their ability to serve as instruments through whom God would save men. It should be noted that this was not original doctrine: Puritans from William Perkins through John Cotton and Solomon Stoddard had insisted upon the need for clergy themselves to have been justified, and only with the liberalization of membership requirements was it possible to question whether a clergyman was indeed a saint. But Tennent, preaching this traditional doctrine at a time of great emotional excitement and encouraging believers to abandon their congregations and parishes in search of effective ministers, laid the groundwork for considerable dissension.

It remained for the next of the major itinerants—John Davenport's great-grandson, James Davenport—to initiate the division of New Englanders into New Lights (supporters of the revivals) and Old Lights (opponents of the revivals). Pastor of a congregation in Southold, Long Island, he had heard Whitefield while attending a synod in Philadelphia and had become an ardent disciple. Indeed, all but a few would have proclaimed him too ardent—an enthusiast in the worse sense of the word. His preaching was shrill, disjointed, loaded with invective. He gyrated on the platform and tore off his clothing above the waist. Worse still was his message. Davenport believed that only the spirit mattered and that learning was its enemy—at one point he presided over the burning of hundreds of books in New London. As religious historian Edwin Gaustad has described him,

Pretending to be able to distinguish infallibly and immediately the elect from the damned, he loudly and publicly greeted the former as brethren, the latter as neighbors. With a special vengeance he denounced his fellow ministers, calling them at random and without proof pharisees, unconverted men, blind guides, and wolves in sheeps' clothing.

Connecticut authorities expelled him from their colony in June of 1742. Massachusetts magistrates declared him insane upon banishing him later in the same year. Davenport eventually repented and brought this spectacular phase of his career to an end, but the damage he had done was irreparable.

The preaching of the itinerants stirred many souls to greater religious sensibility, and some to enthusiasm. But some clergymen, like Boston's Charles Chauncy and Yale's Rector Thomas Clap, emerged as sharp critics of the revivals, singling out extreme enthusiasm, the encouragement of itinerancy (which threatened the important relationship between pastor and congregation), and the disdain for the intellect. The career of James Davenport alone was enough to document their case. By the time George Whitefield returned to New England in 1745 the landscape was dotted with lay exhorters who believed that grace alone qualified them to preach. Increasingly, congregations divided after bitter disputes over the revival. Some of the New Light Separates eventually became Baptists so as to gain tax relief, a development that further alienated the conservatives.

The major itinerants should not be seen as typical of the Awakening. While they were the sparks igniting fires throughout the colonies, it was numerous pastors who kept those fires burning in their congregations and who nurtured the New Light in the souls of the saved. To gain a more accurate and favorable insight into the nature of the Awakening one does best to focus on the work of Jonathan Edwards. Himself an avid student of the Enlightenment, it was Edwards's self-appointed task to capture the essence of Calvinism and explain it in a way compatible with the best thought of the age. The most outstanding theologian since the generation of the founders, he is held by many to be the greatest theologian in American history. During the period of the Awakening he combined his extensive pastoral duties with the preparation and publication of two major evaluations of the nature of the revivals and of religious experience in general—*Some Thoughts concerning the Recent Revival of Religion* (1743) and *A Treatise concerning the Religious Affections* (1746).

Edwards was aware of the extravagance of Davenport and others, and he disapproved of them. The whole, he argued, must not be judged by its parts, but nor should the fact that the whole is good blind one to the evils within it. Examining the positive effects of the Awakening, he pointed to an increase in concern for eternal things, improved moral conduct, awakened consciences, stricter observance of the Sabbath, numerous conversions, and closer attention to the Bible. Without doubt, he concluded, this must be the work of God. The evils existed, but they were not intrinsic to the revivals. Rather, they were the results of human imperfection: "The beam of light, as it comes from the fountain of light upon our hearts, is pure; but, as it is reflected thence, it is mixed." Examining with precision the psychology of conversion in *A Treatise concerning the Religious Affections*, he explained that "true religion consists, in great measure, in vigorous and lively actings of the inclination and will of the soul, or the fervent exercises of the heart," and he contended that true conversion led to human renewal and sanctified behavior. Edwards himself believed that the millennium was to dawn in New England and that the saints had ·a responsibility to prepare for it by purging their society of its corruptions.

In his own preachings Edwards used affective language to reach the hearts of his congregations and kindle their imagination. Occasionally, as in his sermon at Enfield, "Sinners in the Hands of an Angry God," he appears to have acted in a way that supports the contention that he tried to scare men into grace. But if Edwards frequently tried to shake men's assurance by preaching the terrors of the Lord and the tenuousness of man's situation, he almost invariably coupled that with the assurance that "there is a Saviour provided, who is excellent and glorious; who has shed his precious blood for sinners, and is every way sufficient to save them; who stands ready to receive them."

Fiercely as the fires of revival burned, they nevertheless were of short duration. While the New Lights heightened the general concern for moral behavior and their commitment to purifying society continued to influence many, there were limits as to how much of the past the evangelicals could recapture. The secularization and individualism of a half century were not to be stripped away by a series of sermons. Edwards himself learned that lesson in Northampton. His attempt to enforce a strict moral code alienated some of the community's leaders when the behavior of their children was questioned. An attempt to abolish open communion and restrict the sacraments to the elect was almost unanimously rejected. Edwards was forced from his pulpit. He entered into a period of ministering to the Indians at Stockbridge, Massachusetts, where he was sharply critical of the colony's agents who exploited the tribes. It was at Stockbridge that he composed his massive treatises on *Original Sin* and *Freedom of the Will*. Later he was named president of Princeton College, where he died from the effects of an inoculation against smallpox.

Where does the true nature of the Awakening lie? In the career of Jonathan Edwards or in that of a James Davenport? Certainly historian Richard Hofstadter was correct in identifying the potential antiintellectualism in the revivals, a potential that came to the fore as revivalism moved to the American frontier in later generations. But in the theologically educated New England of the 1740s it was Davenport who was the aberration and who was shunned by most of the revivalists. More fundamental is the question of what precipitated the Awakening, what made the citizens of New England receptive to the preachings of Edwards, Whitefield, and the others? A number of historians have, by illuminating various aspects of the period, highlighted some of the factors involved. Philip Greven, Richard Bushman, and J. M. Bumstead have all pointed out that the Awakening had its strongest impact on towns founded in the early years of the eighteenth century. Bushman identifies the source of much of the revivals' appeal as based on guilt and anxiety: social life had become increasingly anticommunal, individualistic, and unethical; for many the Awakening offered a release from guilt in yielding to God. Greven has pointed to the need for further study of the social and particularly the family context in which converted saints moved. Others have pointed out that the revivals were able to build new communities of saints, brought together regardless of class, economic, or political divisions, in a society increasingly fragmented by such forces. Research now in progress will probably add to the completeness of the picture. But whatever forces existed to add to or detract from the appeal, the Great Awakening was essentially a religious phenomenon. The revivalists, like the English Puritans of the sixteenth and early seventeenth centuries, were responding to the needs of the people for reassurance and direction, for release from anxiety and motivation for action. It affected people of all classes and professions, in Boston and on the frontier, dividing families and congregations—again like the early Puritan movement.

The effects of the Awakening were mixed. It fragmented numerous congregations and, concentrated as it was in the Puritan churches, weakened the strength of the religious establishment and lent inadvertent aid to the cause of religious freedom. At the same time the Awakening accentuated the factionalism developing in Connecticut. It minimized the importance of denominational differences for some, making the experience of saving grace seem of greater relevance than quarrels over ecclesiastical structure. The Awakening probably did improve the moral tone of the society. And it revived the religious sense of New England's mission, leading many down a path that would create a revolution and a new nation just as surely as would the natural rights philosophy of other colonists.

SUGGESTIONS FOR FURTHER READING

CHAPTER 1

M. M. Knappen's study, *Tudor Puritanism* (Chicago, 1939), remains the best treatment of the pre-Elizabethan origins of Puritanism, but for Elizabeth's reign has been supplanted by Patrick Collinson's detailed *The Elizabethan Puritan Movement* (Los Angeles, 1967). For those wishing a brief but careful survey of the course of the Reformation in England from the accession of Elizabeth to the Restoration of the Stuarts, H. G. Alexander, *Religion in England, 1558–1662* (London, 1968) is strongly recommended. Specific aspects of the spread and impact of Puritanism may be pursued in Mark Curtis, *Oxford and Cambridge in Transition, 1558–1642* (London, 1959); William Haller, *The Elect Nation: The Meaning and Relevance of Foxe's "Book of Martyrs"* (New York, 1963); Patrick McGrath, *Papists and Puritans under Elizabeth I* (London, 1967); Christopher Hill, *Economic Problems of the Church from Archbishop Whitgift to the Long Parliament* (London, 1956); and Horton Davies, *Worship and Theology in England from Cranmer to Hooker, 1534–1603* (Princeton, 1970). Primary sources for the period are collected in H. C. Porter, *Puritanism in Tudor England* (London, 1971) and Leonard Trinterud, *Elizabethan Puritanism* (New York, 1971).

CHAPTER 2

Comprehending Puritan theology is one of the most important yet one of the most demanding tasks for the student who wishes to understand seventeenth-century England and New England. The best explanation of Puritan religious thought remains that of Perry Miller, particularly as expressed in *The New England Mind: The Seventeenth Century* (New York, 1939) and in selected essays collected in *Errand into the Wilderness* (Cambridge, Mass., 1956) and *Nature's Nation* (Cambridge, Mass., 1967). Charles H. George and Katherine George in *The Protestant Mind of the English Reformation, 1570–1640* (Princeton, 1961) have attempted to minimize the differences between Anglicans and Puritans, while John F. New, *Anglican and Puritan, 1558–1640* emphasizes the theological differences. Geoffrey Nuttall, *The Holy Spirit in Puritan Faith and Experience* (Lon-

232

don, 1946) sheds light on an important dimension of Puritan theology that is significant for an understanding of New England "antinomians" and Quakers as well as of English sectaries. Norman Petit, *The Heart Prepared: Grace and Conversion in Puritan Spiritual Life* (New Haven, 1966) treats a central Puritan doctrine. John Eusden has translated and edited William Ames's *Marrow of Theology* (Boston, 1968), a key text for the Puritans themselves and one that retains its value for modern students of the movement. The attraction that Puritanism held for many is variously dealt with in Michael Walzer, *The Revolution of the Saints: A Study of the Origins of Radical Politics* (New York, 1968); Christopher Hill, *Society and Puritanism in Pre-Revolutionary England*, 2nd ed. (New York, 1967); David Little, *Religion, Order, and Law: A Study of Pre-Revolutionary England* (New York, 1969); and Keith Thomas, *Religion and the Decline of Magic* (New York, 1971).

CHAPTER 3

The combination of religious, social, economic, and political developments that precipitated the Great Migration may be examined in Carl Bridenbaugh, *Vexed and Troubled Englishmen: 1590–1642* (New York, 1968); Allen French, *Charles I and the Puritan Upheaval: A Study of the Causes of the Great Migration* (London, 1955); and John Horton, "Two Bishops and the Holy Brood: A Fresh Look at a Familiar Fact," *New England Quarterly*, 40 (1967), 339–363. T. H. Breen and Stephen Foster have provided new insight into the nature of the migration in "Moving to the New World: The Character of Early Massachusetts Immigration," *William and Mary Quarterly*, Ser. 3, XXX (1973), 189–222. Edmund S. Morgan has edited a collection of primary sources and historical interpretations of the Puritan migration, *The Founding of Massachusetts: Historians and Their Sources* (Indianapolis, 1964).

CHAPTER 4

George Langdon, *Pilgrim Colony: A History of New Plymouth, 1620–1691* (New Haven, 1966) is the best single-volume study of the Pilgrim adventure. The English and Dutch background from which the Plymouth colonists emerged is perceptively treated in B. R. White, *The English Separatist Tradition from the Marian Martyrs to the Pilgrim Fathers* (London, 1971). Plimoth Plantation Inc., which operates the excellent working replica of the Pilgrim settlement, has sponsored three works of value on the colony: Ruth McIntyre, *Debts Hopeful and Desperate: Financing the Plymouth Colony* (Plymouth, 1963); Darrett Rutman, *Husbandmen of Plymouth: Farms and Villages in the Old Colony, 1620–1692* (Boston, 1967); Sydney James, ed., *Three Visitors to Early Plymouth* (Plymouth, 1963). John Demos, *A Little Commonwealth: Family Life in Plymouth Colony* (New York, 1970) and Harry Ward, *Statism in Plymouth Colony* (Port Washington, N.Y., 1973) focus on domestic and political life, respectively.

William Bradford's *Of Plymouth Plantation*, preferably in the edition by Samuel Eliot Morison (New York, 1967), remains one of the best expressions of the colonial mind in its most graceful form.

CHAPTER 5

The formative decade of the Bay Colony has yet to be subjected to a rigorous and well-rounded examination by one of this generation's historians. Political developments can best be traced in the relevant chapters of James Truslow Adams, *The Founding of New England* (Boston, 1921) or John Fiske, *The Beginning of New England* (Boston, 1898), making allowance in each case for the bias of the author. Perry Miller treated the period from a primarily religious perspective in *Orthodoxy in Massachusetts 1630–1650* (Cambridge, Mass., 1933). The crises of the decade have received greater attention. The life of Roger Williams is best set forth in Ola Winslow, *Master Roger Williams: A Biography* (New York, 1957), while his thought is most clearly explained in Edmund Morgan, *Roger Williams: The Church and the State* (New York, 1967). Perry Miller's *Roger Williams: His Contribution to the American Tradition* (Indianapolis, 1953) is still of value but should be read in conjunction with Edmund Morgan's "Miller's Williams," *New England Quarterly*, XXXVIII (1965), 513–523. Emery Battis, *Saints and Sectaries: Anne Hutchinson and the Antinomian Controversy in the Massachusetts Bay Colony* (Chapel Hill, 1962) is the best starting point for an examination of its subject. Articles of value include Ronald Cohen, "Church and State in Seventeenth-century Massachusetts," *Journal of Church and State*, 12 (1970), 475–493, and Edmund Morgan, "The Case against Anne Hutchinson," *New England Quarterly*, X (1937), 635–649. Lyle Koehler has had questionable success in trying to provide a feminist perspective in "The Case of the American Jezebels," *William and Mary Quarterly*, Ser. 3, XXXI (1974), 55–78.

CHAPTER 6

Massachusetts Bay's sister colonies have been slighted by historians, with Langdon's *Pilgrim Colony* representing the only thorough and up-to-date study devoted to one of the other Bible Commonwealths. Scribners' "The History of the American Colonies" series should remedy this gap, with volumes forthcoming on Rhode Island by Sydney James, Connecticut by Robert Taylor, and New Hampshire by Jere Daniell. Benjamin Labaree will write on Massachusetts in the same series. Turning to earlier works, Charles M. Andrews has written on two of the colonies: *The Beginnings of Connecticut, 1632–1662* (New Haven, 1936), and *The Rise and Fall of the New Haven Colony* (New Haven, 1934), which remain standard works. Though not colony histories, Charles Clark, *The Eastern Frontier: The Settlement of Northern New England 1610–1763* (New York, 1970) and James Hedges, *The Browns of Providence Plantation I: The Colonial Years* (Providence, 1974) shed light on areas for which there are no adequate studies.

CHAPTER 7

Stephen Foster, *Their Solitary Way: The Puritan Social Ethic in the First Century of Settlement in New England* (New Haven, 1971) provides an excellent introduction to the foundations of Puritan social and political philosophy. Political thought is best approached through Edmund S. Morgan, ed., *Puritan Political Ideas, 1558–1794* (Indianapolis, 1965) and T. H. Breen, *The Character of the Good Ruler: A Study of Puritan Political Ideas in New England 1630–1730* (New Haven, 1970). Key studies of the franchise include B. Katherine Brown, "Freemanship in Puritan Massachusetts," *American Historical Review*, LIX (1954), 865–883, and "Puritan Democracy: A Case Study," *Mississippi Valley Historical Review*, L (1963), 377–396; Stephen Foster, "The Massachusetts Franchise in the Seventeenth Century," *William and Mary Quarterly*, Ser. 3, XXIV (1967), 613–623; Richard Simmons, "Godliness, Property, and the Franchise in Puritan Massachusetts: An Interpretation," *Journal of American History*, LV (1968), 495–511; Robert Wall, "The Massachusetts Bay Colony Franchise in 1647," *William and Mary Quarterly*, Ser. 3, XXVII (1970), 136–144; and Michael Zuckerman, "The Social Context of Democracy in Massachusetts," *William and Mary Quarterly*, Ser. 3, XXV (1968), 523–544.

CHAPTER 8

Williston Walker, *The Creeds and Platforms of Congregationalism* (Boston, 1960) contains the major platforms of New England church polity, with valuable introductions and annotations that make it an excellent study of the nature of the American Puritan churches. Edmund Morgan, *Visible Saints: The History of a Puritan Idea* (New York, 1963) traces the concept of regenerate membership from English roots to the Half-Way Covenant. Robert Scholz has outlined the relations among the clergy in "Clerical Consociation in Massachusetts Bay: Reassessing the New England Way and Its Origins," *William and Mary Quarterly*, Ser. 3, XXIX (1972), 391–414. Ecclesiastical discipline is well treated in Emil Oberholzer, *Delinquent Saints: Disciplinary Action in the Early Congregational Churches in New England* (New York, 1956). David Hall has studied the evolving relationship between pastors and their congregations in *The Faithful Shepherd: A History of the New England Ministry in the Seventeenth Century* (Chapel Hill, 1972). Important aspects of church life are treated in Alice Earle, *The Sabbath in Puritan New England* (New York, 1900) and Babette Levy, *Preaching in the First Half-Century of New England History* (Hartford, 1945).

CHAPTER 9

Lawrence Stone, *The Causes of the English Revolution, 1529–1642* (New York, 1972) is an excellent introduction to the long-term and short-term causes of the Puritan revolt, while Ivan Roots has surveyed the Interregnum period in *Commonwealth and Protectorate: The English Civil War and Its Aftermath* (New York, 1966). William Haller, *Liberty and Reformation in the Puritan Revolution* (New York, 1955) interprets the religious events of the period. The introductory material in Robert Paul's edition of *An Apologetical Narration* (Boston, 1963) focuses on those English Congregationalists to whom New Englanders were particularly committed. The biography of Cromwell that best illuminates the importance of the religious dimension of his life is Robert Paul, *The Lord Protector: Religion and Politics in the Life of Oliver Cromwell* (London, 1955); it may be supplemented with Christopher Hill's interpretive study, *God's Englishman: Oliver Cromwell and the English Revolution* (New York, 1970). The relation forged between one colony and the Protector is the subject of my brief article, "The New Haven Colony and Oliver Cromwell," *Connecticut Historical Society Bulletin*, 38 (1973), 65–72.

CHAPTER 10

New England domestic affairs in the 1640s can be approached through Edmund Morgan's study, *The Puritan Dilemma: The Story of John Winthrop* (Boston, 1958). Robert Wall, *Massachusetts Bay: The Crucial Decade, 1640–1650* (New Haven, 1972) examines the major political issues of the decade but gives many of them a significance that I do not believe is warranted. Lawrence Shaw Mayo's *John Endecott: A Biography* (Cambridge, Mass., 1936) needs updating and fleshing out, but it offers a worthwhile survey of Endecott's career.

CHAPTER 11

English history from the Restoration to the Glorious Revolution is examined in David Ogg, *England in the Reign of Charles II* (London, 1962) and *England in the Reigns of James II and William III* (London, 1955). The same period is surveyed for the American colonies in Wesley Frank Craven, *The Colonies in Transition, 1660–1713* (New York, 1968). The debate in Massachusetts over reaction to the Restoration is dealt with in Paul Lucas, "Colony or Commonwealth: Massachusetts Bay, 1661–1666," *William and Mary Quarterly*, Ser. 3, XXIV (1967), 88–107.

CHAPTER 12

The most impressive treatment of the struggle of New Englanders to adjust to a changing world remains Perry Miller's *The New England Mind: From Colony to Province* (Cambridge, Mass., 1953). The issue of declension is treated by Edmund S. Morgan in "New England Puritanism: Another Approach," *William and Mary Quarterly*, Ser. 3, XVIII (1961), 236–242, and by Robert Pope in "New England Versus the New England Mind: The Myth of Declension," *Journal of Social History*, III (1969–1970), 301–318. Pope has also thoroughly described *The Half-Way Covenant: Church Membership in Puritan New England* (Princeton, 1969). The schism in Boston's First Church is treated by Richard Simmons in "The

Founding of the Third Church in Boston," *William and Mary Quarterly*, Ser. 3, XXVI (1969), 241–252. The definitive work on sects outside the orthodox consensus and the treatment accorded to them is William McLoughlin, *New England Dissent 1630–1833: The Baptists and the Separation of Church and State* (Cambridge, Mass., 1971). The Puritan roots of New England Quakerism are described in James F. Maclear, " 'The Heart of New England Rent': The Mystical Element in Early Puritan History," *Mississippi Valley Historical Review*, XLII (1956), 621–652.

CHAPTER 13

The mounting challenges to the Massachusetts charter, culminating in its revocation, are dealt with by Michael Hall in *Edward Randolph and the American Colonies* (Chapel Hill, 1970). The best treatment of the Dominion remains Viola F. Barnes, *The Dominion of New England* (New Haven, 1923). David Lovejoy, *The Glorious Revolution in America* (New York, 1972) provides a view of the interrelation between English and American politics in the 1680s, and places the Boston revolt in the context of the general North American reaction to the fall of James II. A solid narrative of the witchcraft crisis can be found in Marion Starkey, *The Devil in Massachusetts* (New York, 1949); Chadwick Hansen does much to convey the force that the hysteria must have had for contemporaries in *Witchcraft at Salem* (New York, 1969); Paul Boyer and Stephen Nissenbaum, in *Salem Possessed: The Social Origins of Witchcraft* (Cambridge, Mass., 1974) analyze the history of sociopolitical divisions in Salem (town and village) and use their findings to suggest reasons for the direction that the accusations took.

CHAPTER 14

The past decade has seen a major revaluation of the communal life of seventeenth-century New Englanders, as various historians have begun to apply the techniques of social anthropology and demographic research to the study of colonial life. These findings are summarized and compared to early scholarship on the New England town by John Waters in his essay "From Democracy to Demography: Recent Historiography on the New England Town," in Alden T. Vaughan and George A. Billias, eds., *Perspectives on Early American History* (New York, 1973). Among the best of the town studies have been Philip Greven, *Four Generations: Population, Land, and Family in Colonial Andover, Massachusetts* (Ithaca, N.Y., 1970); Kenneth Lockridge, *A New England Town, the First Hundred Years: Dedham, Massachusetts, 1636–1736* (New York, 1970); and Sumner Chilton Powell, *Puritan Village: The Formation of a New England Town* (Middleton, Conn., 1963). A more traditional type of community study is the examination of Boston, Newport, and other colonial communities by Carl Bridenbaugh in *Cities in the Wilderness: The First Century of Urban Life in America, 1625–1742* (New York, 1938). T. H. Breen points up the importance of the colonists' English background in the shaping of colonial life in "Persistent Localism: English Social Change and the Shaping of New England Institutions," *William and Mary Quarterly*, Ser. 3, XXXII (1975), 3–28. John Demos has made the family his principal concern in *A Little Commonwealth: Family Life in Plymouth Colony* (New York, 1970). His findings should be compared to those of Levin Shucking, *The Puritan Family: A Social Study from the Literary Sources* (London, 1969) and Edmund S. Morgan, *The Puritan Family* (New York, 1966). Additional light on the family is to be found in James T. Johnson, *A Society Ordained by God: English Puritan Marriage Doctrine in the First Half of the Seventeenth Century* (Nashville, Tenn., 1970) and Roger Thompson, *Women in Stuart England and America: A Comparative Study* (London, 1974). The educational system that complemented the roles of the community and the family has been effectively studied by a number of scholars. Among the key works in the field are Lawrence Cremin, *American Education: The Colonial Experience, 1607–1783* (New York, 1970); James Axtell, *The School upon a Hill: Education and Society in Colonial New England* (New Haven, 1974); Samuel Eliot Morison, *Harvard in the Seventeenth Century*, 2 vols. (Boston, 1936); and Richard Warch, *School of the Prophets: Yale College, 1701–1740* (New Haven, 1973).

CHAPTER 15

An excellent introduction to the broad range of Puritan literary achievement is Sacvan Bercovitch, ed., *The American Puritan Imagination: Essays in Revaluation* (New York, 1974). Other broadly based studies include Everett Emerson, ed., *Major Writers of Early American Literature* (Madison, Wis., 1972); Samuel Eliot Morison, *The Intellectual Life of Colonial New England* (Ithaca, 1956); and Kenneth Murdock, *Literature and Theology in Colonial New England* (Cambridge, Mass., 1949). Specific areas of literary production can be examined in Owen Watkins, *The Puritan Experience: Studies in Spiritual Autobiography* (New York, 1972); Peter Gay, *A Loss of Mastery: Puritan Historians in Colonial America* (Los Angeles, 1966); Elizabeth White, *Anne Bradstreet, 'The Tenth Muse'* (New York, 1971); Norman Grabo, *Edward Taylor* (New York, 1961); and Richard Crowder, *No Featherbed to Heaven: A Biography of Michael Wigglesworth* (East Lansing, 1962). Two of the more striking forms of New England art are examined in Marian Donnelly, *The New England Meeting Houses of the Seventeenth Century* (Middletown, Conn., 1968) and Dickran Tasjian and Ann Tasjian, *Memorials for Children of Change: The Art of Early New England Stonecarving* (Middletown, Conn., 1973). Percy Scholes surveys *The Puritans and Music in England and New England* (London, 1934). Science in the Puritan colonies has been accorded few full-length studies. An excellent survey is Raymond Stearns, *Science in the British Colonies of America* (Urbana, Ill., 1970), while medical science of the period can be approached through Otho Beall and Richard Shyrock, *Cotton Mather: First Significant Figure in American Medicine* (Baltimore, 1954).

CHAPTER 16

Alden T. Vaughan, *New England Frontier: Puritans and Indians, 1620–1675* (Boston, 1965) remains the best study of its subject, though its interpretation has been challenged by Francis Jennings, "Goals and Functions of Puritan Missions to the Indians," *Ethnohist*, 18 (1971), 197–212. Puritan missionary efforts are specifically dealt with in William Kellaway, *The New England Company: 1649–1776* (London, 1961) and Ola Winslow, *John Eliot, "Apostle to the Indians"* (Boston, 1968). King Philip's War is well analyzed in Douglas Leach, *Flintlock and Tomahawk: New England in King Philip's War* (New York, 1966). Lorenzo Greene, *The Negro in Colonial New England, 1620–1776* (New York, 1942) is the only book-length treatment of Puritans and blacks; it should be supplemented with Bernard Rosenthal, "Puritan Conscience and New England Slavery," *New England Quarterly*, XLVI (1973), 62–81 and Robert C. Twombly and Robert H. Moore, "Black Puritan: The Negro in Seventeenth Century Massachusetts," *William and Mary Quarterly*, Ser. 3, XXIV (1967), 224–242.

CHAPTER 17

G. B. Warden, *Boston, 1689–1776* (Boston, 1970) surveys the evolution of New England's leading city in the period between the revolutions of 1689 and 1775, and in the process sheds light on developments in the political life of the colony. Richard Bushman, *From Puritan to Yankee: Character and the Social Order in Connecticut, 1690–1765* (Cambridge, Mass., 1967) stands as a model integration of politics, economics, social organization, and religion in a process of change. Michael Zuckerman's *Peaceable Kingdoms: New England Towns in the Eighteenth Century* (New York, 1970) offers a controversial interpretation of the meaning of political life on the local level.

CHAPTER 18

Joseph Ellis traces the growing appeal of Anglicanism through a biography of its most persuasive exponent in *The New England Mind in Transition: Samuel Johnson of Connecticut* (New Haven, 1973). Carl Bridenbaugh, *Mitre and Sceptre: Transatlantic Faiths, Ideas, Personalities, and Politics, 1689–1775* (New York, 1962) describes the struggle over an Anglican bishop. Conrad Wright analyzes the growth of liberal Puritanism in *The Beginnings of Unitarianism in America* (Boston, 1955). Edwin S. Gaustad, *The Great Awakening in New England* (New York, 1957) introduces its subject well, while Edward Davidson, *Jonathan Edwards: The Narrative of a Puritan Mind* (Boston, 1966) is a good starting place for a study of the men who sparked that revivalist movement.

GUIDE FOR RESEARCH

"Going to the sources" for further insight into colonial New England may be undertaken with varying degrees of success, depending on one's geographical location. Many archival sources of value still remain accessible only to those who can travel to the depositories in which they are held. Nevertheless, a significant and ever-growing amount of source material is available in printed form. What follows is an outline of the principal guides to archives and the major collections of printed and microfilm sources.

GUIDES TO ARCHIVES

Andrews, Charles M., *Guide to the Materials for American History to 1783, in the Public Records Office of Great Britain*, 2 vols. (1912–1914).
———, "Lists of the Journals and Acts of the Councils and Assemblies of the Thirteen Colonies, and the Floridas, in America, preserved in the Public Record Office in London," in American Historical Association, *Annual Report* (1908).
Andrews, Charles M., and Frances Davenport, *Guide to the Manuscript Materials for the History of the United States to 1783 in the British Museum, in Minor London Archives, and in the Libraries of Oxford and Cambridge* (1908).
Billington, Ray A., "Guides to American Historical Manuscript Collections in Libraries of the United States," *Mississippi Valley Historical Review*, XXXVIII (1951).
Cuthbort, Norma B., *American Manuscript Collections in the Huntington Library for the History of the Seventeenth and Eighteenth Centuries* (1941).
Flaherty, David H., "A Select Guide to the Manuscript Court Records of Colonial New England," *The American Journal of Legal History*, II (1967).
Greene, Evarts B., and Richard B. Morris, *A Guide to the Principal Sources for Early American History (1600–1800) in the City of New York* (2nd ed., 1953).

240

Griffin, Grace G., *A Guide to Manuscripts Relating to American History in British Depositories Reproduced for the Division of Manuscripts of the Library of Congress* (1946).

Guide to the Resources of the American Antiquarian Society (1937).

Guide to the Records in the National Archives (1948).

Hamer, Philip M., *A Guide to Archives and Manuscripts in the United States* (1961).

Handbook of the Massachusetts Historical Society (1949).

Hasse, Adelaide R., "Materials for a Bibliography of the Public Archives of the Thirteen Original States," American Historical Association, *Annual Report* (1906).

Historical Records Survey, *Guides to Depositories in Massachusetts* (1939).

Library of Congress, *Manuscripts in Public and Private Collections in the United States* (1924).

National Union Catalogue of Manuscript Collections (1959–   ).

Powers, Z. J., "American Historical Manuscripts in the Historical Manuscripts Room," *Yale University Library Gazette*, XIV (1939).

Worthley, Harold F., *An Inventory of the Records of the Particular (Congregational) Churches of Massachusetts Gathered 1620–1805* (1970).

PRINTED SOURCES: PUBLIC RECORDS AND DOCUMENTARY COLLECTIONS

Abstracts and Index of the Records of the Inferior Court of Pleas (Suffolk County Circuit), Held at Boston 1680–1698 (1940).

Acts and Resolves, Public and Private, of the Province of the Massachusetts Bay, 1692–1780, 21 vols. (1869–1922).

Andros Tracts, 3 vols. (1868–1874).

Bartlett, John R., ed., *Records of the Colony of Rhode Island and Providence Plantation in New England*, 10 vols. (1856–1865).

Batchellor, A.S., and H.H. Metcalfe, eds., *Laws of New Hampshire . . . The Province Period*, 3 vols. (1904–1915).

Bates, S.A., ed., *Records of the Town of Braintree, 1640–1793* (1886).

Bouton, Nathaniel, ed., *Documents and Records Relating to the Province of New Hampshire, 1623–1800*, 49 vols. (1867–1943).

Dexter, F.B., ed., *Ancient Town Records, New Haven Town Records, 1649–1684*, 2 vols. (1917–1919).

Dow, George F., ed., *Records and Files of the Quarterly Courts of Essex County, 1636–1683*, 8 vols. (1911–1921).

Farrand, Max, ed., *The Laws and Liberties of Massachusetts . . . 1647* (1929).

Fernow, B., ed., *Documents Relative to the Colonial History of New York*, 15 vols. (1853–1883).

Firth, C.H., and R.S. Raith, eds., *Acts and Ordinances of the Interregnum, 1642–1660*, 3 vols. (1911).

Force, Peter, ed., *Tracts and Other Papers, Relating Principally to the Origin, Settlement, and Progress of the Colonies in North America*, 4 vols. (1947 edition).

———, *A Documentary History of the North American Colonies*, 9 vols. (1837–1853).

Grant, W.L., and James Munro, eds., *Acts of the Privy Council, Colonial Series, 1613–1783*, 6 vols. (1908–1912).

Hill, D.G., ed., *Dedham Records, 1635–1845*, 5 vols. (1886–1899).

Hoadly, Charles J., ed., *Records of the Colony and Plantation of New Haven from 1638 to 1649* (1857).

———, *Records of the Colony or Jurisdiction of New Haven from May, 1653 to the Union* (1858).

Hutchinson, Thomas, ed., *A Collection of Original Papers Relative to the History of the Colony of Massachusetts Bay*.

Jensen, Merrill, ed., *English Historical Documents, IX: American Colonial Documents to 1776* (1964).

Journal of the Commissioners for Trade and Plantations, April 1704–May 1782, 14 vols. (1920–1938).

Kavenagh, W. Keith, ed., *Foundations of Colonial America: A Documentary History, I: Northeastern Colonies* (1973).

Labaree, Leonard, ed., *Royal Instructions to British Colonial Governors, 1670–1776*, 2 vols. (1935).

Libby, Charles T. and Robert Moody, eds., *Province and Court Records of Maine*, 3 vols. (1928–1947).

MacDonald, W., ed., *Documentary Source Book of American History, 1606–1898* (1908).

———, *State Charters and Other Documents Illustrative of American History, 1606–1775* (1899).

Massachusetts Historical Society, *Journals of the House of Representatives, 1715–1752*, 28 vols. (1919–1953).

Perry, W.S., ed., *Historical Collections Relating to the American Colonial Church*, 5 vols. (1870–1878).

Providence Record Commissioners, *Early Records of the Town of Providence*, 21 vols. (1892–1915).

Reports of the Record Commissioners of the City of Boston, 39 vols. (1876–1909).

Sainsbury, W. Noel, et al., eds., *Calendar of State Papers, Colonial Series, America and the West Indies, 1574–1711*, 20 vols. (1860–1903).

Shurtleff, Nathaniel B., ed., *Records of the Governor and Company of Massachusetts Bay in New England, 1628–1692*, 5 vols. (1853–1854).

———, *Records of the Court of Assistants of the Colony of Massachusetts Bay, 1630–1692*, 3 vols. (1901–1928).

Shurtleff, Nathaniel B., *Records of the Colony of New Plymouth in New England, 1620–1692*, 12 vols. (1855–1861).

Stock, Leo F., ed., *Proceedings and Debates of the British Parliament Respecting North America*, 5 vols. (1924–1941).

Thorpe, Francis N., ed., *Federal and State Constitutions, Colonial Charters, and Other Organic Laws*, 7 vols. (1909).

Thurloe, John, ed., *A Collection of the State Papers of John Thurloe, Esq.; Secretary to the Two Protectors, Oliver and Richard Cromwell* (n.d.).

Trumbull, J. Hammond, ed., *The Public Records of the Colony of Connecticut, 1636–1776*, 15 vols. (1850–1880).

Whitmore, W.H., ed., *Bibliographical Sketch of the Laws of the Massachusetts Colony from 1630 to 1686* (1890).

PRINTED SOURCES: SOCIETY COLLECTIONS

Most of the state and local historical societies of New England have followed a program of regularly printing portions of their holdings. Below are listed some of the major printing projects:

American Antiquarian Society, *Proceedings* (1812–   ).
Colonial Society of Massachusetts, *Publications* (1895–   ).
Connecticut Historical Society, *Collections* (1860–   ).
Massachusetts Historical Society, *Proceedings* (1791–   ).
Massachusetts Historical Society, *Collections* (1792–   ).
Maine Historical Society, *Collections* (1831–1906).
New Hampshire Historical Society, *Collections* (1824–1939).
New Hampshire Historical Society, *Papers* (1865–   ).
Rhode Island Historical Society, *Collections* (1827–1941).
Rhode Island Historical Society, *Publications* (1893–1901).

BIBLIOGRAPHIES OF 17th- AND 18th-CENTURY BOOKS

Evans, Charles, et al., eds., *American Bibliography: A Chronological Dictionary of all Books, Pamphlets, and Periodicals Printed in the United States . . . 1639 . . . to 1820*, 14 vols. (1903–1959).

Pollard, A.W., and G.R. Redgrave, *Short-Title Catalogue of Books Printed in England, Scotland, and Ireland and of English Books Printed Abroad, 1475–1640* (London, 1926).

Shipton, Clifford, and James Mooney, comps., *National Index of American Imprints through 1800. The Short-Title Evans*, 2 vols. (1969).

Wing, Donald, *Short-Title Catalogue of Books Printed in England, Scotland, Ireland, Wales, and British America and of English Books Printed in Other Countries, 1641–1700* (1945).

The books in the Evans Bibliography have all been published on microcard, and the "Evans Microcard Collection" is widely available in libraries. University Microfilms is in the process of making available on microfilm all titles contained in the Pollard-Redgrave and Wing volumes.

INDEX